PowerPoint 2007 for Starters

THE MISSING MANUAL

E. A. Vander Veer

POGUE PRESS™
O'REILLY®

Beijing · Cambridge · Farnham · Köln · Paris · Sebastopol · Taipei · Tokyo

PowerPoint 2007 for Starters: THE MISSING MANUAL

by E. A. Vander Veer

Published by O'Reilly Media, Inc., 1005 Gravenstein Highway North, Sebastopol, CA 95472.

O'Reilly books may be purchased for educational, business, or sales promotional use. Online editions are also available for most titles (*safari.oreilly.com*). For more information, contact our corporate/institutional sales department: (800) 998-9938 or *corporate@oreilly.com*.

Printing History:

January 2007:   First Edition.

 This book uses RepKover™, a durable and flexible lay-flat binding.

ISBN-10: 0-596-52831-0
ISBN-13: 978-0-596-52831-7
[M]

TABLE OF CONTENTS

PART TWO: DELIVERING SLIDESHOWS

PART THREE: BEYOND BULLET POINTS—GRAPHICS AND TRANSITIONS

THE MISSING CREDITS

About the Author

 E. A. Vander Veer started out in the software trenches, lexing and yac-cing and writing shell scripts with the best of them. She remained busy and happy for years writing C++ programs and wresting data from recalcitrant databases. After a stint as an Object Technology Evangelist, she found a way to unite all of her passions: writing about cool computer stuff in prose any human being can understand. Books followed—over a dozen so far— including *Flash 8: The Missing Manual, JavaScript for Dummies, XML Blueprints*, and the fine tome you're holding right now. Her articles appear in online and print publications including Byte, CNET, Salon.com, WEBTechniques, and CNN.com. She lives in Texas with her husband and daughter. Email: *emilyamoore@rgv.rr.com*.

About the Creative Team

Nan Barber (editor) has worked with the Missing Manual series since its incep-tion—long enough to remember booting up her computer from a floppy disk. Email: *nanbarber@oreilly.com*.

Peter Meyers (editor) works as an editor at O'Reilly on the Missing Manual series. He lives with his wife and cats in New York City. Email: *peter.meyers@gmail.com*.

Michele Filshie (copy editor) is O'Reilly's assistant editor for Missing Manuals and editor of *Don't Get Burned on eBay*. Before turning to the world of computer-related books, Michele spent many happy years at Black Sparrow Press. She lives in Sebastopol, CA. Email: *mfilshie@oreilly.com*.

Echo Swinford (technical reviewer) has spent 10 years in the medical presentations and education industry. She's currently finishing her Master's degree in New Media at the Indiana University-Purdue University at Indianapolis School of Informatics. Her first book, *Fixing PowerPoint Annoyances*, was published by O'Reilly Media in February 2006, and she has a string of tech editing credits with other publishers. Echo has been a Microsoft PowerPoint MVP since early 2000. She can be contacted for projects and consulting at *freelance@echosvoice.com*.

Geetesh Bajaj (technical reviewer) has been designing PowerPoint presentations and templates for over a decade and heads Indezine, a presentation design studio based out of Hyderabad, India. His indezine.com site attracts nearly a million page views each month, and it has hundreds of free PowerPoint templates and other goodies for visitors to download. In addition, Geetesh also issues a biweekly Power-Point newsletter on indezine.com that has tens of thousands of subscribers.

Acknowledgements

It takes a team of dedicated, hardworking professionals to turn any manuscript into a finished book, and the O'Reilly team is one of the best in the business. Extra thanks go out to Nan Barber, whose competence, surefootedness, and directness make her the kind of editor every author dreams of; Echo Swinford and Geetesh Bajaj, whose experience and dead-eye accuracy helped shape this book immeasurably; and Pete Meyers, who made sure the trains ran on time (while still managing to be a genuinely nice guy).

—*E. A. Vander Veer*

The Missing Manual Series

Missing Manuals are witty, superbly written guides to computer products that don't come with printed manuals (which is just about all of them). Each book features a handcrafted index and RepKover, a detached-spine binding that lets the book lie perfectly flat without the assistance of weights or cinder blocks.

Recent and upcoming titles include:

Access 2007 for Starters: The Missing Manual by Matthew MacDonald

Access 2007: The Missing Manual by Matthew MacDonald

Digital Photography: The Missing Manual by Chris Grover and Barbara Brundage

Excel 2003 for Starters: The Missing Manual by Matthew MacDonald

Excel 2003: The Missing Manual by Matthew MacDonald

Excel 2007 for Starters: The Missing Manual by Matthew MacDonald

Excel 2007: The Missing Manual by Matthew MacDonald

Google: The Missing Manual, Second Edition by Sarah Milstein, J.D. Biersdorfer, and Matthew MacDonald

iMovie 6 & iDVD: The Missing Manual by David Pogue

iPhoto 6: The Missing Manual by David Pogue

iPod: The Missing Manual, Fifth Edition by J.D. Biersdorfer

PCs: The Missing Manual by Andy Rathbone

Photoshop Elements 5: The Missing Manual by Barbara Brundage

PowerPoint 2007: The Missing Manual by E. A. Vander Veer

Quicken for Starters: The Missing Manual by Bonnie Biafore

The Internet: The Missing Manual by David Pogue and J.D. Biersdorfer

Windows XP for Starters: The Missing Manual by David Pogue

Windows XP Home Edition: The Missing Manual, Second Edition by David Pogue

Windows XP Pro: The Missing Manual, Second Edition by David Pogue, Craig Zacker, and Linda Zacker

Windows Vista: The Missing Manual by David Pogue

Windows Vista for Starters: The Missing Manual by David Pogue

Word 2007 for Starters: The Missing Manual by Chris Grover

Word 2007: The Missing Manual by Chris Grover

INTRODUCTION

- ▶ **What You Can Do with PowerPoint 2007**

- ▶ **What's New in PowerPoint 2007**

- ▶ **The Very Basics**

- ▶ **About This Book**

IF YOU'VE NEVER SEEN A POWERPOINT PRESENTATION, you're in a pretty select group. With legions of folks all over the world pounding out an estimated *30 million PowerPoint slides every day*, PowerPoint's the runaway leader in the field of presentation programs, leaving competitors like Corel Presentations and Apple's Keynote in the dust. PowerPoint has become so ubiquitous that it's even managed to work its way into the English language: *powerpointless*, as many audience members can attest, describes a PowerPoint presentation that has bulleted text, graphics, animated slide transitions—everything except a good reason for existing.

So how do you improve a program that's wildly successful? If you're Microsoft, you completely redesign it. That's right: PowerPoint 2007 looks completely different from its previous incarnation, PowerPoint 2003. Gone are the menus, wizards, and most of the toolbars and panes that a generation of PowerPointilists grew up with. As you see in Figure I-1, Microsoft has replaced all of that with the ribbon. And that's just the tip of the redesign iceberg.

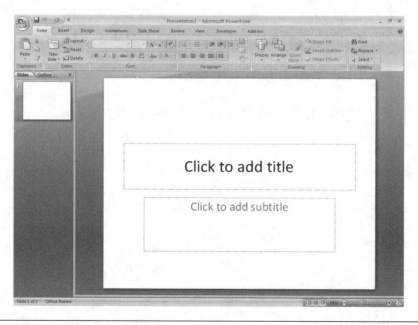

Figure I-1. If you're a PowerPoint 2003 aficionado, expect to be a little shocked when you fire up PowerPoint 2007 for the first time. This version's the biggest wholesale change to the PowerPoint look in nearly a decade, and there's no fallback "classic" mode, either.

The good news is you can still do the same things in PowerPoint 2007 that you could do in earlier versions—and a few more, besides. You can still design beautiful slideshows that contain bulleted lists, pictures, and sound clips. You can still deliver your slideshows in person, on CD, or on an unattended kiosk.

What's new in PowerPoint 2007 is *how* you do all of these things.

Fortunately, you're holding the book that Microsoft should have included in the PowerPoint 2007 box—but didn't. If you're familiar with PowerPoint 2003 or an earlier version of the program, this book will help you make the transition from the old, familiar way of doing things to the new, improved way. (You'll even see tips and tricks that were buried so deep inside menus and toolbars in PowerPoint 2003 that you probably didn't know they were there.)

On the other hand, if you're brand new to PowerPoint—or even to presentation programs in general—then you're in luck, because this book shows you how to build basic to bowl-'em-over presentations for work, school, or whatever you're involved in.

FROM THE FIELD
Presentation vs. Slideshow

Microsoft's help files, as well as most PowerPoint books, use the terms *presentation* and *slideshow* interchangeably. But a very important distinction exists between the two.

A *slideshow* is a collection of slides but a *presentation* is everything that goes into delivering the slideshow to your audience. A presentation includes not just the slideshow, but speaker notes, printed handouts, and—most important of all—*you*, the presenter.

In other words, no matter how cool your slides are, they aren't your presentation. Your slides are nothing more than tools you use to deliver your message. If you keep this distinction in mind, you'll keep your focus on the message—where it belongs—and off the tricky stuff you can do with PowerPoint. For your audience's sake, avoid bringing yet another power-pointless presentation into the world!

What You Can Do with PowerPoint 2007

PowerPoint was originally designed to help business professionals create and deliver electronic slideshows (sales presentations, mostly). But over the years, as Microsoft piled on the options, folks began discovering new ways to use the program.

Here's a short list of what you can create using PowerPoint 2007:

▶ **Multimedia presentations.** Use PowerPoint to create slideshows that you—the presenter—can run in front of an audience on a computer screen (for small groups) or a digital projector (for a packed conference hall). The kinds of presentations that fit into this group include business and sales presentations, workshop and conference sessions, academic lectures, in-class reports, courtroom summations, and church choir programs. The sky's the limit. Anytime you need to stand in front of a group and present information, you can use a PowerPoint slideshow to get your point across.

▶ **Kiosk presentations.** Presentations that run unattended, are perfect for trade shows, department store product demonstrations—even (believe it or not) weddings and funerals.

▶ **Printed documents.** It's not a full-fledged page-layout program like Quark XPress, but PowerPoint 2007 comes with templates for popular printables (like certificates of achievement and calendars). It also gives you more control over layout than earlier versions of the program.

What's New in PowerPoint 2007

Nearly all the changes Microsoft made to PowerPoint 2007 affect the way the program looks and behaves; in other words, the changes affect how you do things in PowerPoint 2007. The most sweeping of these include:

▶ **A completely redesigned interface.** The difference you notice right away is the tabbed *ribbon* (Figure I-2), which replaces all of the old, pre–PowerPoint 2007 menus and toolbars. Instead of wasting time trying to remember if the option you want is hiding on a toolbar or a menu or a pane or a dialog box or somewhere else entirely, in PowerPoint 2007, you reach *all* options from the ribbon.

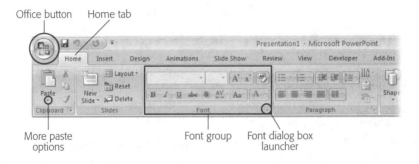

Office button   Home tab

More paste options   Font group   Font dialog box launcher

Figure I-2. You can't make the ribbon larger, nor can you move it around or hide its tabs (although PowerPoint does let you hide the ribbon itself; see page 7). If you're wondering why there's no File tab, it's because the Office button replaces the File menu in all Microsoft Office 2007 programs.

▶ **New file formats.** The files you'll create in PowerPoint 2007 bear a different file extension than the ones you created in earlier versions of the program. The good news is that the new XML-based file formats tend to be smaller and more recoverable than the old ones. The bad news is that you can't edit PowerPoint 2007 files in an earlier version of the program unless you download and install a special converter program (page 13 has details).

▶ **Tighter integration among Office programs.** Microsoft gave all of the Office programs a face lift, not just PowerPoint. The result is that all Office programs share similar elements. For example, the Office button (the old File menu) appears in the same spot in all Office programs, and certain options—like the ones you use to create charts and diagrams—look and behave pretty much the same way in PowerPoint as they do in Word and Excel.

▶ **Improved graphics.** All Office programs share a single, new-and-improved graphics engine that not only makes the charts, diagrams, and other visuals you create in PowerPoint look better (*much* better), but makes them easier to create, too (Figure I-8).

▶ **More look-and-feel options.** PowerPoint 2007 comes with more and better-looking templates and slide layouts than earlier versions of the program.

When Not to Use PowerPoint

It's easy to get caught up in the trappings associated with giving a presentation: the slideshow, the handouts, the speaker notes, and so on. But you can give a fantastic, memorable presentation without any of these supporting tools. *You*—what you have to say and how you say it—are the reason people are filing into the room.

PowerPoint's supposed to *support* your presentation, not *be* your presentation.

So before you even fire up the program, ask yourself these questions:

* **Do I really need slides?** PowerPoint slides are great for keeping key points ("Our company's going down in flames") in front of your audience during your presentation. They're also great for making direct appeals ("Please be happy with your 50 percent pay cut"). What they're *not* good for is delivering a bunch of dense information, such as the in-depth analysis of the last five years' worth of sales activity that led to your conclusion.

* **Do I really need speaker notes?** If you're planning to deliver a lengthy presentation, having your speaker notes cued up to match your slides can save you lots of hair-pulling. But if you're planning a short presentation, you know your material backwards and forwards, or you simply prefer to use 3×5 cards to jog your memory, then speaker notes may not be worth the time it takes to set them up.

* **Do I really need handouts?** Use printouts of your slides when you want to leave lots of specific instructions or actionable items with your audience. If that's not the case, skip the handouts (most end up in the circular file the minute the presentation's over anyway).

A Quick Tour of the New Interface

If you're familiar with PowerPoint 2003, the first sight of PowerPoint 2007 might make you want to run away screaming. Where are the menus? Where are the toolbars? PowerPoint still has everything you need to create killer presentations. Stuff's just organized differently. Remember, the new interface incorporates all the elements you know—buttons, menus, dialog boxes—they're just in different places where, more often than not, you can get to them faster than before.

Ribbon

You can think of the *ribbon* as a big, fat, nonmovable toolbar. It may look as though it's taking up an enormous amount of room on your screen (see Figure I-2), but it doesn't take up any more space than the old menu bar plus a couple of toolbars. Furthermore, the ribbon always appears in the same place, it never gets any bigger, and because you can't customize the ribbon or reposition it the way you could toolbars in PowerPoint 2003, you can't accidentally lose the ribbon.

___ TIP _____

> To temporarily reclaim some screen space, you can hide the ribbon by double-clicking the active tab. When you need to see the ribbon commands again, just click any tab.

Groups

When you launch PowerPoint, the Home *tab* automatically appears selected (Figure I-2), which displays text formatting options organized in sections, or *groups*. For example, options in the Font group of the Home tab let you bold and underline your text; options in the Paragraph group let you align your text and format it as a bulleted or numbered list.

Command buttons

As you'd expect, to select one of the options on a ribbon, just click the button. To underline a heading, select the heading text you want to underline, zip to the Font group, and click the Underline button. To change the color of your text, first select it, and then head to the Font group of the Home tab and click the Font Color button.

A tiny down-arrow icon means you can click the arrow to see additional options. For example, clicking the down-arrow that appears beneath Paste (Figure I-2) displays a menu of paste-related options. Clicking the button (instead of the down-arrow next to it) lets you bypass the menu and go straight to the most popular menu command. Clicking the Paste button triggers the same result as choosing Paste → Paste: Both immediately paste the contents of the Clipboard onto your slide.

Dialog box launchers

To give you complete control over every element of your slideshow while sticking to their design philosophy of offering all options on the ribbon, the PowerPoint 2007 designers placed a tiny *dialog box launcher* button in the bottom-right corner of many ribbon groups. When you click a dialog launcher, PowerPoint pops up a dialog box related to that group. Clicking the Font dialog box launcher, for example (Figure I-2), displays the Font dialog box in Figure I-3.

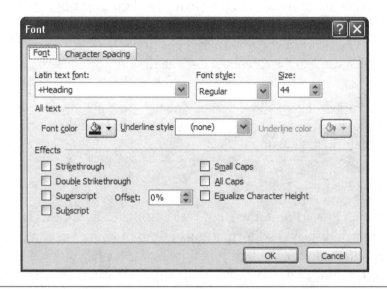

Figure I-3. If you're familiar with PowerPoint 2003, you'll recognize the dialog boxes that let you customize every aspect of your slideshow.

Tabs

Microsoft organized the ribbon's *tabs* in the order they figured most people would create slideshows. They believe most folks begin by adding text to their slides, so they displayed the Home tab first, followed by the Insert tab (which lets you insert charts, diagrams, pictures, and other stuff), followed by the Slide Show tab (which lets you rehearse your timing and record voiceover narration), and so on.

Contextual tabs are tabs that let you work with specialized kinds of objects, such as pictures or charts. They appear above the ribbon, and in this book you'll see them written with a vertical bar after the contextual part of the name: Chart Tools | Format. Contextual tabs appear only when you need them to and automatically disappear when you're finished with them. For example, when you select a chart on your slide, the Chart Tools | Design, Chart Tools | Layout, and Chart Tools | Format tabs appear. Then, when you select a hunk of text, PowerPoint recognizes that you're finished formatting your chart and hides the Chart Tools tabs.

Live Previews

One of the coolest new things in PowerPoint 2007 is the *Live Preview* feature. Imagine you want to apply a design theme to your slideshow. You click the Design tab to see a bunch of different design-theme thumbnails (Figure I-4). As you mouse over each thumbnail, PowerPoint previews the theme right there, on your slide, by temporarily applying it to your slide's content.

If none of those themes grabs you, you can click More to see an entire gallery of options—each of which you can preview, live on your slide, by mousing over each option (see Figure I-4). Live preview galleries save time and hassle by letting you instantly see how an effect looks on your slide before you commit to it. (In the old days, you had to select an option to see how it looked; then, if you didn't like it, you had to select Undo and start all over again).

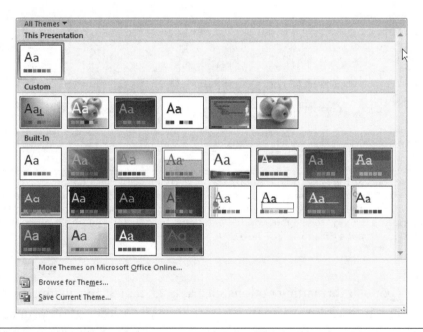

Figure I-4. The Themes gallery, shown here, is just one of many galleries you find in PowerPoint. Mousing over a gallery option automatically previews that option on your slide.

Live previews aren't for everybody. For one thing, galleries can appear on top of the slide element you're trying to modify, which means you can't see the preview. For another thing, some folks don't like the idea of PowerPoint changing their slide's appearance—even temporarily—unless they tell it to by clicking something. To turn off gallery previews, choose Office button → PowerPoint Options → Popular and then turn off the checkbox next to Enable Live Preview.

Mini Toolbar

PowerPoint 2007 did away with most of the toolbars that appeared in earlier versions of the program, but not all of them. One that remains is the pop-up Mini Toolbar shown in Figure I-5.

Figure I-5. Technically, the Mini Toolbar breaks the PowerPoint 2007 design team's commitment not to have stuff come out of nowhere and then disappear, but because so many people spend a lot of time formatting text, they decided it was worth keeping. The Mini Toolbar appears slightly transparent, and disappears immediately if you ignore it and begin typing. You can turn it off completely if it bugs you (the tip on page 88 shows you how).

Packed with popular formatting options such as bold, italics, and alignment, the Mini Toolbar springs into action automatically each time you select text on your slide. The Mini Toolbar duplicates formatting options you find on the Slide ribbon, so technically you don't need it to get your work done. (Still, some folks find it handy.)

Keytips

If you're familiar with an earlier version of PowerPoint, you may recall the Ctrl+<*letter*> keyboard shortcuts that appeared after most menu options. To display the Save As dialog box, you could choose File → Save As, or press Ctrl+S.

Although the old-style keyboard shortcuts still work, PowerPoint 2007 introduces a groovy new way to avoid using your mouse: keytips. *Keytips*, shown in Figure I-6, are tiny letters that appear next to ribbon options after you've pressed Alt. They're much like the underscores that appeared under menu options when you pressed Alt in PowerPoint 2003, but they're easier to spot. To see keytips, press Alt; to hide them, press Alt again.

Clicking a keytip displays additional keytips. Clicking a tab keytip displays group keytips, and clicking a group keytip displays option keytips. Here's how it works. If you want to show a ruler on you slide, you can click View → Ruler, or you can press Alt, then W, and then R (Figure I-6).

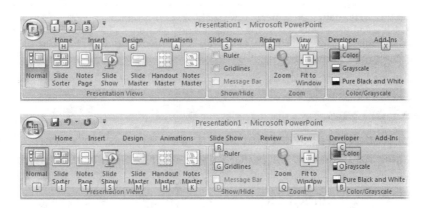

Figure I-6. Top: Just as keyboard shortcuts let you "walk" through menus by pressing keys instead of clicking your mouse, keytips let you step through ribbon commands by pressing keys.

Bottom: Clicking a ribbon group keytip such as J (Show/Hide) displays keytips for the options associated with that particular group (R for Ruler, G for Gridlines, and so on).

Improved screen tip help

In previous versions of PowerPoint, letting your mouse linger over a toolbar option automatically displayed a curt pop-up description of the option such as *Print*

Preview, Spelling, or *Research.* But in PowerPoint 2007, mousing over a ribbon button displays a description that's actually useful. See Figure I-7 for details.

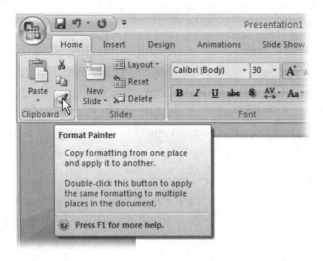

Figure I-7. The screen tip help in PowerPoint 2007 shows you expanded descriptions, outlines the scenarios in which using the command or menu can be useful and lists keyboard shortcuts (if any). For even more information, press F1 to display PowerPoint's help window with a help article describing the option in blow-by-blow detail.

New File Formats

The files you create using PowerPoint 2007 bear different file extensions than the files you created using PowerPoint 2003 or an earlier version of the program. The "x" in the new PowerPoint 2007 file names reflects the new, XML-based file format. Table I-1 shows you the differences.

Table I-1. Old and New File Extensions for the Files You Create in PowerPoint

PowerPoint 2007 File Extension	Description	Old (pre-2007) File Extension
.pptx	Presentation	.ppt
.potx	Template	.pot
.ppsx	Show	.pps

Table I-1. Old and New File Extensions for the Files You Create in PowerPoint (continued)

PowerPoint 2007 File Extension	Description	Old (pre-2007) File Extension
.ppam	Add-in	.ppa
.pptm	Macro-enabled presentation	.ppt

NOTE

This book is based on *PowerPoint 2007: The Missing Manual* (O'Reilly). That book is a comprehensive reference covering every program feature, including geeky pursuits like adding video and animations to your slides and writing macros (mini-programs that automate your slide-shows). Although you'll probably never need to do these things—and never want to—*PowerPoint 2007: The Missing Manual* has everything you need to know.

The implications of the new file formats are twofold:

▶ **Because the new file formats are based on XML, they tend to be more compact than PowerPoint 2003.** A smaller file is good news if you intend to deliver your presentation by email or on CD. Also, these new files are easier to recreate in the event of a computer crash.

▶ **The files you create with PowerPoint 2007 *can't* automatically be edited in earlier versions of the program.** Fortunately, Microsoft offers a compatibility pack that lets folks running Office 2003 open PowerPoint 2007 files; to download and install it, visit *www.microsoft.com/office/preview/beta/converter.mspx*. PowerPoint 2007 also gives you the option to save files compatible with PowerPoint 2003 and earlier versions of the program (see page 53).

Improved Graphics

Microsoft overhauled the part of Microsoft Office that lets you create charts, diagrams, and pictures in PowerPoint, Word, and other Office programs. Not only is creating graphics easier in PowerPoint, the results, as you see in Figure I-8, are much more impressive.

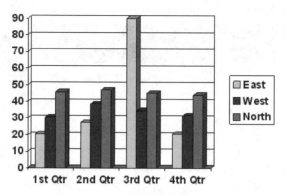

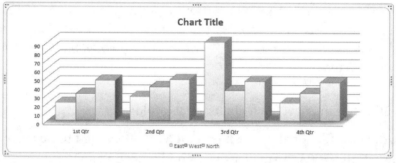

Figure I-8. Top: The charts and other graphics you could create using PowerPoint 2003 got the point across, but they weren't exactly what you'd call inspiring.

Bottom: Not only do graphics look great out of the box in PowerPoint 2007, you can change the way they look with the click of a button by applying professionally designed Quick Styles.

More Theme Options

Like harvest-gold stoves and avocado shag carpeting, the design templates that came with PowerPoint 2003 were beginning to show their age. So Microsoft created a bunch of new design templates (they're called *Office themes* now) that look a little more up-to-date. Unlike the old PowerPoint-only design templates, you can apply the Office themes to any file you create using an Office program, from a PowerPoint slideshow to a Word document or Excel spreadsheet. (That's good news for folks who want to create matching backup reports in Word and matching spreadsheets in Excel to hand out at the end of their PowerPoint presentations.) Also new in PowerPoint 2007 is the ability to create multiple slides with the same layout faster with reusable slide masters (Chapter 5).

The Very Basics

You'll find very little jargon or techno-geek terminology in this book. You will, however, see a few terms and concepts that you'll encounter frequently in your computing life:

▶ **Clicking.** This book gives you several kinds of instructions that require you to use your computer's mouse or trackpad. To *click* means to point the arrow cursor at something on the screen and then—without moving the cursor at all—to press and release the clicker button on the mouse (or laptop trackpad). To *double-click*, of course, means to click twice in rapid succession, again without moving the cursor at all. To *drag* means to move the cursor while pressing the button continuously. To *right-click*, click as described above, but press the mouse button on the right.

When you see an instruction like *Shift-click* or *Ctrl-click*, simply press the key as you click.

▶ **Keyboard shortcuts.** Every time you take your hand off the keyboard to move the mouse, you lose time and potentially disrupt your creative flow. That's why many experienced computer fans use keystroke combinations instead of menu commands wherever possible. Ctrl+B is a keyboard shortcut for boldface type in Power-Point 2007 (and most other programs). When you see a shortcut like Ctrl+S, which saves changes to the current document, it's telling you to hold down the Ctrl key, and, while it's down, type the letter S, and then release both keys. When you see Alt+F, S (the new Save keyboard shortcut), press Alt, then F, and then S.

▶ **All roads lead to Rome.** PowerPoint 2007 usually gives you several ways to choose the same option—by clicking a ribbon option, by right-clicking an object on a slide and then choosing from the shortcut menu that appears, or by pressing a key combination. Some folks prefer the speed of keyboard shortcuts; others like the satisfaction of a visual command array available in menus or toolbars. This book lists the alternatives so that you experiment to see which you like best.

About This Book

PowerPoint was never exactly known for its wonderful documentation. And while the whole point of PowerPoint 2007's radical interface overhaul was to make the program easier to use, "easier" doesn't mean you're going be able to sit down with the new program and bat out a presentation without some help. Fortunately, there *is* help—and you're holding it in your hands.

This is the book that *should* have come in the PowerPoint box. It explains all the ribbons and options and shows you step-by-step how to create slideshow from scratch. You'll learn tips and shortcuts for making PowerPoint easier to work with, as well as guidelines for making your slideshows support your presentation (as opposed to letting it take over your presentation).

PowerPoint 2007 for Starters: The Missing Manual is designed for readers just starting out with presentations. If PowerPoint 2007 is the first presentation program you've ever used, you'll be able to dive right in using the explanations and examples in this book.

About the Outline

PowerPoint 2007 for Starters: The Missing Manual is divided into three parts, each containing several chapters:

▶ **Part 1: Creating Slideshows** guides you through the creation of your very first slideshow in PowerPoint 2007, from adding and editing text, basic charts, diagrams, and tables, to reordering slides and creating reusable slide masters.

▶ **Part 2: Delivering Slideshows** outlines your options for getting your slideshow in front of your audience. You'll see how to run presentations onscreen and on an overhead projector, and package them up for email or CD. You'll also learn everything you need to know about printing slides, speaker notes, and handouts.

▶ **Part 3: Beyond Bullet Points—Graphics and Transitions** shows you how to add pictures, spreadsheets, sound and video clips, and macros to your slides to create compelling, audience-controlled presentations. You'll learn how to draw on your slides, record voice-over narration, add professional-looking slide transitions, and more.

At the end of the book, an appendix explains how to find your way around PowerPoint's built-in and online help pages. It also shows you how to get assistance from a vast online community of fans and experts.

About → These → Arrows

Both throughout this book specifically and the Missing Manual series as a whole, you'll find sentences like, "Click Start → All Programs → Microsoft Office → Microsoft Office PowerPoint 2007." Consider this shorthand to save you lots of extra words to describe how to get there—to a specific file or program or feature—from where you are. Otherwise, you'd have to read through, "Click on this button, and then choose this menu, then scan through the options on this sub-menu to find this which helps you get to this place over there." You've got better things to do with your time than read all those extra words—like putting together the next Great American presentation.

PowerPoint Examples

As you read the book's chapters, you'll encounter a number of step-by-step tutorials. You can work through them using any PowerPoint document of your own, or just begin a new PowerPoint document and start fresh.

About MissingManuals.com

At the missingmanuals.com Web site, you'll find articles, tips, and updates to this book. In fact, you're invited and encouraged to submit such corrections and updates yourself. In an effort to keep the book as up-to-date and accurate as possible, each time we print more copies of this book, we'll make any confirmed corrections you've suggested. We'll also note such changes on the Web site, so that you can mark important corrections into your own copy of the book, if you like. (Click the book's name, and then click the Errata link, to see the changes.)

In the meantime, we'd love to hear your own suggestions for new books in the Missing Manual line. There's a place for that on the Web site, too, as well as a place to sign up for free email notification of new titles in the series.

Safari® Enabled

 When you see a Safari® Enabled icon on the cover of your favorite technology book, that means the book is available online through the O'Reilly Network Safari Bookshelf.

Safari offers a solution that's better than e-books. It's a virtual library that lets you easily search thousands of top tech books, cut and paste code samples, download chapters, and find quick answers when you need the most accurate, current information. Try it for free at *http://safari.oreilly.com*.

PART ONE: CREATING SLIDESHOWS

CREATING A BASIC PRESENTATION

1

▶ Beginning a New Presentation

▶ Choosing a Theme for Your Presentation

▶ Adding Text

▶ Adding More Slides

▶ Moving Around Inside a Presentation

▶ Adding Speaker Notes

▶ Creating and Printing Handouts

▶ Saving and Closing a Presentation

▶ Running a Presentation

THIS CHAPTER WILL FAMILIARIZE YOU WITH POWERPOINT 2007 by walking you through the creation of a basic bullets-and-background slideshow presentation. You'll learn how to create a new slideshow, choose a look and feel, add text and slides, print speaker notes and handouts, and finally, how to unveil your masterpiece.

Beginning a New Presentation

You've got two basic choices when it comes to creating a new presentation:

▶ **You can start from scratch, using a blank canvas.** If you're familiar with earlier incarnations of the PowerPoint program, or if you're interested in learning the ins and outs of PowerPoint quickly, then you'll probably want to choose this option. (As daunting as "from scratch" sounds, you don't have to do all the work yourself; page 31 shows you how to apply a canned look and feel—or *theme*—to your new presentation.)

▶ **You can create a new presentation based on an existing template, theme, or presentation.** A *template* is a generic presentation file designed for you to reuse. Complete with themes (see the box on page 32), background images, and even generic content (such as page numbers and placeholder text), templates let you jump-start your presentation by giving you everything you need *except* your specific content. If you're creating a presentation for your local school board, for example, then you'll need to add the content that describes your findings, conclusions, and suggestions.

Templates are the better option when you need to crank out a presentation in a jiffy. PowerPoint comes with a handful of professionally designed templates and themes, but you can also create presentations based on a template, theme, or presentation that you've previously created, or one that you've found online and downloaded onto your computer.

Creating a New Presentation from Scratch

When you launch PowerPoint, the program starts you off with a brand-new presentation cleverly named Presentation1 (Figure 1-1).

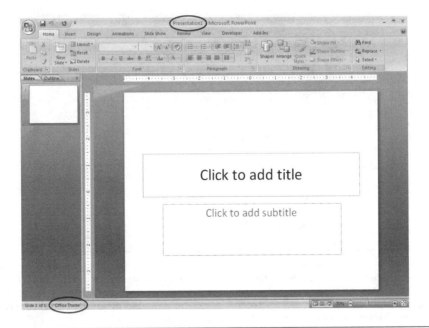

Figure 1-1. PowerPoint calls this a "blank" presentation even though technically it's not blank at all: It contains placeholders for the first slide's title and subtitle. Page 36 shows you how to change the Office theme that PowerPoint hands you to something more colorful and more artfully laid out.

Typically, you dive right in, adding a look and feel, text, pictures, and so on to the blank presentation PowerPoint hands you. But if you've closed or saved your freebie, here's how you create an additional blank presentation:

1. **Select Office button → New.**

   The New Presentation window (Figure 1-2) appears.

2. **On the left side of the New Presentation window, make sure the "Blank and recent" option is selected.**

   If it's not, click it to select it.

3. **In the New Presentation window, double-click Blank Presentation (Figure 1-2). Or you can click Blank Presentation and then click Create.**

   Either way, a new blank presentation named Presentation2 (or Presentation3, or Presentation4 depending on how many new presentations you've created since you launched the program) appears in your PowerPoint workspace.

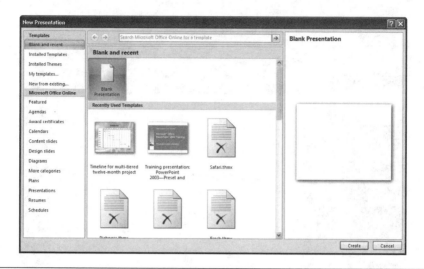

Figure 1-2. Because folks typically want to create a new presentation either from scratch or based on a favorite (and, therefore, recently used) template, the "Blank and recent" option is automatically selected. But you can choose instead to create a presentation based on an existing presentation, or on a theme or template you've created or downloaded from the Web.

TIP

To create a new blank presentation without going through the New Presentation window, press Ctrl+N.

To find out how to add content and design elements to your newly created presentation, zip down to page 39. Page 53 shows you how to save your new presentation.

Creating a Presentation from an Existing Template, Theme, or Presentation

PowerPoint lets you get a jump on your new presentation by starting with an existing template, theme, or presentation and then filling in your content. You can choose from the many templates and themes that come with PowerPoint, or you can go online and search for a specific template or theme that matches your needs. You can also reuse any of the templates, themes, or presentations that you (or your co-workers) have previously created. The following sections describe each of your options.

From an existing template

A *template* is a generic presentation designed (by Microsoft, by a third-party vendor, by you, or by whoever created the template) to be used again and again. Templates help you crank out presentations quickly, because all the design work has been done for you. All you have to do is add your content: the text, charts, graphics, and other elements that convey your particular message.

Templates vary widely, but all contain predefined *themes* (color schemes, background images, title and bullet point layouts, and text fonts). Some templates contain additional format and design elements and even some generic or placeholder content. Some templates are businesslike, with sober colors and artwork; some are whimsical, with wacky fonts and brightly colored balloons all over the place. The template motifs you can find are nearly endless, which makes it relatively easy to choose a template that fits the mood and structure you want to create for your presentation.

WORD TO THE WISE

The Trouble with Templates

The downside to using PowerPoint's pre-built templates is that you can end up with a presentation that looks exactly like the one Bob in Accounting presented last week. If that happens, then not only do you look bad, but your audience may tune out, assuming they've heard the same message before.

Another potential downside to using templates is that you may be tempted to shoehorn your presentation into the template—which is almost never a good idea.

Just keep in mind that to create an effective presentation, you need to focus first and foremost on your message, and *then* choose a template (or a theme, described on page 36) that supports your message. You may also want to consider tweaking the template—adjusting the font or replacing the background image with a tasteful gradient, for example—both to fit your message and to help ensure your presentation is as original and memorable as you are.

PowerPoint gives you four different options for creating a new presentation using an existing template: Recently used templates, Installed Templates, "My templates" (templates you've saved yourself), and Microsoft Office Online. The option you choose depends on where you want PowerPoint to hunt for the template, as described in the following sections.

Recently used templates. PowerPoint keeps track of the templates you apply to your presentations and displays the last few in a list. So if you tend to use the same two or three templates to create all your presentations, chances are you'll find this option the easiest.

Here's how to create a new presentation using a template you recently applied to another presentation:

1. **Select Office button → New.**

    The New Presentation window appears.

2. **In the left side of the New Presentation window, make sure the "Blank and recent" option is selected. (If it's not, click to select it.)**

3. **In the middle of the New Presentation window, scroll through the template thumbnails.**

    — TIP
    Mousing over a template briefly displays the location of the template (for example, *C:\Program Files\Microsoft Office\Templates\QuizShow.potx* for a built-in template stored on your computer, or Office Website for a template located on Microsoft's Web server). You might find this information useful if, for example, you're hunting for a template you remember finding online.

4. **Click to select the template you want to base your new presentation on.**

    In the right side of the New Presentation window, a preview appears (see Figure 1-3). Depending on whether the selected template is stored on your computer or on Microsoft's Web server, PowerPoint displays a Create or Download button, respectively, at the bottom of the New Presentation window.

5. **Click Create (or Download).**

    The New Presentation window disappears. (If you clicked Download, then a Downloading Template message flashes briefly on the screen.) PowerPoint then loads the selected template into a new presentation it names Presentation1 (or Presentation2, or Presentation3, depending on how many presentations you've created since you launched PowerPoint).

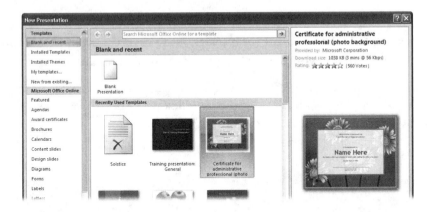

Figure 1-3. To see a larger version of a tiny template thumbnail—as well as to display any available identifying information, such as the template's file size and popularity rating—simply click to select the template.

Installed templates. When you installed PowerPoint, you automatically installed a handful of professionally designed templates, including templates that let you set up photo albums (Classic Photo Album and Contemporary Photo Album), corporate-style slideshows (Corporate Presentation), layouts for print publications (Pitchbook), animated question-and-answer tutorials (Quiz Show), and big-screen slideshows (Wide Screen Presentation 16×9).

To use one of these built-in templates to create a new presentation, follow these steps:

1. **Select Office button → New.**

   The New Presentation window appears.

2. **In the left side of the New Presentation window, click Installed Templates.**

   Several template thumbnails appear in the middle of the New Presentation window.

3. Click a template to select it.

A larger version of the template appears in the preview area (the right side) of the New Presentation window.

4. Click Create.

The New Presentation window disappears, and you see a new presentation file based on the template you selected. Figure 1-4 shows you an example.

— TIP ——————————————————————————————

Instead of clicking a template and then clicking Create, you can save a step by simply double-clicking the template.

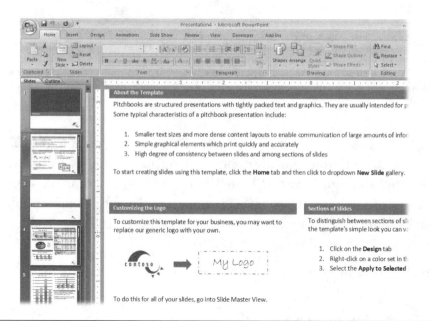

Figure 1-4. Templates are nothing more than presentations for which someone (the template author) has defined Slide and Title masters. Masters, which you'll learn all about in Chapter 5, define the way your slides look overall (like this crisp, clean background) as well as the way your text looks (the color and font). Templates also typically include helpful slide layouts and content, like the attractive section headings and replaceable text shown here.

My templates. Each time you create your own template (page 54) or download a template from Microsoft's Web site (page 30), PowerPoint automatically stores the template in a special directory on your computer similar to this one: *C:\Documents and Settings\[Your Name]\Application Date\Microsoft\Templates.*

To use one of these templates to create a new presentation, follow these steps:

1. **Select Office button → New.**

   The New Presentation window appears.

2. **On the left side of the New Presentation window, click "My templates."**

   The New Presentation window vanishes, and the New Presentation dialog box shown in Figure 1-5 appears.

3. **In the New Presentation dialog box, select the template you want to use and click OK.**

   The New Presentation dialog box disappears, and PowerPoint displays a new presentation file based on the template you selected.

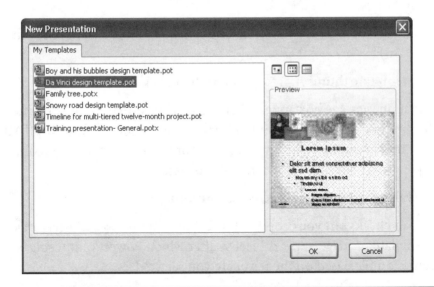

Figure 1-5. PowerPoint stores the templates you create—or that you download from Microsoft's Office Online Web site—in a special folder so that you won't confuse them with PowerPoint's built-in templates. To change how the template icons appear, choose from Large Icons (which makes the template names easier to read), List (shown here), and Details (which displays the date the template was created).

Online. Although lots of Web sites offer PowerPoint templates for download, you should check Microsoft's Office Online Web site first for a couple of reasons. One, Microsoft's templates are free; and two, checking Microsoft's site is one-click easy, as described next.

> **TIP**
>
> Because Microsoft lets its customers upload templates willy-nilly, the quantity and quality of the templates you find on its site can vary widely. Figure 1-6 shows how to weed out customer-submitted templates, leaving only those designed by official Microsofties.

1. **Select Office button → New.**

   The New Presentation window appears.

2. **On the left side of the New Presentation window, under Microsoft Office Online, choose the type of template you're looking for, such as Brochures or Content Slides.**

   Template thumbnails appear in the center of the New Presentation window (Figure 1-6).

3. **Click a template thumbnail to select it; then click Download.**

   A validation message box appears, letting you know that Microsoft is gearing up to check your copy of PowerPoint to make sure it's not bootlegged. (If Microsoft doesn't find a legitimately purchased copy of PowerPoint on your computer, then you won't be able to download templates.)

4. **In the validation message box, click Continue.**

   Microsoft checks out your copy of PowerPoint. If it passes muster, a Downloading Template message appears briefly, after which PowerPoint displays a new presentation file based on the template you selected.

The rest of this chapter shows you how to add text and change the look of your newly created presentation.

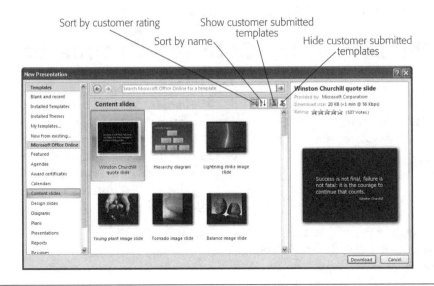

Sort by customer rating

Sort by name

Show customer submitted templates

Hide customer submitted templates

Figure 1-6. For finer control over the templates you see, select Rating Sort (which displays the most popular templates first, as determined by other PowerPoint fans), Name Sort (which displays named templates in alphabetical order), Show Customer Submitted (which displays all templates, including the ones other PowerPoint folks have uploaded), or Hide Customer Submitted (which shows only those templates created by Microsoft).

From an existing (built-in) theme

If you know which theme you want to apply to the new presentation you're creating, then you can save a click or two by applying it when you create the presentation file. (The alternative is to create the presentation file and *then* apply the theme, as described on page 36.)

To create a new presentation based on one of the themes that comes with Power-Point:

1. **Select Office button → New.**

    The New Presentation window appears.

2. **On the left side of the New Presentation window, click Installed Themes.**

    Several theme thumbnails appear in the middle of the New Presentation window.

The Difference Between Templates and Themes

In PowerPoint 2007, you have two separate and distinct ways to customize your presentations—*templates* and *themes*.

* **Templates.** A template is any presentation you plan to reuse. You tell PowerPoint—and remind yourself and your coworkers—that you plan to reuse it by saving it in the special template file format, .potx. Templates typically define custom slide layouts and, in some cases, generic content. Every template has a theme.

* **Themes.** A theme tells PowerPoint what color to use for your slides' titles, subtitles, body text, background, and so forth. It also describes which fonts and graphic effects to use; for example, some themes automatically add shadows to title text and blurring to the shapes you add to your slides.

3. **Click a theme to select it.**

   A larger version of the theme appears in the preview area (the right side) of the New Presentation window.

4. **Click Create.**

   The New Presentation window disappears and you see a new presentation based on the theme you selected. Figure 1-7 shows you an example.

— TIP —

Instead of clicking a theme and then clicking Create, you can save a step by simply double-clicking the theme.

From an existing presentation

If you've already got a presentation on your computer—created in any version of PowerPoint—then you can load that presentation into PowerPoint 2007 and use it as the basis of a new presentation.

Figure 1-7. Unlike applying a template to a newly created presentation, applying a theme doesn't start you out with custom slide layouts or content. Instead—as you can see by the single slide shown here—themes give you coordinated color, font, and background effects. PowerPoint automatically applies these effects to each new slide you create.

You've got two options for loading an existing presentation: the New From Existing Presentation window, which is a good choice if you've never used PowerPoint before; and the Open window, which is handy if you're familiar with PowerPoint.

NOTE

A third, quickie alternative exists for creating a new presentation from an existing one—but this alternative works only if you've recently edited the existing presentation. To try it out, click the Office button and then, from the list of Recent Documents that appears, choose an existing document. After PowerPoint opens the document, immediately save it (Office button → Save As) with a different name.

The New from Existing Presentation window

If you're new to PowerPoint, then you'll appreciate the New from Existing Presentation window, which simplifies the process of opening an existing presentation. And unlike using the Open window, using the New from Existing Presentation window automatically generates a new file name, so you don't have to worry about accidentally overwriting your original presentation.

To create a presentation using the New from Existing Presentation window:

1. **Select Office button → New.**

   The New Presentation window appears.

2. **Click "New from existing."**

   The New from Existing Presentation window appears.

3. **Select the file you want to open, as described in Figure 1-8, and then click Create New.**

   The New from Existing Presentation window disappears, and the presentation you selected appears in your PowerPoint workspace. PowerPoint gives the presentation a new, generic name (PowerPoint2, PowerPoint3, and so on) to remind you to rename the file before you save it. (Page 54 shows you how to rename files.)

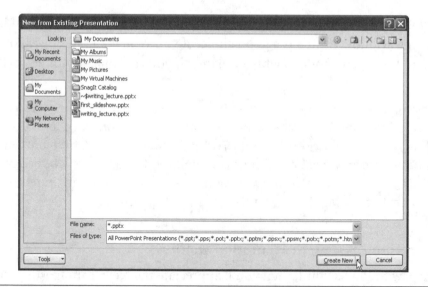

Figure 1-8. To browse your computer for an existing PowerPoint file, either click the folder icons you see on the left side of the window, or click the "Look in" drop-down menu. When you see the Power-Point file you're looking for, click it to select it. Then click Create New to load it into PowerPoint under a new name.

The Open window

The Open window gives you more options for opening an existing presentation than the New from Existing window does. You'll find these options useful in certain situations, such as when you want to protect an existing presentation by opening it in read-only mode, read through all the slides to make sure it's the one you want, and *then* save a copy.

To open an existing presentation using the Open window:

1. **Choose Office button → Open (or press Ctrl+O).**

    The Open window shown in Figure 1-9 appears.

2. **Select the file you want to open, either by clicking the folder icons you see on the left side of the window, or by clicking the "Look in" drop-down menu. When the PowerPoint file you're looking for appears in the list, click it to select it.**

> **TIP**
> To see a preview of each file on the right side of the Open window as you select it, click the Open window's Views icon (Figure 1-9) and select Preview.

3. **Choose one of the following options:**

    ▶ **Open.** Opens the selected file.

    ▶ **Open → Open Read-Only.** Opens a protected version of the file that lets you make changes to the presentation, but doesn't let you save them unless you specify a new filename.

    ▶ **Open → Open as Copy.** Opens the presentation file, but renames it *Copy(1)filename.pptx*.

    ▶ **Open → Open in Browser.** Opens the selected HTML file in Internet Explorer (or your default browser).

    ▶ **Open → Open and Repair.** Tells PowerPoint to fix a corrupted file before it tries to open it.

    The file you selected appears in your PowerPoint workspace.

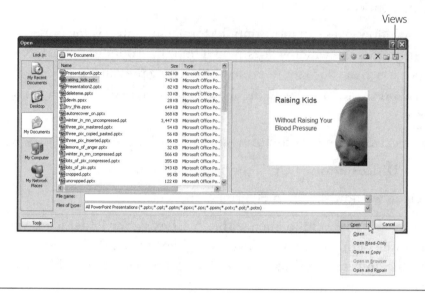

Views

Figure 1-9. To open a file quickly, double-click it (instead of selecting it and then clicking Open or one of the Open options).

Choosing a Theme for Your Presentation

No matter which approach you use to create a presentation—from scratch, from an existing presentation, from a template, or from a built-in theme—once you have a presentation, you can change how it looks in one fell swoop by changing its *theme*.

A *theme* is a collection of characteristics including colors, fonts, and graphic effects (such as whether the shapes you add to your slides have drop shadows). For example, applying the built-in Deluxe theme turns your background a tasteful shade of blue and displays your title text (which appears in the Corbel font) in an attractively contrasting, gently shadowed shade of yellow—all thanks to the theme. You can change all of these characteristics individually, of course, as you'll see in Chapter 4. But applying themes gives you more bang for your buck in several important ways:

▶ **Using themes is quicker than changing individual settings one at a time.** Applying a theme is a two-click proposition. Changing the dozen-plus settings controlled by a theme would exercise your click finger a lot more than that. And themes save you time you'd otherwise spend figuring out which colors look good together.

▶ **Using themes helps ensure a decent-looking, readable slide.** Consistency is an important design principle: it sets the tone for your presentation and lets your audience focus on your message. When you change settings manually, you can end up with a distracting mishmash of colors and fonts on a single slide or across slides. Not so with themes. Once you apply a theme, the theme takes control of your settings. If you change the background color of your slides, then the theme automatically changes the title and subtitle fonts to compatible colors—colors that aren't just readable against your new background, but attractive, too.

▶ **Using themes lets you create a consistent look and feel across Microsoft Office-produced materials.** You can use the same themes you use in PowerPoint in Word and Excel, too. When you apply the same theme to your Word documents, Excel spreadsheets, and PowerPoint slides, you end up with a consistently presented, harmonious whole.

Here's how to apply a theme to a PowerPoint presentation:

1. **Click the Design tab.**

   The Design ribbon appears, complete with a Theme gallery (Figure 1-10). (For more on PowerPoint 2007's new ribbons, check out page 7.)

Figure 1-10. The Themes section of the Design ribbon contains just a snippet of the Themes gallery; to see more themes, you need to click the More icon.

2. **Click the More icon at the bottom-right corner of the Themes section (Figure 1-10).**

   Additional themes appear in the gallery, as shown in Figure 1-11.

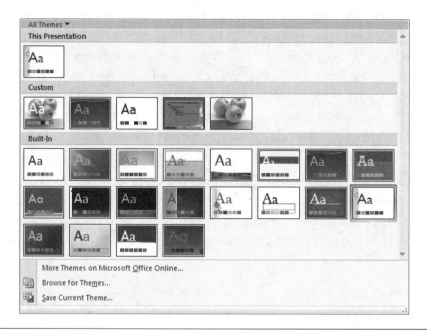

Figure 1-11. You can find additional themes on the Web and download them into PowerPoint by clicking "More Themes on Microsoft Office Online."

3. **Mouse over the themes in the gallery one by one.**

PowerPoint previews each theme as you mouse over it (Figure 1-12) so you can get an idea of how each will look applied to your presentation's content and layout.

NOTE

If you mouse over a theme and PowerPoint doesn't immediately preview it on your slide, wait a few seconds: the process is quick, but it's not instantaneous.

---

4. **Click a theme to select it.**

PowerPoint applies the selected theme to all of the existing slides in your presentation, as well as all the new slides you create.

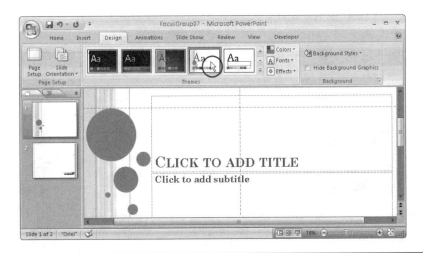

Figure 1-12. No more clicking Preview or Apply and waiting around: simply mousing over a theme temporarily applies it to your presentation. To apply the theme for good, click the theme to select it. If you change your mind, you can revert back to your presentation's original theme by applying the Office Theme theme.

___ **TIP** ___

> PowerPoint lets you apply a theme to only selected slides. Applying more than one theme to a slideshow is useful when you're creating a distinct before-and-after presentation or other multi-section slideshow and want each section to look distinct. For details, check out Chapter 4.

Adding Text

You'll want to add at least some text to most, if not all, PowerPoint presentations you create. (See the box on page 42 for advice on how much prose to add to your presentation.) Knowing that, the PowerPoint designers made it easy for you to add text to your slides. The following sections show you how.

Adding Text to an Existing Text Box

When you start to work with a new presentation, the ribbon displays the Home tab (Figure 1-13).

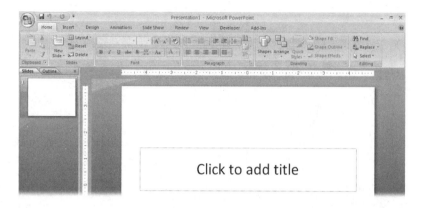

Figure 1-13. Until you click a text box, most of the options appear grayed out, meaning you can't use them. See Figure 1-14 for a glimpse of the subtitle box.

Blank presentations come complete with title and subtitle placeholder text boxes. To replace the placeholder text in either of these two text boxes with your own text, simply click inside the placeholder and begin typing. When you do, two things happen:

▶ **PowerPoint displays the Drawing Tools | Format tab and, on the Home ribbon, activates many of the text formatting options (Figure 1-14).** You can use these options to change the font, size, and color of your text, turn your text into a right-justified paragraph or a bullet point, and much more. (Chapter 3 describes your options in detail.)

▶ **Resize and transform handles appear at the corners and edges of the text box (Figure 1-14).** Tiny white *resize handles*, which are square on the edges of the text box and circular on the corners, let you stretch or shrink your text box by dragging them. The circular green *transform handle* appears above the top of your text box and lets you tilt it. Drag the handles to tilt or resize your text box.

Adding a New Text Box

You're not limited to the placeholder text boxes PowerPoint starts you off with: you can add as many additional text boxes to your slides as you like.

Figure 1-14. As soon as you click a text box, PowerPoint activates the text formatting and drawing tools and reveals the Drawing Tools | Format tab. Now, in addition to typing your text, you can format it, change its color, or add an effect (such as a glow or bevel). Drag any of the eight white resize handles to resize your text box; drag the circular green transform handle to rotate the text box. Chapter 3 covers text manipulation in more detail.

To add a new text box to a slide:

1. **Click the Insert tab.**

   The Insert ribbon (Figure 1-15) appears.

Figure 1-15. As you can see in the Text section of the Insert ribbon, PowerPoint makes it easy to add not just text boxes, but headers, footers, date- and timestamps, and more.

2. **On the Insert ribbon, click Text Box.**

   In the status bar at the bottom of the screen, PowerPoint displays a helpful hint ("Click and drag to insert a text box"). When you mouse over your slide, you notice that your cursor looks like a tiny down arrow.

The Evils (or Not) of Text

There are two schools of thought when it comes to using text in PowerPoint presentations. One says text is king; the other advises PowerPointers to use as little text as possible. Here's the rationale for each approach:

* **Text rules—always has, always will.** According to the more-bullets-the-better crowd, a presentation *is* text. Period. It's how we think, it's what we're used to, and it helps us organize our thoughts, reactions, and questions.

* **Text distracts.** The other school of thought is that it's nearly impossible for audiences to read more than a couple of words on a slide, even if they're sitting up front and wearing their glasses. And if your audience *does* read your slides, that means they're busy reading and forming opinions instead of paying attention to the actual presentation (which is *you*). Using a lot of text may result in ineffective and boring brain dumps disguised as presentations.

So which approach should you take? In a perfect world, you'd have time to create super-compelling graphics that beautifully complement your presentation. You'd deliver the message of your presentation by engaging your audience with your wit, knowledge, body language, and persuasive powers. You'd use text sparingly and appropriately: to pose questions (which you'd answer in your talk) and to hammer home main points.

Ultimately, you get to make the call. As long as you choose an approach that supports your presentation goals, you're golden.

3. **On the slide, click where you want your new text box to appear.**

   A text box appears with the cursor handily positioned inside (Figure 1-16). The Drawing Tools | Format tab pops up, and on the Home ribbon, PowerPoint activates most of the formatting options, ready for you to format your text.

   — NOTE
   Alternatively, you can click and drag to draw the outline of your text box before you begin typing. It's another step, but it'll help you get an idea of how much space your text will take up on your slide *before* you actually type it in.

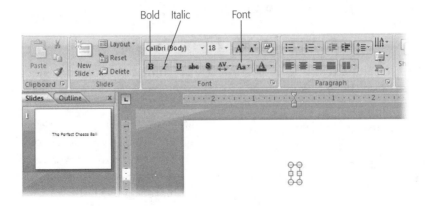

Figure 1-16. Choosing one or more formatting options (such as Bold, Italics, or Font) before you begin typing tells PowerPoint to apply those options to your text automatically as you type. (You'll find more on formatting in Chapter 3.)

4. **Type your text.**

   The text box expands automatically to accommodate your text.

Adding More Slides

When you create a new blank presentation, PowerPoint spots you one slide. But in most cases, you'll want your presentation to contain a lot more slides than that. Fortunately, adding a new slide is easy, as you'll see in the following sections.

PowerPoint gives you two options: adding a slide with layout identical to the current slide, and specifying a different slide layout. A *slide layout* is a description of what content appears where on a slide. For example, applying a Title Slide layout to a slide positions title and subtitle text placeholders near the middle of your slide, and nothing else. Applying a Title and Content layout positions a title text placeholder near the top of a slide, and an object placeholder beneath that.

To add a slide with a layout identical to the current slide:

1. **Select any non-title slide.**

   PowerPoint doesn't automatically duplicate title slides for a pretty obvious reason: 99 percent of the time, you don't want two title slides in a single presentation. For the one percent of the time when that's exactly what you want, add a slide, and then change the slide's layout to Title Slide as shown on page 116.

Using Text Effectively

If you choose to include text in your presentation, then keep these tips in mind:

✳ **Distill.** Your audience's eyes will glaze over if you hit them with a barrage of text on every slide, so you want to distill your message into as few words as possible. (Three to six bullets and a dozen or so words per slide is a good guideline.) In other words, reserve text for the few salient points you want your audience to take home with them. When you need back-up documentation, examples, supporting facts and figures, and so on, distribute hard-copy handouts—don't try to cram the information onto your slides.

✳ **Carefully consider word placement.** The Space Shuttle Columbia disaster a few years back put PowerPoint in the limelight for a sobering reason: In a PowerPoint presentation delivered to NASA officials *before* the disaster, engineers mentioned the problem that, ultimately, contributed to the tragic breakup of the shuttle over Texas in 2003. But the crucial information was buried in an avalanche of bullet points near the end of a long presentation, and none of the decision-makers in the audience realized its significance. Moral of the story: reserve the first and last slides of your presentation for critical information.

2. **Click the Home tab.**

   The ribbon you see in Figure 1-17 appears.

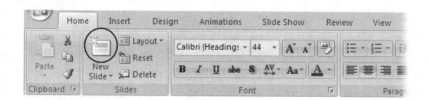

Figure 1-17. Clicking the New Slide button is the quickest way to add a slide to your presentation. You can always change the layout, of course, but when you want to add a different kind of slide—say, one with a subtitle or columns—you can save yourself some time by choosing a new slide layout right off the bat, as shown on page 45.

3. **Click the New Slide button.**

    PowerPoint inserts a new slide after the current slide. If that's not what you want (for example, if you want to add a slide to the beginning of your presentation), then you can easily change the order of your slides. Page 142 shows you how.

TIP

PowerPoint gives you another way to add a new slide with a layout similar to the current slide. In the Slides pane (at the left side of your workspace, as shown in Figure 1-16), you can right-click the page after which you want to create a new slide. Then, from the menu that appears, select Duplicate.

To add a slide with a different layout:

1. **On the Home ribbon, click the down-arrow next to New Slide.**

    A menu similar to the one you see in Figure 1-18 appears.

2. **Click to select the slide layout you want. Your choices include Title Slide, Title and Content, Section Header, Two Content, Comparison, Title Only, Blank, Content with Caption, and Picture with Caption.**

    PowerPoint adds your new slide after the current slide.

TIP

To make an exact copy of the current slide—content and all—make sure you have the slide selected in the Slides pane, and then press Ctrl+D.

Moving Around Inside a Presentation

Moving around your presentation when you only have one slide isn't much of an issue. But once you start adding slides, you'll want a way to hop quickly from your first slide to your last. You'll also want to jump to specific slides in the middle of your presentation; for example, to tweak a particular slide's layout, to add content, or to delete it.

PowerPoint gives you several ways to flip through your presentation. This section acquaints you with the easiest and most useful options: using your workspace scroll bar, using the View pane on the left side of the screen, and using the Home ribbon's Find function.

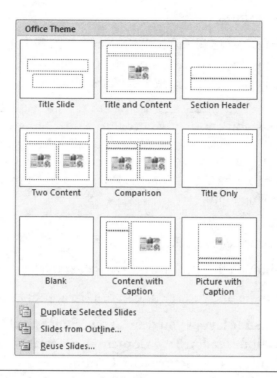

Figure 1-18. The appearance and number of slide layouts you see in this menu depend on the theme (and template, if any) you've applied to your presentation. If you add a slide and then change your mind, you can either click Undo (Ctrl+Z), or delete the slide by choosing Home → Delete.

Navigating with the Scroll Bar

In PowerPoint, you see a scroll bar on the right side of your workspace similar to the one in Figure 1-19.

To scroll through your presentation, all you need to do is click the scroll bar and drag up (to scroll toward the beginning of your presentation) or down (to scroll toward the end). As you go, PowerPoint displays each slide in turn.

TIP

To flip forward (or back) through your presentation one slide at a time, click the Next Slide (or Previous Slide) arrow shown in Figure 1-19.

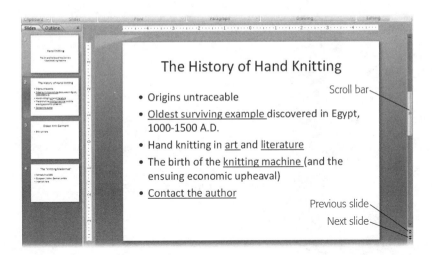

Figure 1-19. If you've got more than one slide, the vertical scroll bars always appear in PowerPoint, no matter which tab you select or which ribbon appears at the top of your workspace. Scrolling tells PowerPoint to display slides not just in the main workspace, but also to display thumbnail versions in the Slides pane.

Navigation with the Slides and Outline Tabs

Slides and Outline tabs are not views (they both appear in Normal view) but are tabs that let you see slide thumbnails or an outline of your slideshow, respectively, in the Slides (Figure 1-20) or Outline (Figure 1-21) pane.

PowerPoint assumes you want to use Slides view until you tell it otherwise. To change views, click the Outline tab shown in Figure 1-21. To switch back to Slides view, click the Slides tab.

> **NOTE**
>
> If you don't see the View pane at all, select View → Normal (or click the Normal icon shown in Figure 1-20) to display it.

Using Find

When you've got a lot of slides and you're looking for one containing a specific word or phrase, you'll want to bypass Views in favor of the Find function. Similar to

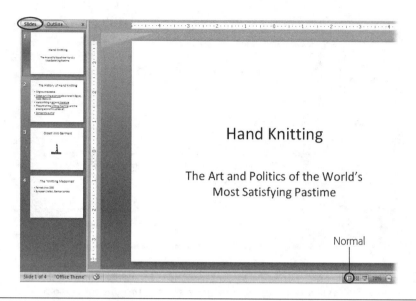

Figure 1-20. Here, the Slides tab is selected. You're viewing the contents of the first (selected) slide.

the Find feature in other Windows programs, PowerPoint's Find function lets you search for specific words quickly and easily. Here's how to use it.

1. **Press Ctrl+F.**

   The Find dialog box appears (Figure 1-22).

2. **In the "Find what" box, type in the text you want to find (in Figure 1-22, the text is *marshmallow*).**

   If you like, you can click to turn on the "Match case" checkbox (which tells PowerPoint to look for *marshmallow* but not *Marshmallow*, *MARSHMALLOW*, or *MaRsHmAlLoW*) or the "Find whole words only" checkbox (which tells PowerPoint to look for *marshmallow* but not *chocolatemarshmallowgraham*). When you finish, click Find Next.

   PowerPoint displays the slide containing your text. If it doesn't find a match, it shows this message: "PowerPoint has finished searching the presentation. The search item wasn't found."

Figure 1-21. Here's the same presentation in outline form. To banish the View pane altogether, click the X in the upper-right corner. To resize it, simply drag the resize handle on the right side of the pane. (In keeping with its new-and-improved design philosophy, PowerPoint doesn't let you make the View pane larger than one-quarter of the total interface.)

Figure 1-22. Another way to display this Find box is to head to the Editing section of the Home tab and then click the Find button. Chapter 2 shows you how to use the more advanced Find functions, including Replace, which lets you automatically replace the text you find with different text.

Adding Speaker Notes

Speaker notes are optional text notes you can type into PowerPoint. You can associate a separate speaker note with each slide of your presentation. Your audience can't see speaker notes, but you can. You may find speaker notes useful:

▶ **While you're putting your presentation together.** If you know you need to add a graphic to slide six and a couple of bullet points to slide 33, then you can jot down reminders to yourself in the Speaker Notes pane (Figure 1-23). Then, before you put your presentation to bed, you can view your speaker notes and double-check that you've caught everything.

▶ **While you're delivering your presentation.** You can set up your presentation so that your audience sees your slideshow on the screen while you see your notes (on your own computer monitor). Or, if you're the tactile type, you may prefer to print out your speaker notes and keep them with your during your presentation.

To add speaker notes for a particular slide, click in the Speaker Notes pane (Figure 1-23) and type away.

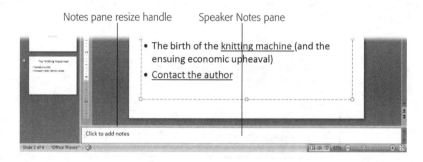

Figure 1-23. Speaker notes are specific to individual slides, so when you select a new slide, PowerPoint displays a fresh, clean Speaker Notes pane. You can make the pane bigger by dragging the resize handle.

___ NOTE ___

If you don't see the Speaker Notes pane, then click the Speaker Notes pane's resize bar at the bottom of the workspace and drag upward, as shown in Figure 1-24.

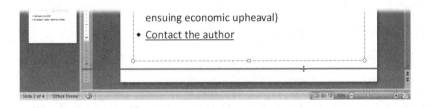

Figure 1-24. Depending on the view you choose, the Speaker Notes pane doesn't always appear automatically—and it's not obvious that you can drag the resize bar at the bottom of the workspace to display it. Fortunately, you can. The farther you drag, the larger the notes display (and the smaller the slide display).

Creating and Printing Handouts

You don't have to do anything special to create handouts in PowerPoint. That's because *handouts* in PowerPoint are nothing more than slides printed one or more to a page.

FROM THE FIELD

Handouts: Killing Trees Unnecessarily?

If you think your audience will benefit from printouts of your slides, then by all means, go for it. Say your presentation slides consist of graphic images accompanied by a few well-placed questions. What you want is a participatory, interactive presentation. Your audience should listen to you and jot down the answers to those questions—and what better way to encourage this interaction than to pass out hard copies of each slide?

But for some presentations, slide printouts are pretty worthless. Instead, you're going to want to give your audience printouts containing facts, figures, contact information, and other in-depth supporting information that you didn't have room for in your actual presentation.

One way to jump-start the process of creating truly useful handouts is to pull your PowerPoint presentation text into Word 2007 (assuming you have a copy installed on your computer). Using your presentation text as a starting point, you can add information until you've built handouts your audience will actually take back to their homes and offices.

To pull your slides into a Word document, click Office button → Publish → Create Handouts in Microsoft Office Word.

To print handouts:

1. **Select Office button → Print → Print Preview.**

    The Print Preview ribbon appears, and PowerPoint's best guess at how you want your handouts printed appears in the workspace.

2. **Click the "Print what" drop-down box and then, from the menu that appears, choose how you want PowerPoint to print your handouts (Figure 1-25).**

    PowerPoint redisplays the handouts preview based on your selection.

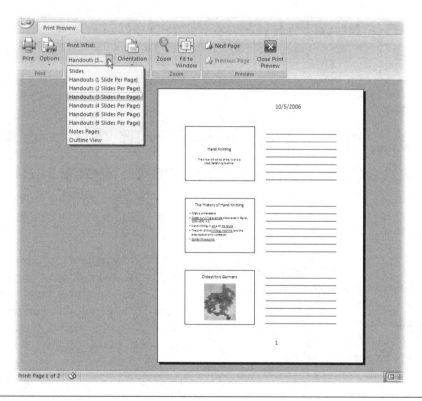

Figure 1-25. You can tell PowerPoint to print up to nine slides per page. Here, you see the effect of printing three per page, which is a nice compromise: large enough to read the slides, but roomy enough for note taking.

3. Click Print.

The familiar Print dialog box appears.

NOTE _____

Chapter 8, which shows you how to print your presentation, walks you through the Print dialog box step by step.

_____

4. Click OK.

PowerPoint prints your handouts.

5. Click Close Print Preview (Figure 1-25) to dismiss the Print Preview ribbon and return to your workspace.

Saving and Closing a Presentation

Lightning storms hit, coffee cups spill, and power cords work themselves out of walls (especially if you have a dog who likes to chase squeaky toys). After you've created a new presentation file and spent some time working on it, you'll want to save it every so often so that when your system crashes, you can recover your work. And if you're like most folks, you'll also want to save and close your presentation each time you wrap up a work session.

Saving and closing a PowerPoint presentation are both straightforward tasks. If you're familiar with any other Windows programs, then you'll recognize most of the steps.

To save a newly created presentation:

1. Select Office button → Save.

The Save As dialog box appears (Figure 1-26).

NOTE _____

Alternatively, you can press Ctrl+S or click the Save button (the little diskette icon) that appears in the Quick Access toolbar.

_____

2. **Click the "Save in" drop-down box to choose a directory to store your file in. In the File name field, type a new name for your file.**

Shoot for short, unique, and memorable; you don't want to have to spend a lot of time hunting for your file a week from now.

3. **Click the "Save as Type" drop-down box to select a file format. Most of the time, you'll choose the .pptx format.**

The box on page 55 explains your options. For example, to save your presentation as a template that you can use over and over, choose .potx.

4. **Click Save.**

The Save As dialog box disappears and PowerPoint saves the file in the format you specified.

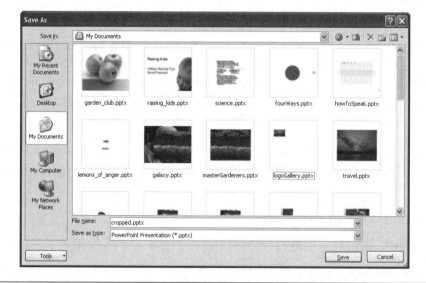

Figure 1-26. Most of the time, when you're ready to save your presentation, you'll choose the .pptx file type (a plain-vanilla PowerPoint 2007 presentation) or .ppt (the old, pre-2007 PowerPoint format). But you've got about a dozen choices, including the template (.potx) and show (.ppsx) formats.

To *close* a presentation, simply select Office → Close. When you do, PowerPoint closes your presentation with no fanfare. If you've never saved this particular file, however, a dialog box pops up asking you if you want to save the changes you made. Click Yes to display the Save As dialog box shown in Figure 1-26 and proceed as described above.

PowerPoint 2007 File Types

PowerPoint 2007 (and Office 2007 more generally) introduces a slew of new file types, complete with unfamiliar file extensions. Here they are, in a nutshell:

* **.pptx** (PowerPoint 2007 presentation). Most of the time, you want to save your file in this format.

* **.potx** (PowerPoint 2007 template). Lets you save a presentation as a reusable design template.

* **.potm** (PowerPoint 2007 macro-enabled design template). Lets programmers save a macro-filled presentation as a design template.

* **.ppsx** (PowerPoint 2007 show). Lets you save this file as a PowerPoint show that folks can run using the PowerPoint viewer, as described in Chapter 7.

* **.ppsm** (PowerPoint 2007 macro-enabled show). Lets programmers save a macro-filled presentation as a show.

* **.ppam** (PowerPoint 2007 add-in). Lets programmers save presentations that actually add to PowerPoint's interface.

* **.pptm** (PowerPoint 2007 macro-enabled presentation). Lets programmers save presentations that contain macros.

* **.thmx** (Microsoft Office Theme). Lets you save your presentation as a reusable collection of colors, fonts, and graphic effects so that you can apply it to another PowerPoint slideshow, Word document, or Excel spreadsheet.

* **.ppt** (PowerPoint 2003—and earlier—presentation). Lets you save your presentation in a form that folks running PowerPoint 2003 can edit.

PowerPoint 2007 also handles the same file types as earlier versions, including .ppt, .pps, .htm, and so on.

Running a Presentation

Chapter 7 shows you everything you need to know about setting up and running special types of presentations: for example, recording narration, hiding certain slides, and creating stand-alone presentations that run on kiosks. But for running through a basic presentation on your very own computer, the process is simple:

1. **Press F5 or click the Slideshow icon you see at the bottom of the screen, as shown in Figure 1-27.**

    PowerPoint replaces your workspace with a full-screen version of your slideshow, beginning with the currently selected slide.

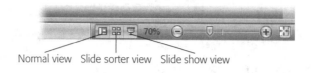

Normal view   Slide sorter view   Slide show view

Figure 1-27. Clicking the Slideshow icon at the bottom of your workspace is one of the easiest ways to run your presentation.

TIP

> Pressing Shift+F5 and clicking the Slideshow icon both tell PowerPoint to run your slideshow beginning at the current slide (not necessarily the *first* slide). To run your slideshow from the beginning, you have three choices: press F5, click the Slideshow icon, or select Slide Show → Start Slide Show → From Beginning.

---

2. **Click the forward and backward arrows that appear at the bottom of the screen (Figure 1-28) to step through your presentation. (Figure 1-28 describes how to end the presentation before the last slide.)**

   After the last slide, PowerPoint displays a black screen containing the words "End of slide show, click to exit."

Back   Ink   Slide   Next

Figure 1-28. PowerPoint displays ghosted controls (Back, Ink, Slide, and Next) when you run a presentation. Mousing over these controls highlights them so you can see where to click. To end your slideshow immediately without having to flip through every last slide, you have two choices: either hit Esc or click the Slide icon and then, from the menu that appears, choose End Show.

---

3. **Click anywhere on the screen (or press the Space bar or Enter).**

   PowerPoint returns you to your workspace.

EDITING SLIDES

▶ Editing Text

▶ Reversing an Action (Undo)

▶ Finding and Replacing Text Automatically

▶ Checking Spelling

▶ Adding Special Characters

TEXT IS THE HEART AND SOUL of an effective PowerPoint presentation. But coming up with just the right words—and organizing them in just the right way—isn't always easy. Just as you would if you were constructing a presentation using a flip chart or overhead transparencies, you jot down a few bullet points, read through what you've written, think of a few additional points, change your mind, and end up deleting, rearranging, and editing your material over and over again until you've got every word on every page (*slide*) exactly right.

Fortunately, PowerPoint can help. In addition to the standard cut, copy, and paste operations, this chapter shows you how to use PowerPoint's Search and Replace feature to find words and phrases buried in long presentations and change (or delete) them quickly. And if spelling's not your speciality, PowerPoint can help you check it.

Editing Text

When you change the text on a PowerPoint slide—when you cut it, copy it, replace it, or move it around—what you're doing is *editing* your text. To see most of the editing tools PowerPoint offers, all you have to do is take a look at the ribbon's Home tab (Figure 2-1). The following sections describe each editing tool in detail.

> **NOTE**
>
> In contrast, when you change the way your text *looks*—when you make it bold, italicize it, choose a different font or background color for it, and so on—what you're doing is *formatting*. Chapter 3 tells you all you need to know about formatting text.

Selecting Text

Before you can do anything to the text on your slides, you first have to select it. Text can appear in any of three places on a slide: in one of the title or subtitle place-holder text boxes that PowerPoint automatically adds to your slide; in a text box that you've added to a slide (page 40), or in a shape that you've added to a slide (page 261).

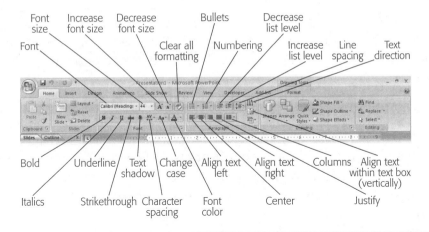

Figure 2-1. Clicking the Home tab shows you your editing options, but you can't actually use any of them until you click inside a text box. When you do, PowerPoint activates the text editing options (except Paste and Clipboard, which remain grayed out until you cut or copy text; in other words, until you have something to paste from the Clipboard) and the Drawing Tools | Format tab appears.

To select text:

1. **Click anywhere in an existing text box, placeholder text box, or on a shape.**

   PowerPoint highlights the outline of the text box you clicked in. In addition, PowerPoint displays the Drawing Tools/Format context tab and activates the text-related options in the Home tab—underlining, font size, alignment, and so on.

   > **NOTE**
   >
   > When you click in a placeholder text box (one that says *Click to add title* or *Click to add subtitle*), PowerPoint erases the placeholder text. (Placeholder text doesn't appear in Slide Show view, nor does it appear when you run your slideshow; it's just there to remind you to type your own text.)

2. **Drag to select as much text as you like.**

   Alternatively, you can press Shift and use the arrow keys (or click again). Or double-click to quickly select a single word. To select *discontinuous* words or phrases, press Ctrl while you select each word or phrase.

   Whichever method you use, PowerPoint highlights the text you select.

Cutting Text

As you edit and reorganize the content of your slideshow, you may run into a situation where you want to remove text from one slide and either ditch it permanently or reserve it so that you can paste it back into your slideshow later (on a different slide, perhaps).

Cutting text was designed for just such situations. When you cut text, you remove it from your slide and stow it away for safekeeping on the Office Clipboard. You can then choose to paste the cut text back onto the original slide or another slide; if you don't, eventually the Office Clipboard simply discards it. The box on the next page tells you more about the Clipboard.

To cut text:

1. **Select the text you want to cut (see the previous section).**

   PowerPoint highlights the selected text.

2. **Choose Home → Clipboard → Cut (the Cut icon looks like a tiny pair of scissors, as shown in Figure 2-1), or press Ctrl+X.**

   PowerPoint removes the selected text from your slide and adds it to the Clipboard.

Copying Text

When you *copy* text, you tell PowerPoint to place a copy of the text on the Office Clipboard so that you can replicate it later—either by pasting it onto the same slide, onto another slide, or into another document (such as a Word document)

The Ins and Outs of the Office Clipboard

The Office Clipboard that PowerPoint uses is the same clipboard that all the other Microsoft Office programs use: Word, Excel, Access, and so on. The Clipboard acts as a kind of virtual shoebox. Its job is to store the bits of information you've cut or copied from all of your Office programs (up to 24 pieces of information total) so that you can paste them in later, should you want to.

For example, say you copy some text from a Word document. Because Word automatically stores all cut and copied text on the Office Clipboard, you can paste that copied text onto a PowerPoint slide quickly and easily. You can go the other way, too, copying content from a PowerPoint slide and pasting it into a Word or Excel document.

You paste information from the Clipboard using Paste, Paste Special, and Clipboard options (as described in this chapter).

altogether. Copying text is useful for those times when you need to repeat lengthy or tricky-to-spell words or phrases throughout your presentation.

To copy text:

1. **Select the text you want to copy (page 58).**

   PowerPoint highlights the selected text.

2. **Choose Home → Clipboard → Copy (the Copy icon looks like two tiny identical documents, as shown in Figure 2-1), or press Ctrl+C.**

   PowerPoint adds the selected text to the Clipboard.

— TIP

> Another way to copy text is to right-click your selection and then, from the menu that appears, choose Copy.

Pasting Text

When you *paste* text, what you're actually doing is telling PowerPoint to take a hunk of information you've already placed on the Clipboard—either by cutting or copying—and slap that information onto your slide. So in order to paste something, you must first cut or copy it.

The Clipboard can hold up to 24 separate pieces of information, so you have two options when it comes to pasting: You can quickly paste the last thing you cut or copied, or you can hunt through the entire contents of the Clipboard and choose what you want to paste. After you cut or copy a chunk of text once, you can paste it into your presentation as many times as you like.

Automatically pasting the last chunk of text you cut (or copied)

Like a lot of Microsoft programs, PowerPoint gives you a super-quick way to paste the last thing you cut or copied to the Clipboard. This procedure is one of the All Time Most Popular Office Tricks.

Here's how you do it:

1. **Click to position your cursor in the text box where you want your pasted text to appear.**

    PowerPoint highlights the outline of the text box you clicked in.

2. **Either click the Paste icon (which looks like a little clipboard behind a document, as shown in Figure 2-2), or choose Home → Paste → Clipboard → Paste. Keyboard jockeys save time by pressing Ctrl+V.**

    PowerPoint pastes the last thing you cut or copied onto your slide, and a tiny Paste Options icon appears briefly near your cursor.

Choosing what to paste

Use this option when you want to paste multiple bits of information, or when you can't remember how long ago you cut (or copied) the text you want to paste.

To choose the text you want to paste into a slide:

1. **Click in the text box where you want your pasted text to go.**

   PowerPoint highlights the outline of the text box you clicked in.

2. **Click the Clipboard dialog box launcher.**

   The Clipboard task pane appears on the left side of your screen as shown in Figure 2-2.

3. **In the Clipboard task pane, click to select the text you want to paste.**

   PowerPoint pastes the selected text onto your slide.

4. **To close the Clipboard task pane, click the X in the upper-right corner of the pane.**

Choosing how to paste

In most situations, simply pasting text onto your slides the standard way is what you want. But PowerPoint gives you a few additional options for pasting certain types of information onto your slides. For example, when you want to be able to use Power-Point's picture-formatting options to edit the pasted text, you'll want to paste it directly onto your slide as a picture.

To choose how to paste text onto your slides:

1. **Click the down arrow next to Paste and then, from the menu that appears, choose Paste Special.**

   The Paste Special window (Figure 2-3) appears.

2. **Choose how you want to paste the information onto your slide. Your options depend on the type of information you're pasting, but they include:**

   ▶ **Pasting the information directly.** Turning on the radio box next to Paste, as shown in Figure 2-3, lets you choose one of several options including pasting the text as document object, pasting it as a picture, and pasting it as formatted

Figure 2-2. If you've been busy copying and cutting, then you may have filled up the Clipboard. In that case, you'll need to use the scroll bars to scroll down through the contents of the Clipboard and find what you're looking for. Clicking Paste All pastes the entire contents of the Clipboard to wherever you've positioned your cursor, beginning with the first cut (or copied) item and ending with the last.

text. Which option you want to choose depends on how you plan to format the text. For example, pasting text as a picture lets you use the options on Power-Point's Picture Tools | Format contextual tab to format the text.

▶ **Pasting a link to the information.** Turning on the radio box next to Paste Link lets you paste the text onto your slide, with a twist: double-clicking the pasted text lets you edit it not in PowerPoint, but in the program you used to create the text.

After you've made your choice, click OK.

PowerPoint pastes the most recently cut or copied text based on your selection.

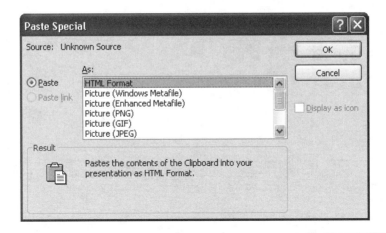

Figure 2-3. The options the Paste Special window displays depend on the kind of information you cut (or copied), the program you were in when you cut (or copied) it, and whether or not the program you cut (or copied) it from is still running on your computer.

Moving Text

When all you want to do is move a bit of text from one spot on your slide to another spot on the same slide, you can certainly choose to cut the text and then paste it. But PowerPoint offers an easier way to accomplish the same thing: moving the text.

To move text:

1. **Select the text you want to move (page 58). Then, click your selection (but don't let go of your mouse button just yet).**

    The "moving" box you see in Figure 2-4 appears beneath your cursor.

2. **Drag the selection and drop it where you want it to appear.**

    The "moving" box disappears, and PowerPoint moves the text.

Deleting Text

Unlike cutting text (page 60), which tells PowerPoint to save the text on the Clipboard in case you want to reuse it later, *deleting* text erases it completely. The only way to get deleted text back is to click Undo (see the next section).

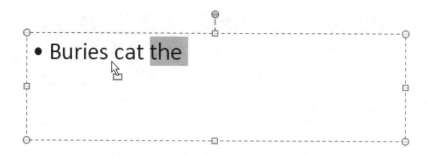

Figure 2-4. After you've selected a chunk of text, clicking your selection displays the "moving" box you see here. Now all you have to do is drag the selection to where you want it and let go of your mouse.

To delete text:

1. **Select the text you want to delete (page 58).**

   PowerPoint highlights the selected text.

2. **Do one of the following:**

   ▶ Press Delete. (PowerPoint deletes the selected text.)

   ▶ Type some new text. (PowerPoint deletes the selected text and replaces it with your new text.)

   ___ TIP _____

   To delete individual characters, position your cursor *after* the character you want to delete and press Backspace, or *before* the character you want to delete and press Delete.

Reversing an Action (Undo)

Undo is great for recovering from those slip-of-the-finger goofs everyone makes from time to time. Clicking the Undo button you see in the Quick Access toolbar (Figure 2-5) tells PowerPoint to reverse the last action you told it to take. If you cut some text and then select Undo, for example, PowerPoint puts the cut text back where it was (and removes the cut text from the Clipboard). If you paste some text and then select Undo, then PowerPoint removes the pasted text. If you just prefer pressing keys to using the mouse, you can reverse the last action by pressing Ctrl+Z.

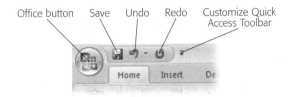

Office button   Save   Undo   Redo   Customize Quick
                                          Access Toolbar

Figure 2-5. As useful as Undo is, don't rely on it too much. Out of the box, PowerPoint only keeps track of the last 20 actions you took since the last time you opened your presentation, so you're out of luck if you want to undo the thing you did 21 keystrokes ago. Another reason not to rely on Undo is that, when you close your presentation, PowerPoint erases all record of the actions you took when the file was open.

___ NOTE ___

If you click Undo and then change your mind, you can undo the effects of Undo and reapply your action. To do so, just head to the Quick Access toolbar and click Redo or press Ctrl+Y.

Finding and Replacing Text Automatically

Imagine you're just putting the finishing touches on your presentation when you decide to check your email. There, in your virtual inbox, you see it: a memo informing you that Marketing just renamed the product you referred to throughout your presentation as "Sunny's Tomato Juice" to "Sunny's All-Natural Lycopene Infusion."

Fixing every occurrence by hand would take you forever, and you'd likely miss a few.

Fortunately, there's a better way. PowerPoint's Replace option can find all the occurrences of a particular word or phrase and replace them automatically with the text you specify.

___ NOTE ___

If you want to use Find without Replace—for example, if all you want to do is check to make sure that you've included a specific phrase in your presentation and don't want PowerPoint to swap it out for you—check out page 47.

To search for and replace text automatically:

1. **Press Ctrl+H or select Home → Editing → Replace.**

   The Replace dialog box shown in Figure 2-6 appears.

2. **In the "Find what" box, type in the word or phrase you want to search for.**

   For example, *Tomato Juice.*

3. **In the "Replace with" box, type in the text you want PowerPoint to substitute for the occurrences of "Find what" text it may (or may not) find.**

   All-Natural Lycopene Infusion, in this example.

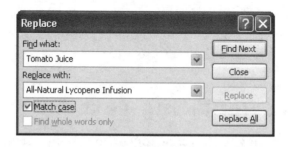

Figure 2-6. Be sure to turn on the "Match case" checkbox as shown here if you want PowerPoint to look for a phrase that matches your "Find what" text exactly, capitalization and all.

___ **WARNING** _____

PowerPoint doesn't find occurrences of text buried inside pictures, charts, or diagrams, because these occurrences aren't text at all (to PowerPoint, at least). Using PowerPoint's Find and Replace options only helps you find (and replace) text in text boxes and shapes.

4. **Repeat Steps 2–4 for every word or phrase you want to replace.**

5. **If you repeat the steps until PowerPoint reaches the end of your presentation, the message "PowerPoint has finished searching the presentation" appears. Click OK to dismiss message.**

6. **When you're finished finding and replacing text, click Close.**

   The Replace dialog box disappears.

Replacing Fonts

In addition to letting you replace text, PowerPoint also lets you swap the fonts you've applied to text. Replacing fonts is useful when you're trying to match a font you've used in your slideshow to the font you've used in an Excel chart, or to the font your company (or client) uses in its marketing materials.

There's only one small caveat: Replacing fonts is a one-shot deal. You can't tell PowerPoint to replace a font only in certain text passages or certain slides. Instead, the program replaces the font wherever it finds it, from your first slide to your last.

To replace fonts:

1. Select Home → Editing → Replace → Replace Fonts.

2. From the "Replace" drop-down list that appears, choose the font you want to replace.

3. From the "With" drop-down list, choose the new font you want to apply to your slideshow text.

4. Click Replace. When you do, PowerPoint searches your entire slideshow for text formatted using the "Replace" font and applies the "With" font to that text.

Click Replace All to tell PowerPoint to find and replace all occurrences of *Tomato Juice* (the text you typed in the "Find what" box) with *All-Natural Lycopene Infusion* (the contents of the "Replace with" box) in one fell swoop. Or click Find Next to tell PowerPoint to flip to the first slide in your presentation containing the "Find what" text and select it. If you want to replace the text, click Replace. To search for additional occurrences, click Find Next again.

Checking Spelling

Spelling errors are never a good thing. At best, they can give your audience the impression that you don't pay attention to details. At worst, they can actually prevent your audience from understanding what you're talking about. And make no mistake about it: the typo that no one but the former English teacher noticed when it appeared on a hard-copy handout is obvious to everyone when it's four feet high and splashed across a projector screen.

Spell checkers' suggestions aren't always right, and they can miss errors, too. What's more, studies suggest that some folks actually make *more* mistakes when they use spell checkers than when they don't because they rely on the tool instead of their own proofreading skills. A spell checker can be a timesaver, but it's no substitute for carefully reading through your presentation.

PowerPoint gives you two choices when it comes to spell checking your presentation. You can check as you go, automatically, or wait until you're finished with your presentation and then run the check manually.

Setting up spelling

Whether you choose automatic spell checking or manual, you want to give PowerPoint a heads-up on what kinds of special words to look out for—words like company-specific acronyms, passwords, or other non-words that you want PowerPoint to skip during a spell check. To set spelling options:

1. **Select Office button → PowerPoint Options.**

    The PowerPoint Options window appears.

2. **On the left side of the PowerPoint Options window, click the Proofing category to select it.**

3. **Turn on the checkbox next to one or more of the following:**

    ▶ **Ignore words in UPPERCASE.** You want to choose this option if you use a lot of acronyms, like FUBAR.

    ▶ **Ignore words that contain numbers.** This option is useful if, say, you're a system administrator who peppers presentations with passwords like *edgar123*.

    ▶ **Ignore Internet and file addresses.** This option tells the spell checker not to flag computer-era "words" such as *www.oreilly.com* and *myFile.txt*.

    ▶ **Flag repeated words.** Catches mistakes mistakes that the human eye often misses.

4. **Click OK.**

    The PowerPoint Options window disappears, returning you to your slides.

Contextual Spelling (And Why It's Not Reliable, Either)

Spell checking is great for catching mis-spelled words (such as *mispelled*). But it's useless when it comes to catching *misused* words, which are at least as common as—and can tarnish your well-polished presentation even more than—glaring typos.

Take, for example, the phrase *more then this*. Because *then* is a legitimate, cor-rectly spelled word, the PowerPoint spell checker doesn't flag it and suggest the correct word for this phrase, *than*.

PowerPoint does offer an option called *contextual spelling* which can help catch this sort of grammar error.

When you turn on contextual spelling, the PowerPoint spell checker examines words in the context of their neighbors to see if it can spot common grammar mistakes. For example, the spell checker correctly flags *then* in the phrase *More then this*. It even suggests *than*, which is in fact the correct spelling. As long as you're aware that no contextual spell checker can catch every grammatical error.

Here's how to turn it on: Choose Office → PowerPoint Options → Proofing, turn on the checkbox next to "Use contextual spelling," and then click OK.

Automatic (continuous) spell checking

Out of the box, PowerPoint assumes you want it to flag misspelled words automati-cally, as you type, by underlining them with a wavy red line. Figure 2-7 shows you an example.

> **NOTE**
>
> If you see an obvious misspelling on a slide but don't see a wavy under-line, someone turned off automatic spell checking. To turn it on again, select Office → PowerPoint Options → Proofing. Then make sure the radio box next to "Check spelling as you type" is turned *on,* and the one next to "Hide spelling errors" is turned *off.*

To correct a misspelling, right-click the misspelled word.

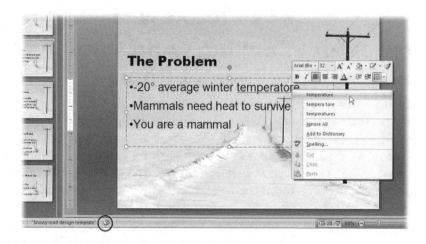

Figure 2-7. The misspelling icon in the status bar and the wavy line you see underneath "tempera-tore" is PowerPoint's way of letting you know that it doesn't recognize the word. (In other words, "temperatore" doesn't appear in PowerPoint's built-in dictionary.) To tell PowerPoint to recognize a particular spelling in the future, or to display any of the other options you see here, right-click the misspelled word.

___ NOTE _____

PowerPoint's spell checker examines WordArt and charts, but ignores misspellings in any pictures (such as bitmaps) or graphs that you add to your slides.

_____

From the context menu that appears (Figure 2-7), click to choose one of the following options:

▶ **One of the suggested correct spellings.** (In the example in Figure 2-7, the suggested correct spellings are *temperature*, *tempera tore*, and *temperatures*). Power-Point's built-in dictionary contains quite a few common words, so unless you're using trademarked names or jargon, chances are good you'll find the correct spelling listed for the word you've misspelled.

When you choose a word, the context menu disappears. On the slide, PowerPoint replaces the misspelled version with the corrected version you chose.

▶ **Ignore All.** Tells PowerPoint to ignore this misspelled word each time it encounters it in this presentation. Choose this option when you're using an "illegitimate" word that you don't want PowerPoint to recognize a year from now, such as company-specific code name you know will be retired after the presentation you're currently working on.

When you choose this option, the context menu disappears, as does the red wavy line beneath the misspelled word. PowerPoint doesn't flag additional occurrences of the misspelling (if it encounters them) in this presentation.

▶ **Add to Dictionary.** Tells PowerPoint to ignore this particular spelling when it appears in any presentation (technically, any presentation to which you've attached a custom dictionary; see the box on page 74 for more information). This is the option you want to use for teachers' names, company acronyms, and other words you know you'll be using in more than one presentation.

When you choose this option, the context menu disappears, as does the red wavy line beneath the misspelled word. PowerPoint doesn't flag additional occurrences of this new word (assuming it encounters them) in *any* presentation.

▶ **Spelling.** Tells PowerPoint to display the Spelling dialog box shown in Figure 2-8.

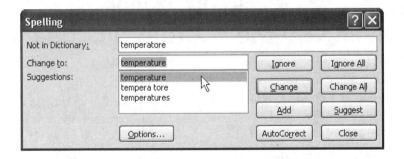

Figure 2-8. The options you can choose from in this dialog box change depending on whether or not you've selected a suggested spelling. Here, the suggested spelling temperature is selected, so Power-Point activates all of the options. If you don't select a suggested spelling, then the only available options are Resume, Ignore All, Add, Suggest, Options, and Close.

In the Spelling dialog box, you tell PowerPoint how to handle the misspelled word. Your options include:

▶ **Ignore.** Tells PowerPoint to ignore this particular occurrence of the misspelling, but to highlight any additional occurrences it finds in this presentation.

▶ **Ignore All.** Tells PowerPoint to ignore every existing occurrence of the misspelling in this presentation.

- **Change.** Tells PowerPoint to swap the selected suggestion (in Figure 2-8, *temperature*) for this particular occurrence of the misspelling.

- **Change All.** Tells PowerPoint to swap the selected suggestion for every existing occurrence of the misspelling.

- **Add.** Tells PowerPoint to add the "misspelled" word to the custom dictionary you choose (see box below).

- **Suggest.** Tells PowerPoint to cough up additional suggested spellings.

- **AutoCorrect.** Tells PowerPoint to keep an eye out for this misspelling in the future, and automatically substitute the selected suggestion if you misspell the same word the same way again.

- **Close.** Closes the Spelling dialog box without taking any additional action.

- **Options.** Tells PowerPoint to display the PowerPoint Options window, which lets you customize the way PowerPoint checks spelling.

POWER USERS' CLINIC

Cleaning up the Custom Dictionary

PowerPoint uses two separate dictionaries to check your spelling: a "real" dictionary (one that you can't change) and a custom dictionary (one called *custom.dic* that you *can* change).

Say, for example, that you accidentally added the word *persnicketty* to the custom dictionary when what you wanted to add was *persnickety*.

In PowerPoint 2007, the process of cleaning up erroneous custom spellings is easier than in previous versions. To delete a word from *custom.dic*, follow these steps:

1. Choose Office button → PowerPoint Options.

2. In the PowerPoint Options window that appears, click Proofing to select it.

3. Select Custom Dictionaries.

4. In the Custom Dictionaries dialog box that pops up, make sure the checkbox next to the custom dictionary you want to use is turned on, and then click Edit Word List.

5. In the dialog box that appears, click to select the word(s) you want to delete, and then click Delete to get rid of the word and OK to dismiss the dialog box.

Manual spell checking

Some folks find automatic spell checking (page 71) more distracting than helpful. They either resent those wavy red underlines distracting them while they're busy trying to concentrate, or they just get so used to seeing the underlines that they ignore them and end up leaving in misspellings.

If either of these reactions sounds familiar, you'll want to turn off automatic spell checking and run the tool yourself, when you've finished composing your text and are ready to begin proofreading in earnest.

To turn off automatic spell checking:

1. **Select Office button → PowerPoint Options → Proofing.**

   The PowerPoint Options window (Figure 2-9) appears showing all the spelling and automatic spelling options.

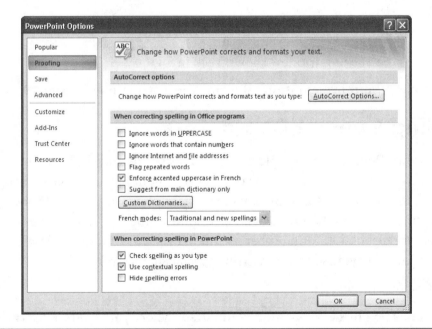

Figure 2-9. The options you set here in the PowerPoint Options window are divided into labeled sections. Some settings (such as whether or not you want the spell checker to flag repeated words) affect all Microsoft Office programs; others (such as whether or not you want automatic spell checking turned on) affect PowerPoint only.

2. **Turn off the checkbox next to "Check spelling as you type" and then click OK.**

The PowerPoint Options window disappears.

To check the spelling of your presentation manually:

1. **Click the Review tab.**

The reviewing tools appear (Figure 2-10).

Figure 2-10. The Review tab shows you all the options you're likely to need after you've finished creating your presentation, when you're ready to read through and tweak it. To bypass the Review tab altogether and skip directly to the Spelling window, press F7.

2. **Click Spelling.**

Up pops the Spelling window shown back in Figure 2-8.

3. **Spell check your presentation following the instructions on page 70.**

Adding Special Characters

Because PowerPoint comes complete with a slew of fonts and character sets, you can add all kinds of special characters to your slides without having to have a souped-up keyboard. Mathematical signs, foreign currency symbols, umlauts, schwas, superscripted characters, and happy faces are just some of the special characters—or *symbols*—at your disposal. If for no other reason than to accent those *e*'s in résumé, you want to familiarize yourself with inserting special characters.

Here's how you do so:

1. **Click in a text box and position your cursor where you want to insert the special character. Select Insert → Text → Symbol.**

The Symbol dialog box appears (Figure 2-11).

2. **From the Font drop-down menu, choose a font.**

   The special characters you see vary depending on the font you choose, not just in appearance but in number.

3. **From the Subset drop-down menu, choose the type of symbol you're interested in.**

   Alternatively, you can scroll through the symbol window to find the symbol you're looking for.

4. **Choose the symbol you want to insert, and then click Insert.**

   PowerPoint inserts the selected symbol.

5. **Click Close to dismiss the Symbol dialog box.**

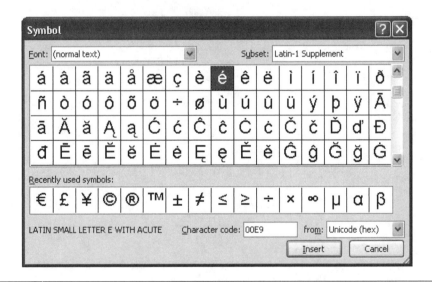

Figure 2-11. Not all fonts are created equal. The Webdings and Wingdings dingbat fonts, for example, eschew the business, mathematical, and linguistic (shown here) in favor of vector art: telephones, hearts, buildings, and other stylized drawings you can enlarge to create clean, simple graphics.

FORMATTING AND ALIGNING YOUR TEXT

▶ **Automating Text Formatting**

▶ **Manually Formatting Text Appearance**

▶ **Manually Aligning and Indenting Text**

▶ **Formatting Text Boxes**

CONTENT MAY BE KING, BUT PRESENTATION IS QUEEN. You're going to spend a lot of time choosing just the right text to add to your slides, so don't blow all that hard work by ignoring the way your text looks. If your text is hard to read or conveys a message counter to the point you're trying to make—if you choose whimsical, candy-colored fonts for a presentation introducing your company's expanded line of funeral services, for example—you're going to confuse (or even lose) your audience.

This chapter shows you how to format your text effectively. You'll find out how to choose fonts, colors, and special effects (such as underlining and shadowing) that support and strengthen your message (Figure 3-1), and how to avoid the effects that detract from it (Figure 3-2).

Figure 3-1. Effectively formatted text is easy to read and it subliminally reinforces the message you're trying to drive home. Here, a solid, "respectable" font, a sober blue-and-tan-and-white color scheme, and spare, businesslike layout all contribute to the seriousness of the message.

Automating Text Formatting

PowerPoint gives you more options for formatting text than a normal human being will ever need—everything from the basic (bold, italics, underlining) to the wacky

Figure 3-2. Anyone who's spent time in corporate America has suffered through at least one presentation like this. While it's true that your message (and your audience) should dictate the formatting choices you make, getting carried away is never a good idea. Too many formatting bells and whistles can affect your message more negatively than no formatting at all.

(beveling, stacking, 3-D rotation). And it gives you two ways to take advantage of these options: automatically, and manually.

▶ **Automatic.** If you haven't finished adding text to your slides, you can turn on one or more of PowerPoint's automatic formatting features to tell the program to catch basic formatting and punctuation goofs for you as you type.

▶ **Manual.** If you've already added text to your slides or want to apply fancy effects, you'll need to format your text manually—either by applying individual effects one at a time, or by applying one of PowerPoint 2007's predesigned styles.

In most cases, you'll want to use both automatic and manual formatting. The following sections show you how.

Less Is More

As you format your presentation, make sure you keep the following three goals in mind:

Readability.

Readability.

Readability.

Specialty formatting—like drop-shadows, bevels, and text that runs up and down instead of left to right—is the PowerPoint equivalent of swearing: If you use it sparingly and appropriately, it gets your audience's attention. Use it frequently or indiscriminately, and it'll turn your audience off and reflect poorly on your skills as a communicator.

One way to keep your slides readable is to remember that your slides should *aid* you in giving your presentation; they shouldn't *be* your presentation.

Instead of automatically typing out a bunch of bullet points, consider displaying something on your slide that grabs your audience's attention, such as a drawing, a photo (*www.istockphoto.com* is a great source), or a provocative question. Then let your audience focus on this simple, powerful visual while you explain how it relates to your message—using as many words as you need to. (Chances are your audience will remember a striking photo or a single, stark, provocatively worded question much better than a bunch of text.)

If you *do* decide to go the text route, keep it readable by sticking to three or four bullet points per slide; try to limit each bullet point to five or six words; and size the text at 32 points or larger.

Using AutoFormat

You can tell PowerPoint to catch certain formatting errors—like typing a hyphen when you meant to type a dash—and replace them with the correct punctuation or symbol automatically. You can also tell the program to automatically format text that threatens to spill over its bounding placeholder box.

> **NOTE**
>
> AutoFormat isn't retroactive. In other words, turning on AutoFormat options doesn't affect existing text; it affects only the text you add to your slides *after* you turn on AutoFormat. To see how to manually format existing text, flip to page 87.

To turn on automatic formatting options:

1. **Choose Office button → PowerPoint Options (it's at the bottom of the Office menu).**

   The PowerPoint Options window appears.

2. **Select the Proofing panel, and then click the AutoCorrect Options button.**

   The AutoCorrect dialog box opens (Figure 3-3).

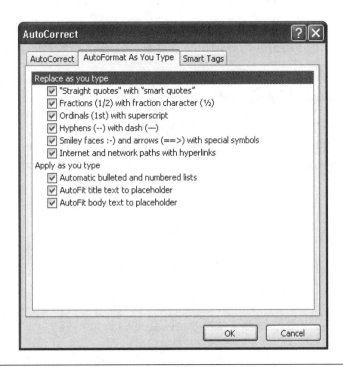

Figure 3-3. Out of the box, PowerPoint assumes you want all of the AutoFormat options turned on, and you probably will—except for the automatic bulleted/numbered lists and AutoFit options, which is annoying if you like to control your own formatting.

3. **Click the AutoFormat As You Type tab.**

   This tab is where you control which items PowerPoint fixes on the fly. Turn on the checkbox next to one or more of the options that are described in the list that follows.

- ▶ "Straight quotes" with "smart quotes." Popular with perfectionists, this option tells PowerPoint to substitute slightly curved quotation marks for the usual straight ones. (Here's where the "smart" part comes in: If you type "A dog named 'Sam,'" the first single and double smart quotes curve attractively to the right, and the final single and double smart quotes curve left. Plain old straight quotes, on the other hand, don't change their appearance based on position.)

- ▶ **Fractions (1/2) with fraction character (1/2).** Turns the serviceable *1/2* (or *1/4*, or *3/4*, and so on) into a tiny, easier-to-read ½ (or ¼, or ¾) symbol.

- ▶ **Ordinals (1st, 2nd, and so on) with superscript.** Tells PowerPoint to super-script the *st*, *nd*, *rd*, and *th* portions of *1st, 2nd, 3rd, 4th, 5th*, and so on.

- ▶ **Hyphens (--) with dash (—).** Tells PowerPoint to turn two short hyphens in a row into a single long *em* dash.

- ▶ **Smiley faces :-) and arrows ==> with special symbols.** Tells PowerPoint to turn homemade smiley emoticons and arrows into actual smiley and arrow symbols, as shown in Figure 3-4.

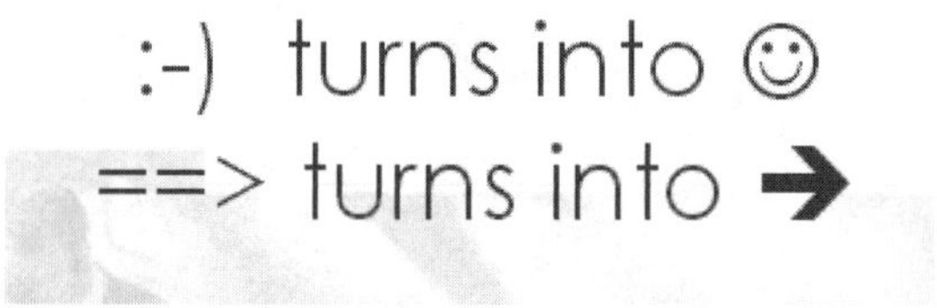

:-) turns into ☺
==> turns into →

Figure 3-4. The standard substitutions you see here work for most folks, but if you prefer, you can turn them off by unchecking their boxes (Figure 3-3).

- ▶ **Internet and network paths with hyperlinks.** Tells PowerPoint to automatically turn any Web and email addresses you add to your slides (like *http:// www.oreilly.com, www.missingmanuals.com*, and *yourEmail@yourISP.net*) into clickable hyperlinks.

- ▶ **Automatic bulleted and numbered lists.** Tells PowerPoint to format your text as a bulleted or numbered list automatically when you type in a sentence begin-ning with either * or 1. (You find out all about lists on page 102.)

▶ **AutoFit title text to placeholder.** Tells PowerPoint to try to keep your title text inside its placeholder bounds. Typically, you want to select this option for two reasons: Overflowing text boxes are hard to select, and wordy titles don't do your presentation any good. When you do select this option, PowerPoint shrinks your font size and squeezes your line spacing automatically as soon as the text you type overflows your title placeholder box.

NOTE

Because titles, by definition, are supposed to stand out and be read-able, PowerPoint doesn't automatically reduce your font size lower than the smallest size allowed by whoever designed the theme you're using (usually somewhere around size 40)—no matter how much title text you type in. But *you* can reduce your type as small as you want. Page 91 shows you how.

▶ **AutoFit body text to placeholder.** Tells PowerPoint to restrict your subtitle text to its placeholder bounding box, no matter how much text you type. If you type so much text that you spill over the placeholder, PowerPoint automatically shrinks the text font and line spacing to make it fit. Don't choose this option if you tend to be wordy, because as long as you keep typing, PowerPoint keeps shrinking your text until it's too small to read. Because the auto-shrunken text fits neatly into its placeholder box, you may not notice how small it's become. Thirty-two-point text is about as small as you want on a slide.

Using AutoFit

PowerPoint's AutoFit options let you control how you want your text to fit into the title and text placeholders you add to your slides. (Do you want your text to spill over? Shrink to fit?) AutoFit options also let you control whether you want to split giant wads of text into multiple columns, or break it up and put it on multiple slides.

Whether you've turned the automatic AutoFit options for title and body text on or off, PowerPoint always recognizes when text overflows its bounding box and lets you choose how you want to handle it by popping up the AutoFit Options icon shown in Figure 3-5.

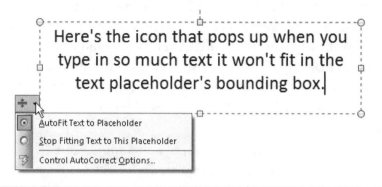

Figure 3-5. There are two kinds of people in the world: those who appreciate the AutoFit Options icon springing to life every few minutes, and those who hate it. If you're the latter, simply click outside the text box to dismiss the icon. Otherwise, take advantage of the suggestions that this icon's menu provides. After all, the icon appears only when your text is running amok.

To select an AutoFit option:

1. **Click in a title or subtitle placeholder. Begin typing and continue until the text overflows the placeholder (the bounding box).**

   PowerPoint displays a tiny AutoFit Options icon at the lower left of your place-holder (see Figure 3-5).

2. **Click the AutoFit Options icon.**

   A menu similar to the one in Figure 3-5 appears. The actual options you see depend on the kind of text box you're working with, as well as how much text you've typed in and how you've formatted it.

3. **Choose one of the following options:**

   ▶ **AutoFit Text to Placeholder.** Tells PowerPoint to shrink the text until it all fits neatly inside its bounding box (for text placeholders), or—if you're working with a title placeholder—to reduce the font size no lower than size 30. Choosing this option helps you keep your text within PowerPoint's suggested layout bounds (which, in turn, helps make sure your text is both readable and attractively laid out).

- **Stop Fitting Text to This Placeholder.** Springs the font size of your text back to its original point size. You want to choose this option in cases where you're trying to create a specific, nontraditional effect. Maybe you want to display a simple drawing using an extra-large character from a dingbat font (such as Webdings).

- **Split Text Between Two Slides.** Tells PowerPoint to create a new slide and move half of the text to a similar placeholder on the new slide.

- **Continue On a New Slide.** Tells PowerPoint to create a new blank slide. As you continue to type, the new text flows onto the newly created slide in an unbroken stream.

- **Change to Two Columns.** Tells PowerPoint to reformat your text as a two-column layout. (For more on columns and slide layouts, zip down to page 99.)

- **Control AutoCorrect Options.** Displays the AutoCorrect dialog box you saw back in Figure 3-3, which lets you change your AutoFit settings.

TIP

If you want to change (or just look at) your AutoFit settings without waiting for PowerPoint to kick up the AutoFit Options icon, no problem—just right-click your text box. Then, from the context menu that appears, choose Format Text Effects to display the Format Text Effects dialog box. In the Format Text Effects dialog box, click the Text Box tab. Figure 3-6 shows you the result.

Manually Formatting Text Appearance

While PowerPoint's automatic formatting options help with the grunt work of formatting the text on your slides, you should do some of the formatting yourself. After all, the program has no way of knowing which words or phrases you want to emphasize—which, when you get right down to it, is what formatting is all about.

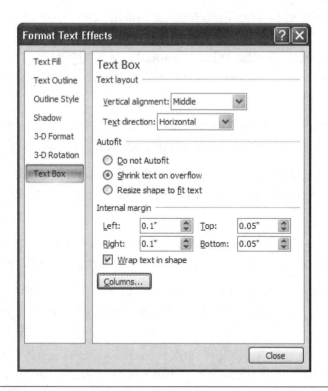

Figure 3-6. The handiest way to deal with a ton of text is to wait until it overflows your text box and take one of PowerPoint's AutoFit suggestions. But if you're the impatient type—or if you know you're going to be adding a lot of text and want to resize the text box sooner rather than later—then the Format Text Effects dialog box, shown here, offers some of the same AutoFit options.

PowerPoint conveniently displays all of its text formatting options on the Home tab (Figure 3-7). A handful of the most commonly used formats also appear when you right-click text or when you select it, as shown in Figure 3-8.

NOTE

If you're the kind of person who simply can't stand pop-ups, you can turn off the Mini Toolbar. To do so, select Office button → PowerPoint Options and then, in the PowerPoint Options window that appears, select Popular and turn off the "Show Mini Toolbar on selection" check-box.

Chapter 3: Formatting and Aligning Your Text

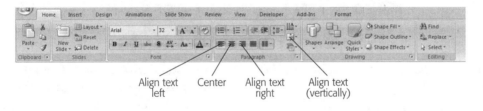

Figure 3-7. Most of PowerPoint's text formatting options appear on the Home tab.

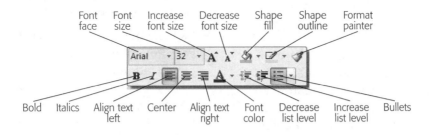

Figure 3-8. As soon as you right-click or select text, PowerPoint pops up the semi-transparent, or ghosted, Mini Toolbar shown here. Mouse over the Mini Toolbar and it becomes active, giving you a quick way to apply the most common formatting options (bold, italics, and so on).

Using the options you find on the Home tab, you can format individual characters and words by changing their color, font size, font, underlining, shadowing, and so on. You can format paragraphs by indenting them, turning them into bulleted or numbered lists, and by applying effects to them, such as rotating them or turning them into diagrams. The following sections show you how.

Changing the Font

PowerPoint's *fonts* (what printers used to call *typefaces*) determine how text looks: spidery, staid, clunky, old-fashioned, funky, and so on. Arial, Helvetica, and Times Roman are three common fonts, although PowerPoint offers a lot more than that. (The actual number of fonts you can apply to your text in PowerPoint depends on how many fonts you have installed on your computer. For more information, see the box on page 90.)

Troubleshooting Fonts

Can using exotic fonts cause problems in PowerPoint?

Yes. Say you create a presentation using the SuperFancy font you downloaded from the Web and installed on your computer. You copy your presentation to your laptop and hop on a plane. When you arrive at your client's office, ready to give your spiel, you discover that the text of your presentation appears totally different from the way you created it. The problem? You forgot to install SuperFancy on your laptop, so Power-Point substituted a *system font* (one of the factory-installed fonts that come with all operating systems). To avoid this problem, you've got two choices:

✳ **Use a standard font such as Arial, Times New Roman, or Courier New.** These fonts are pretty run-of-the-mill, it's true, but they're 99.9 percent likely to be installed on every computer—and at least *you're* the one choosing them (and not PowerPoint).

✳ **Embed your special font directly into your PowerPoint presentation.** This option lets your audience see exactly what you intended them to see. On the downside, embedding swells the size of your PowerPoint presentation, which becomes an issue if you intend to deliver it over the Web, and may cause problems in older versions of the program. Chapter 7 (page 222) shows you how to embed a font.

To change the font:

1. **Click in a text box.**

    The Drawing Tools | Format contextual tab appears, and PowerPoint activates the formatting options on the Home tab.

2. **Select the characters you want to format.**

    The characters appear highlighted, and you see a ghosted Mini Toolbar.

3. **Choose Font, either in the Home → Font group or from the Mini Toolbar.**

    A list of fonts similar to the one you see in Figure 3-9 appears.

4. **Select a font.**

    PowerPoint automatically reformats the selected text.

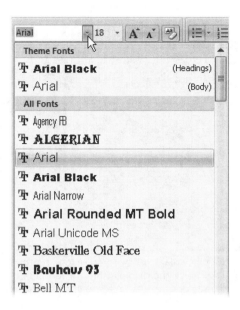

Figure 3-9. PowerPoint doesn't raise a fuss if you choose a different font for every single character on your slide, but you should stick with one or two fonts per presentation (unless you like the ransom note look). Out of the box, the program assumes you want to use the Calibri font.

__ NOTE _____

Although they're common in the print world, *serif* fonts (fonts with fancy little feet on the letters) tend to be harder to read on computer screens than *sans-serif* (literally, "without serif") fonts. Sans-serif fonts—like Calibri—look clearer onscreen.

Changing Font Size

PowerPoint gives you two different ways to change the size of your font: You can increase or decrease your font by choosing from a list, or you can type a specific font size (such as 38). If you're like most folks, you'll want to increase or decrease your font size, eyeball the result, and repeat until you achieve the look you want. But when you need to match the font size on one slide to the size on another, the quickest approach is to specify the number directly using the drop-down menu shown in Figure 3-10.

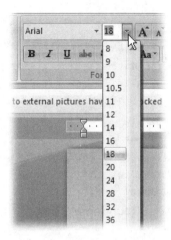

Figure 3-10. If you don't see the particular font size you're looking for, no problem. Instead of clicking the arrow next to the Font box, click the displayed font (here, 18), type your own font size, and press Return. PowerPoint obediently applies any size you specify, from ridiculously small (1) to ridiculously large (999).

TIP

Have pity on the folks in the back row (or, if you'll be delivering your slideshow over the Web, the folks with small monitors) and keep your font size as large as possible. A quick way to tell if your font's big enough is to print out a slide and drop it face-up on the floor. If you're standing over it and can't read it easily, your font is too small.

To change font size:

1. **Click in a text box.**

   The Drawing Tools | Format context tab pops up, and PowerPoint activates the formatting options on the Home tab.

2. **Select the characters you want to format.**

   The characters appear highlighted, and the Mini Toolbar appears.

3. **In either the Home → Font group or on the Mini Toolbar, choose a font size option.**

You have three choices:

▶ **Increase font size.** Clicking this option (the one with the "A" followed by the up-arrow) bumps up the font size to the next-highest size on the list.

▶ **Decrease font size.** Clicking this option (the "A" followed by the down-arrow) shrinks font size to the next-lowest size on the list.

▶ **Font size menu.** Clicking this option (a drop-down box displaying a number) shows the list you see in Figure 3-10, from which you can choose the precise font size you want. Rolling your mouse over the list shows you immediately, right on the slide, what your text looks like in each font. When you find the size you want, click it to apply the previewed changes to your slide.

POWER USERS' CLINIC

The New Font Dialog Box

The Font dialog box offers a one-stop shop for all font-related settings described in this chapter: font and size, bolding and underlining, coloring and shadowing, superscripting and sub-scripting, and more.

Using the Font dialog box saves you time if you're used to using it in older versions of PowerPoint, or if you want to make a bunch of font changes all at once.

To display the Font dialog box, either click the Font dialog launcher (the little down-arrow in the bottom right corner of the Home tab's Font section, as shown in Figure 3-7) or right-click in a text box and then, from the context menu that appears, choose Font.

To use the Font dialog box to change an underline from a solid to a dashed one, click the Font tab, and then choose the dashed style you want from the "Under-line style" drop-down box. To change the color of an underline, from the Font tab, head to the "Underline color" drop-down box and choose a color.

Bolding, Italicizing, and Underlining Text

Three of the easiest and most common ways to draw attention to text are to bold, italicize, or underline the text (Figure 3-11). These effects look and behave pretty much the same in PowerPoint as they do in most word-processing programs, including Microsoft Word.

Figure 3-11. Whether you choose them from the Home tab or the Mini Toolbar, Bold and Italicize are toggle options. Click once to apply them, and click the same option again to remove them. Although these basic formatting effects are among the oldest known to humankind, they're also the most effective—as long as you use them sparingly.

To bold, italicize, or underline text:

1. **Click in a text box.**

   The Drawing Tools | Format contextual tab pops up, and PowerPoint activates the formatting options on the Home tab.

2. **Select the characters you want to format.**

   The characters appear highlighted, and the Mini Toolbar appears.

3. **Choose one or more of the formatting options in the Home → Font group or from the Mini Toolbar: Bold, Italicize, or Underline. (The Underline option isn't available on the Mini Toolbar.)**

Changing Text Color and Background Color

PowerPoint lets you change the color of your text (and its background) from basic black to puce, chartreuse, chocolate mousse, or any other hue you come up with. You can color all of it, just a word or two for emphasis, or change the background color of the text box. You can also apply a gradient effect that makes your text look as though a light's shining on it (the following section shows you how).

To change text and text background color:

1. **Click in a text box.**

   The Drawing Tools | Format context tab pops up, and PowerPoint activates the formatting options on the Home tab.

2. **Select the characters you want to format.**

   The characters appear highlighted, and the Mini Toolbar appears.

3. **Click the drop-down arrow next to the Font Color icon that appears in the Mini Toolbar or in the Home → Font group.**

   The color picker you see in Figure 3-12 appears.

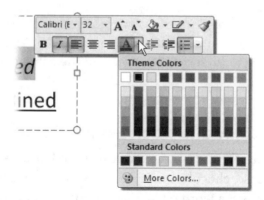

Figure 3-12. Here, you see the basic color picker that appears when you choose Font Color from the Mini Toolbar, or when you select Font from the Font section of the Home tab. Most of the time, these basic options are all you need. But if you like, you can apply a special text effect, as described below.

4. **Choose a color from either the Theme or Standard sections of the color picker.**

   Choosing a color from the Theme section makes sure the color of your text coordinates attractively with the other colors in your theme, like the background color of your slide. If you choose a color from the Standard section, there's no guarantee it will look good with the other elements on your slide.

Adding Special Text Effects

In addition to basic bolding, italicizing, and underlining, you can add all kinds of special effects to your text, as you can see in Figure 3-13. You find the special effects options on the Font and WordArt Styles sections of the Home tab.

To add a special effect to your text, simply select the text, and then click the effect on the ribbon.

▶ **Add a superscript or subscript.** If your presentation covers chemistry or some other scientific field, you'll need to subscript and superscript characters (think H_2O). On the Home tab, click the Font dialog launcher and then, in the Font dialog box that appears, make sure the Font tab is selected and then turn on the checkbox next to Superscript or Subscript.

▶ **Add a shadow.** Select Home → Font → Text Shadow. When you do, PowerPoint automatically adds a shadow to your text. For a more sophisticated shadow effect, right-click your selection, choose Format Text Effects, and then, in the Format

Bevel (3-D)

3-D Rotation

warp

Figure 3-13. Special text effects like these can add zing to your presentation—as long as you use them sparingly and remember not to sacrifice readability for coolness.

Text Effects dialog box that appears, click Shadow (see Figure 3-14). Click Presets to choose from a handful of standard shadows; then, if you want, you can use the other options to tweak the standard shadow.

- **Change text case.** You can tell PowerPoint to format the case of your text automatically, which is useful for fixing capitalization goofs. Click Home → Font → Change Case (the "AAa" button). From the menu that appears, choose one of the following: "Sentence case" (uppercases the first word of each line and adds a period after last word); "lowercase" (changes all characters to lowercase), UPPERCASE (changes all characters to uppercase); Capitalize Each Word (uppercases first letter of each word); or "tOGGLE cASE" (reverses the existing capitalization). This last option is rarely useful *unless* you just typed in a bunch of text with the caps lock key on by mistake).

- **Apply a pre-crafted effect (Quick Style).** The Quick Styles section of the Home tab offers a gallery of text effects including outlined fonts, glows, and reflections. To see them all, click the down arrow next to the Quick Styles option. The result is the full gallery of effects shown in Figure 3-15. Clicking an effect applies it directly to your text.

- **Add a beveled (3-D) effect.** To get the most out of applying a 3-D effect, make sure your text is large and blocky. 3-D doesn't do much for skinny, light-colored characters. Then go to Home → Drawing → Quick Styles → Text Effects → Bevel and, from the gallery that appears, click to choose a bevel option.

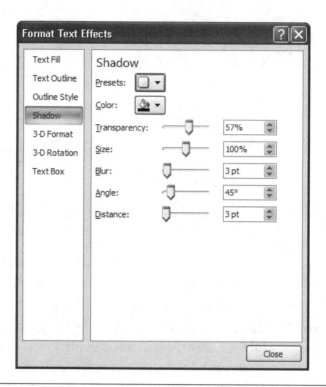

Figure 3-14. Shadows tend to make skinny fonts unreadable, but they can effectively draw attention to short headings displayed in plump, bold fonts. Click Presets to choose from a gallery of attractive, predesigned shadow options; then click Size, Angle, Distance, or any of the other options shown here to customize the predesigned look.

▶ **Add a 3-D rotation effect.** Another effect that looks better applied to shapes than to text, the 3-D rotation effect reformats your text in 3-D form and then slants it based on the perspective you choose. On the Drawing section of the Home tab, select Shape Effects → 3-D Rotation and then, from the gallery that appears, click to choose the option you want.

Manually Aligning and Indenting Text

To effectively convey your message on a slide, your text must above all be readable. After all, your audience may have to read it across a large conference room, or on a small laptop monitor. Make things easier on your audience's eyes by making sure your words are neatly and attractively lined up.

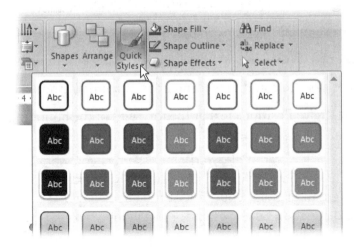

Figure 3-15. PowerPoint offers a quick-pick gallery of the most popular text effects, including outlines, colored fills, and 3-D beveling.

Aligning Text and Creating Columns

Neatly arranged text can mean the difference between an easy-to-read, professional-looking slide, and a jumbled mess.

PowerPoint gives you two ways to align text:

▶ **You can align text with respect to its bounding placeholder box.** For example, you can center heading text inside its box or position it flush left or flush right. If you've got a paragraph's worth of text, you can *justify* it (add spaces between the words so the ends of each line up) or turn it into two or more columns.

▶ **You can align a text placeholder box with respect to the slide it's on.** This type of alignment's called *layout*, and it's covered on page 119.

This section shows you how to align text with respect to its bounding placeholder box.

To align text:

1. **Click in a text box.**

    The Drawing Tools | Format contextual tab pops up, and PowerPoint activates the formatting options on the Home tab.

2. **Go to Home → Paragraph and choose an alignment option.**

   You can see examples in Figure 3-16, left:

   ▶ **Align Text Left.** Positions text at the top left of the bounding box.

   ▶ **Center.** Positions text at the top center of the bounding box.

   ▶ **Align Text Right.** Positions text at the top right of the bounding box.

   ___ NOTE _____

   Unless you tell it different, PowerPoint assumes you want to align text at the top of the bounding box. Choosing Align Text Left, for example, has the effect of aligning your text at the left *and top* of the bounding box. (The distinction becomes important when your text box is really big.)

   _____

   ▶ **Justify.** Adds spaces between your words so that the left and right edges of your sentences line up nicely.

   ▶ **Columns.** Lets you split your text into one, two, or three columns. Simply click the number of columns you'd like, and PowerPoint reformats your text immediately. Clicking More Columns lets you choose four or more columns, and lets you adjust the space between your columns.

   ___ TIP _____

   If you need absolutely precise layouts (because, for example, you're mocking up a program interface or a printable brochure), you can align text in a text box by setting internal margins (left, right, top, and bottom). To do so, in the Home tab, click Alignment → More Options to display the Format Text Effects dialog box with the Text Box option selected.

   _____

   ▶ **Align Text.** Click Align Text to position text at the top, middle, or bottom of a bounding box.

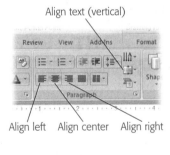

Align text (vertical)

Align left   Align center   Align right

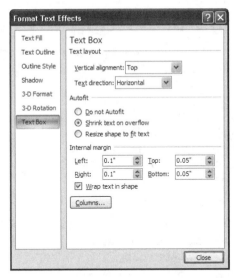

Figure 3-16. Left: Align Text Left, Center, and Align Text Right refer to horizontal alignment. To specify vertical alignment (top, middle, or bottom), click the Align Text (vertically) icon.

Right: If you need absolutely precise layouts (because, for example, you're mocking up a program interface or a printable brochure), you can align text in a text box by setting internal margins (left, right, top, and bottom). To do so, in the Home tab, click Alignment → More Options to display the Format Text Effects dialog box with the Text Box option selected.

TIP

PowerPoint offers one additional, seldom-used alignment option, the Distributed alignment option, which (like Justify) lines up the left and right edges of your text, but (unlike Justify) stretches out the last (*orphaned*) line so that it, too, lines up left and right. To apply the Distributed alignment option, first select your text. Then, on the Home tab, click the Paragraph dialog launcher and, in the Paragraph dialog box that appears, head to the Alignment drop-down box and choose Distributed.

Copying Formatting with the Format Painter

You've spent half an hour tweaking, testing, and perfecting, and at long last, your slide headings are perfectly formatted. PowerPoint gives you an easy way to copy your formatting and apply it to new headings using the Format Painter (the icon shaped like a little paintbrush that appears both on the Home → Clipboard group, and on the Mini Toolbar).

To copy formatting using the Format painter:

1. Click anywhere on the text that has formatting you want to copy.

2. Click the Format Painter. (Notice that, when you mouse over your slide, your cursor turns into a little paintbrush).

3. Click the text you want to format.

To copy formatting to a bunch of different text elements in one fell swoop:

1. Click anywhere on the text that has formatting you want to copy.

2. Double-click the Format Painter. (Once again, your cursor turns into a little paintbrush).

3. Click-drag or double-click to select the text element. As you select, PowerPoint applies the copied formatting to that element. You can repeat this step as many times as you like.

4. When you're finished, click the Format Painter icon again or press Esc. Your icon turns back into a pointer.

Creating Lists

For better or worse PowerPoint slides and bulleted lists are practically synonymous. The fact is, lists (both bulleted and numbered) like the ones you see in Figure 3-17 are a natural fit for PowerPoint because they let you organize information clearly and concisely.

In fact, when you find yourself adding a lot of lists to your slides, let PowerPoint format them for you automatically. After you do, each time you type in an asterisk or a number followed by some text and then the Enter key, PowerPoint automatically changes the asterisk to a basic bullet and types in a new bullet (or number). To turn on automatic list formatting, select Office → PowerPoint Options → Proofing → AutoCorrect Options → AutoFormat As You Type and then turn on the checkbox next to "Automatic bulleted and numbered lists."

Of course, you can always turn a series of sentences into a list manually. Here's how:

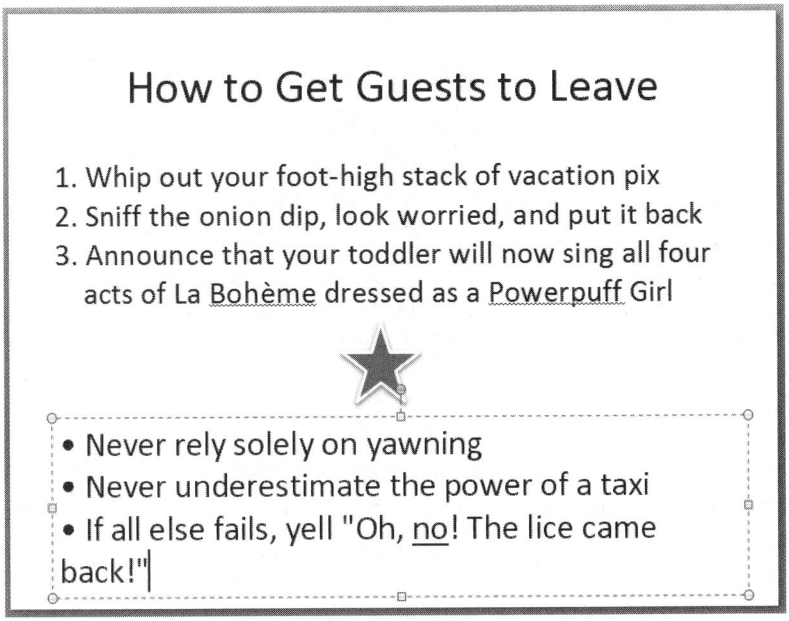

How to Get Guests to Leave

1. Whip out your foot-high stack of vacation pix
2. Sniff the onion dip, look worried, and put it back
3. Announce that your toddler will now sing all four acts of La <u>Bohème</u> dressed as a <u>Powerpuff</u> Girl

- Never rely solely on yawning
- Never underestimate the power of a taxi
- If all else fails, yell "Oh, <u>no</u>! The lice came back!"

Figure 3-17. Here they are, the bread and butter of PowerPoint slides the world over: numbered lists and bulleted lists. You can choose different bullet and numbering schemes, as shown in Figure 3-19.

1. **Click in a text box.**

   The Drawing Tools | Format context tab pops up, and PowerPoint activates the formatting options on the Home tab.

2. **Select the text you want to turn into a list. Then, go to Home → Paragraph and click one of the list buttons shown in Figure 3-18.**

   These buttons are toggles. Clicking once adds the bullets or numbering; clicking again removes it.

   ▶ **Bullets.** The program applies bullets to the beginning of each selected word or sentence.

   ▶ **Numbering.** The program applies sequential numbers (beginning with number 1) to the beginning of each selected word or sentence.

Bulleted list   Numbered list

Figure 3-18. Clicking either the Bullets or Numbering option automatically applies a standard bullet (or numbering) scheme to the text you've selected. If you prefer to customize the standard scheme, instead of clicking the button itself, click the tiny down arrow beside it to see a menu of different styles.

TIP

An alternative—and faster—way to display bullet and numbering options is to right-click your text and then, from the menu that appears, choose Bullets or Numbering.

Customizing bulleted lists

PowerPoint lets you customize your bulleted lists by choosing one of several built-in bullet graphics, or by using your own image for the bullet. You can also resize and recolor your bullets. Here's how.

1. **Select the list you want to customize. Go to Home → Paragraph, and then click the down arrow next to the Bullets button.**

   A list of bullet options appears (Figure 3-19).

2. **Click a bullet option.**

   PowerPoint automatically reformats your list based on the option you chose.

3. **If you don't see a bullet you like, from the option list, choose Bullets and Numbering.**

   The Bullets and Numbering dialog box appears with the Bullets tab already selected (Figure 3-20).

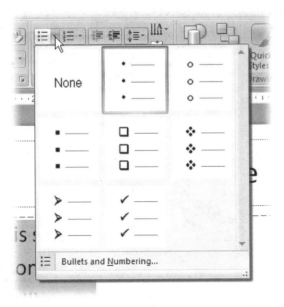

Figure 3-19. Most of the time, one of these standard bullet options will fit the bill. But for those times when you want to substitute an itty-bitty globe or daisy for the standard dot, choose Bullets and Numbering to see additional options.

4. **In the Bullets and Numbering dialog box, click Customize. In the Symbol dialog box that appears, select a symbol and click OK, and then Close.**

   The Symbol dialog box disappears and PowerPoint returns you to the Bullets and Numbering dialog box, where a new bulleted option appears featuring the symbol you selected. Click OK to apply the new bullet to your selection.

   After you click OK, you're back in the Bullets and Numbering dialog box. If you like, you can now change the color and size of your bullets, as described in the next two steps.

5. **To change the color of your bullets, click Color. Select a color swatch from the color picker.**

   The Bullets and Numbering dialog box redisplays all the bullet options using the color you just selected.

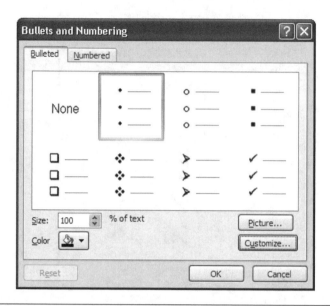

Figure 3-20. The Bullets and Numbering dialog box, shown here, lets you change the way standard bullets and list numbers appear.

6. **If you like, you can change the size of your bullets. In the Bullets and Numbering dialog box, click to increase and decrease the "Size % of text" counter, or type your own number.**

   100% means the bullet appears the same size as the largest upper-case letter of text, 50% means the bullet appears half that size, and so on.

7. **When the Bullets and Numbering dialog box displays the precise bullet option you want, click OK.**

   PowerPoint applies your customized bulleting scheme to your selection.

Customizing numbered lists

This procedure is a lot like customizing a bulleted list.

1. **Select the numbered list you want to tweak. Go to Home → Paragraph → Numbering and click the down arrow.**

   A slew of numbering options appears (Figure 3-21).

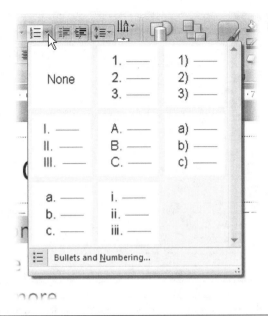

Figure 3-21. Here are the most popular numbering schemes. (If you're wondering, choosing "None" just indents the list.) Click Bullets and Numbering to color, resize, or choose a new starting number for your list.

2. **Click a numbering option.**

   PowerPoint automatically reformats your list based on the option you chose.

3. **To change the color of a list number, select Bullets and Numbering. When the Bullets and Numbering dialog box appears (Figure 3-22), click Color, and then select a color swatch from the color picker that appears.**

   The Bullets and Numbering dialog box redisplays all of the list number options using the color you just selected.

4. **If you like, you can specify how large you want your number to appear in relation to your text: In the Bullets and Numbering dialog box, select the numbering option you want to resize, and then click to increase and decrease the "Size % of text" counter, or type your own number.**

   100% means the number appears the same size as largest uppercase letter of text; 50% means the number appears half that size; and so on.

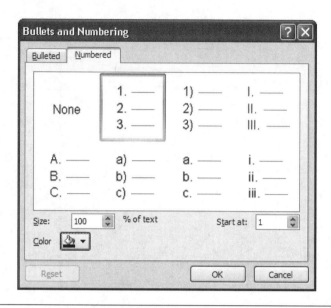

Figure 3-22. Because details matter, PowerPoint lets you choose from a variety of list-numbering options.

5. **If you like, you can change the first number in your list from 1 to something else. From the Bullets and Numbering dialog box, click the "Start at" box and then click the counter or type in your own starting number.**

    The options in the dialog box change automatically.

6. **When the Bullets and Numbering dialog box shows the customized numbering option you want, click to select it, and then click OK.**

    PowerPoint applies your customized numbering scheme to your selection.

Changing Indents

Unlike a word processing program, the text you add to your slides typically doesn't need a whole lot of special indenting. After all, one of the first rules of creating a great PowerPoint presentation is to keep your text brief—which means multiple paragraphs are out (and with them, the need to fiddle with your indents).

But if you *do* need to change the indentation—if you want to adjust the spacing between a bullet and its associated list item, for example—then you can.

Here's how it works: An *indent* is the space PowerPoint automatically leaves before the first line of every paragraph you add to a slide. Out of the box, PowerPoint assumes an indent of half an inch, but the program gives you three ways to change that setting:

▶ **Choose Home → Paragraph → Decrease List Level or Home → Paragraph → Increase List Level.** Selecting Home → Paragraph → Decrease List Level decreases the indent for the currently selected text box by one-half inch (or whatever you've set the indent to; see the third bullet below). Home → Paragraph → Increase List Level increases the indent by one-half inch (or whatever you've sent the indent to). Your text redisplays automatically. PowerPoint doesn't apply your changes to any unselected text or any other text boxes on your slide.

___ **NOTE** _____

If you select a list item and then choose Home → Paragraph → Decrease List Level or Home → Paragraph → Increase List Level, PowerPoint demotes or promotes the list item, adjusting text size as appropriate.

_____

▶ **Turn on rulers and drag your indents where you want them.** Figure 3-23 shows you the rulers, indents, and tab stops you see when you turn on rulers (View → Ruler). Selecting text and then dragging an indent tells PowerPoint to redisplay your selected text automatically based on the new indent. (PowerPoint doesn't apply your changes to any unselected text, or to any other text boxes on your slide.)

▶ **Use the Paragraph dialog box to specify a numeric value (in percentages of inches) for indentations.** To see the Paragraph dialog box shown in Figure 3-24, click the dialog box launcher at the bottom of the Paragraph group (or right-click selected text and then chose Paragraph from the shortcut menu. The indentation options include:

—**Before text.** Indents the entire paragraph from the left margin.

—**Special.** Lets you apply your indents to the first line only, to every line but the first line (hanging), or to none of the text.

—**By.** Lets you choose the width of the indent. PowerPoint displays width options in tenths of an inch, but you can type in hundredths of an inch if you like.

First-line indent   Left margin

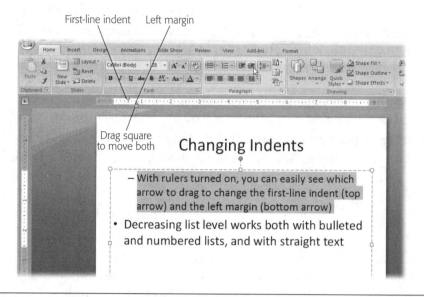

Figure 3-23. In this example, the top paragraph has just been demoted. The top triangle you see in the ruler is the first line indent; the bottom arrow is the indent for the remaining lines in the paragraph. Drag the square to move both in one fell swoop.

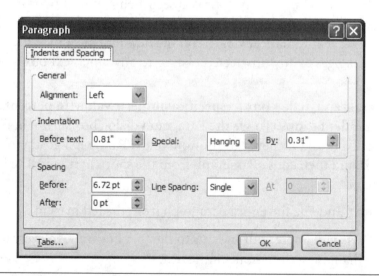

Figure 3-24. The alignment you choose affects your indents. If you set the Alignment field to Left, for example, your indents start at the left; if it's set to Center, your indents start from where your text is centered.

Changing Tab Stops

A *tab* is the amount of space PowerPoint leaves when you press the Tab key. For example, you can scoot the first sentence of a paragraph over by clicking in front of the first word in the paragraph and pressing Tab, and you can scoot an entire list over by selecting the list and pressing Tab. You can also use tabs to create columns.

> **NOTE**
>
> You don't *have* to use tabs to create columns; in fact, PowerPoint has a special columns option you can use (page 99), and it's a lot easier to work with for columns.

Out of the box, PowerPoint sets tab stops every inch, but you can set your tab stops wherever you like. PowerPoint gives you two ways to do that:

▶ **Turn on rulers and drag your tab stops where you want them.** Figure 3-23 shows you the rulers, indents, and tab stops you see when you turn on rulers (View → Show/Hide → Ruler). Selecting text and then dragging a tab stop tells PowerPoint to redisplay your selected text automatically based on the new tab stop. (PowerPoint doesn't apply your changes to unselected text, or to any other text boxes on your slide.)

▶ **Use the Tab dialog box to specify a numeric value (in percentages of inches) for tab stops.** To see the Tabs dialog box shown in Figure 3-25, click the Home → Paragraph dialog box launcher and then, in the Paragraph dialog box that appears, click Tabs. The tab options you can set include:

—**Add a tab stop.** Click to choose a number in the Tab stop position field, and then click Set.

—**Delete a tab stop.** Select the tab stop you want to delete, and then click Clear.

—**Delete all the tab stops for this slideshow.** Click Clear All.

—**Change how far apart PowerPoint places its built-in tab stops.** Change the number in the Default tab stops field.

—**Change a custom tab stop.** Delete the tab stop and create a new one.

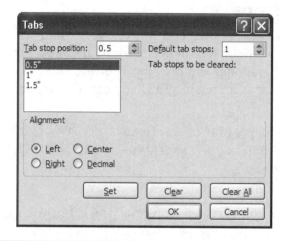

Figure 3-25. After you add, change, or delete a tab stop, click OK to apply the change and dismiss the dialog box.

Changing Text Direction

Most languages read left to right, so most of the time, that's the way you want to display your text. But PowerPoint lets you rotate your text so that it reads top-to-bottom, right-to-left, left-to-right, upside down—pretty much any direction you like. PowerPoint gives you two options for changing the direction of your text: using the Text Direction option, and using the Size and Position dialog box.

Using the Text Direction option

This option is the one to use if you want to rotate text all the way to the left or all the way to the right, or to stack your text from the top of your text box to the bottom. (Typing your text first and *then* changing its direction is much easier than changing the direction of a text box and then typing in your text.)

1. **Click anywhere in a text box. Choose Home → Paragraph → Text Direction (the A with arrows icon). From the menu that appears, choose one of the following options (see examples of each in Figure 3-26):**

   ▶ **Horizontal.** Basic left to right.

   ▶ **Rotate all text 90°.** Positions text on the right side of the slide, rotating each letter so that the text reads from top to bottom.

- **Rotate all text 270°.** Positions text on the left side of the slide, rotating each letter so that the text reads from bottom to top.

- **Stacked.** Stacks letters on top of each other, from top to bottom, without rotating any letters.

2. **Because PowerPoint doesn't automatically change the size of your text box when it repositions your text, you may have to resize your text box yourself to make your text readable in its jaunty new position.**

   If you don't remember how to resize a text box, see page 41.

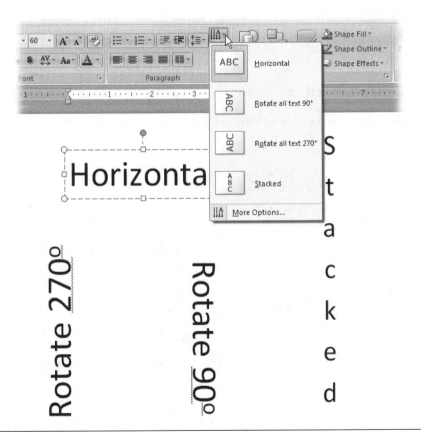

Figure 3-26. Changing the direction of your text makes your text harder to read. So unless you want to use one of these effects as a graphic design element, you can safely skip this trick.

Formatting Text Boxes

In addition to formatting the *text* on your slides, you can also format the text *boxes* that surround the text by applying options such as visible borders, colored backgrounds, and 3-D effects. These options don't change the text inside the text boxes, just the text boxes themselves. Formatting a text box is a good way to draw your audience's attention to a specific bit of text.

To format a text box:

1. **Click anywhere in the text box you want to format. Choose Home → Drawing → Quick Styles.**

    The gallery of effects you see in Figure 3-27 appears. As you mouse over each effect, PowerPoint previews the effect for you on your slide.

2. **Click to choose the effect you want.**

    On your slide, PowerPoint automatically formats your text box.

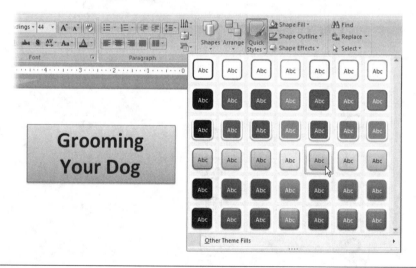

Figure 3-27. Clicking Home → Drawing → Quick Styles lets you turn an ordinary text box into a 3-D button with the click of a mouse—great for emphasizing headings. For a more subtle effect, choose one of the outline options.

FORMATTING AND LAYING OUT YOUR SLIDES

- ▶ Changing Slide Layout
- ▶ Changing Background Color
- ▶ Reapplying Themes, Colors, and Fonts

IN THE PREVIOUS CHAPTER, YOU LEARNED HOW TO MASSAGE TEXT into perfectly indented paragraphs, columns, and lists. Now it's time for the big picture. This chapter shows you how to format slide using *layouts,* and how to reapply a *theme* (see page 36) or *color scheme* (a list of coordinating font colors). Finally—and most important when you're in a time crunch—you'll learn how to turn on PowerPoint's automatic formatting options.

Changing Slide Layout

Each time you create a slide—by creating a new presentation, or by adding a slide to an existing presentation—PowerPoint gives that slide a layout such as the Title Slide layout, with one title text placeholder near the top and one subtitle text placeholder near the middle of the slide. But you can change the layout of your slide at any time, either before you've added content to it or after. PowerPoint gives you several options for changing slide layout:

▶ **Apply canned layouts to your slides.** You can tell PowerPoint to put a title at the top of a slide and two content placeholders (for text, pictures, and so on) side-by-side in the body of the slide.

▶ **Change orientation.** You can change a *landscape* orientation (where the slide's wider than it is tall) to a *portrait* orientation (where the slide's taller than it is wide).

▶ **Reposition elements.** You can drag text boxes and other objects (such as pictures) around on your slide to reposition them.

Applying a Canned Layout

PowerPoint offers nine canned layouts you can use. Most of the time, you're going to want to apply these layouts before you add text to your slides, but you can apply them after, as well.

To apply a canned layout to your slide:

1. **Create a new slide (page 43). Click any blank spot on your new slide.**

    Make sure you don't click a text placeholder, picture, diagram, or other object.

2. **Choose Home → Slides → Layout.**

   A layout gallery based on the template or theme you've applied to your slide-show appears. (You can also display the layout gallery by right-clicking the slide or the slide thumbnail you see in the Slides pane and then, from the context menu that appears, mousing over the Layout option.)

3. **From the layout gallery, click to choose the layout thumbnail you want to apply to your slide (Figure 4-1).**

   Mousing over any thumbnail in the gallery pops up the name of that thumbnail option. Typically, your options include:

   ▶ **Title Slide.** One title placeholder near the top of the slide, and one subtitle placeholder.

   ▶ **Title and Content.** One title placeholder and one large content placeholder.

   ▶ **Section Header.** Similar to the Title Slide layout, but with a contrasting background. (Useful for alerting your audience that you're starting a new section of your slideshow.)

   ▶ **Two Content.** One title placeholder and two content placeholders, each containing an icon you can click to add a diagram, chart, picture, or other content.

   ▶ **Comparison.** Similar to the Two Content layout, but with extra placeholders for headings.

   ▶ **Title Only.** One title placeholder.

   ▶ **Blank.** No text placeholders at all.

   ▶ **Content with Caption.** One title placeholder and one placeholder containing an icon you can click to add a diagram, chart, picture, or other content (see Figure 4-1).

   ▶ **Picture with Caption.** One title placeholder and one placeholder you can click to add a picture.

   PowerPoint automatically applies the layout to your slide.

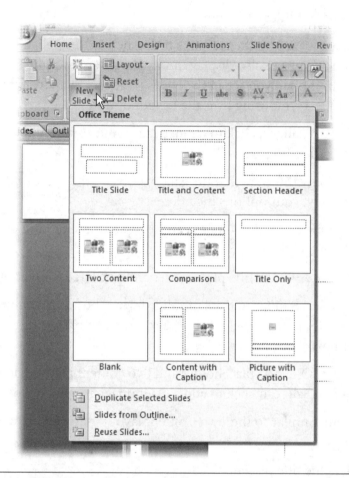

Figure 4-1. Unfortunately, the layout options don't automatically preview—you have to apply one to see how it'll affect your slide. PowerPoint never deletes any of the content you already have on your slide when you apply a new layout; it simply rearranges your content as best it can.

Switching Orientation from Landscape to Portrait (and Back)

Unless you tell it otherwise, PowerPoint assumes you want your presentation to appear in *landscape* form; that is, with slides that appear wider than they are tall. But you can change this orientation to *portrait* if you like. For example, if you intend to print your presentation, staple the pages, and hand it out to your audience, then you may want to switch to portrait so your audience can flip through the pages more easily.

To choose an orientation, go to Design → Page Setup → Slide Orientation and choose either Portrait or Landscape. Figure 4-2 shows you an example of each.

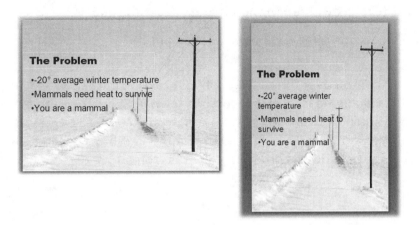

Figure 4-2. Left: Here, you see a slide in landscape orientation, which is the standard orientation for PowerPoint slides.

Right: Here's what a slide looks like in portrait orientation. You can't change the orientation of a single slide or group of slides; it's all the slides in a presentation, or none.

Repositioning Text Boxes

PowerPoint gives you different ways to reposition the text boxes (and other objects) on your slides. You can either drag objects where you want them, or use the Size and Position dialog box.

Dragging typically works best when you have only a few objects on your slide. If you've got a bunch of objects (especially if they're overlapping), or if the text box you want to move is so completely filled with text you think you'll have trouble selecting its border to drag it, you'll want to use the Size and Position dialog box and save yourself some aggravation.

To reposition a text box by dragging:

1. **Click inside the text box you want to reposition and mouse over the outline of the text box.**

   PowerPoint changes your cursor from an arrow to the double-arrow cross you see in Figure 4-3.

2. **Click the text box outline.**

The dashed outline turns solid.

3. **Drag the text box where you want it and release the mouse.**

PowerPoint redraws the text box where you put it.

> **TIP**
>
> For finer control over the position of your text box: As soon as you see both the double-headed arrow cursor shown in Figure 4-3 and a solid text box outline, press the arrow keys on your keyboard to move the text box up, down, left, or right. To move the text box in even tinier increments, hold down Ctrl while you press the arrow keys.

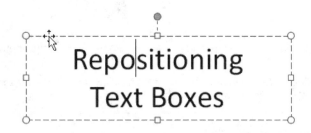

Figure 4-3. When you click in a text box, the text box outline appears dashed. When you click the outline itself—which you need to do to reposition the text box—the outline changes from dashed to solid. If you're having trouble finding the right spot to click, look for the double-headed arrow cursor. When you see it, you know you're in the right spot to drag.

> **TIP**
>
> If you drag a bunch of stuff around on a slide and then change your mind and want to put it back the way it was, there's an easy way to revert to your original. Choosing Home → Slides → Reset tells Power-Point to change your slide back to its original layout.

To reposition a text box using the Size and Position dialog box:

1. **Click anywhere inside the text box you want to reposition. Go to Drawing Tools | Format, and click the Size dialog launcher.**

The Size and Position dialog box pictured in Figure 4-4 appears.

2. **On the Position tab, use the Horizontal box to tell PowerPoint how many inches to position the top-left corner of the text box from the left edge of the slide.**

   PowerPoint moves your text box left and right so you can gauge the effects on your slide in real-time.

3. **Use the Vertical box to tell PowerPoint how many inches to position the top-left corner text box from the top of the slide.**

   PowerPoint moves your text box up and down so you can gauge the effects on the slide in real-time.

4. **When you're satisfied with the position of your text box, click Close.**

   The Size and Position dialog box disappears.

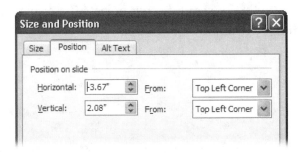

Figure 4-4. The Position tab of the Size and Position dialog box lets you specify precisely how you want to position your text boxes and other elements, which is especially useful if you're using Power-Point to create a program interface mock-up. If you like, you can tell PowerPoint to calculate the Horizontal and Vertical amounts you specify based on the center of your slide (instead of the top-left corner).

Help for Positioning Text Boxes: Zoom, Guides, and Grid

Whether you prefer dragging or using the Size and Position dialog box, there are times you'll need a little help positioning your text boxes and other objects—especially if your eyesight's not the best. PowerPoint offers that help in the form of the zoom, guides, and grid.

- **Zoom.** The *zoom* tool magnifies your slide, making it easier for you to distinguish between the boundaries of different objects on a cluttered slide. To use this tool, drag the zoom slider in the status bar at the bottom of the PowerPoint window. You can also click the + or - signs to zoom in or out, respectively.

- **Guides.** *Guides* in PowerPoint consist of two movable (draggable) crosshairs, one horizontal and the other vertical (Figure 4-5). Guides don't show up when you run your presentation; they appear only when you're working with your slides, to help you align text boxes and other objects. To display the guides, click Alt + F9. To make them disappear, click Alt + F9 again.

  As you drag a guide, PowerPoint pops up a little direction arrow and the number of inches the guide currently is away from the center of your slide, helping you align stuff exactly 2.5 inches left of center, for example.

- **Grid.** PowerPoint's *grid* (Figure 4-5) gives you a bunch of visual reference points you can use to line up text boxes and other objects. To display the grid, select View → Show/Hide → Gridlines.

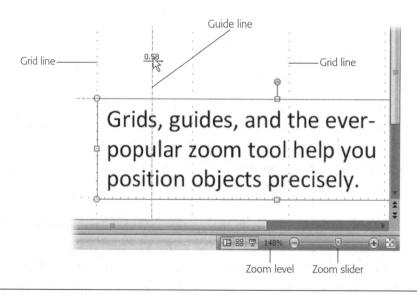

Figure 4-5. The grid helps when you're positioning text boxes; guides are more useful when you're lining up a bunch of objects. Clicking the zoom tool blows up your slide (here, to a whopping 148%) so you can position objects more precisely.

Changing Background Color

In most cases, you won't want to change the background color of your slides. Instead, you'll rely on the professionally designed themes that come with Power-Point, which coordinate text and background color and effects into an aesthetically pleasing package.

Of course, there's an exception or two to every rule. In the case of background color, one exception to the don't-change-it rule is when you need to match your presentation to a specific (non-PowerPoint) corporate or organizational palette, such as the one your Marketing department uses for brochures and four-color ads.

WORD TO THE WISE

Building a Better Background

You're the boss when it comes to choosing a background color and effect for your slides. But keep these tips in mind:

✳ **Go dark—and be consistent.** Dark backgrounds tend to look good in presentations delivered onscreen, while light (or white) backgrounds are best saved for printed materials. Whichever you choose, though—light or dark—just make sure you stick with it. Changing backgrounds from slide to slide is one of the quickest ways to confuse your audience. (In the interest of free choice, you'll find instructions in this section for changing individual slide backgrounds. But it's still not a good idea.)

✳ **If you apply a background gradient, be careful how you arrange your text on top of it.** Few things shout "this is my first PowerPoint presentation" louder than text spanning a background that ranges from light to dark. No matter what color you make your text, part of it will be unreadable. If you *do* decide on a funky background, think like a book- or CD-cover stylist and confine your text to the area of the slide that contrasts best with your text.

Another exception is if you've monkeyed with your font color as described on page 95. Because the human eye sees color in a relative context, black text (for example) appears different depending on whether you set it against a white background, a pink background, or a dark blue background. So when you change the color of your text, you may want to adjust the background color of your slide, too, until you find a combination that looks good to you.

To change the background color of one, some, or all of the slides in a presentation:

1. **In the Slides pane (see Figure 4-6), Ctrl-click to select the slides you want to change.**

   You can skip this step if you want to change the background of the currently selected slide only. To select all of the slides in a presentation press Ctrl+A.

Figure 4-6. If you don't see the Slides pane on the left side of your PowerPoint window, you—or someone else who has access to your computer—may have turned it off. In that case, head down to the Status bar and click Normal (or select View → Presentation Views → Normal). If your Slides pane doesn't look similar to this one, make sure the Slides tab is selected.

2. Choose Design → Background Styles.

A gallery of background color options, complete with cool gradient effects, appears (Figure 4-7).

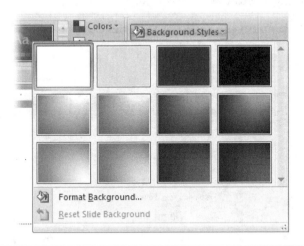

Figure 4-7. The background options PowerPoint offers are ones that coordinate with the theme you've applied to your presentation.

NOTE

Another way to see basic background options is to right-click a blank spot on your slide and then, from the menu that appears, choose Background Styles.

---

3. From the gallery, click to choose an option.

The gallery disappears, and PowerPoint applies the new color-and-gradient background to all the currently selected slides.

NOTE

PowerPoint doesn't police you. If you apply a black background to a slide containing black text, your text becomes unreadable—and Power-Point doesn't warn you in advance.

If you don't see a color option you like in the gallery, you can choose from a broader selection:

1. **In the Background Styles gallery, choose Format Background.**

   The Format Background dialog box opens.

2. **On the Fill tab, turn on the radio button next to "Solid fill."**

   The options you see in Figure 4-8 appear.

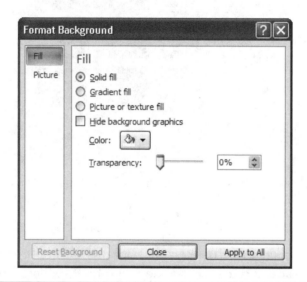

Figure 4-8. Click Color to display a color picker that lets you choose a new background color (see Figure 3-12 for an example). Most of the time, you'll want to stick with one of the Theme colors PowerPoint offers. After all, the whole point of themes is to help you create tasteful presentations. But if you prefer, you can always head to the bottom of the color picker and click "More colors" to apply your own custom-blended background color.

3. **Click the Color drop-down box to display a color picker, from which you can choose the color you want.**

   In most cases, you should stick with a color in the Themes Colors section, so that your background color coordinates with the theme you've applied to your presentation. (You can see how to reapply a theme on page 131.)

4. **If you want to vary the tint of your color, drag the transparency slider. You can also change the percentage in the Transparency box.**

   Whether you drag the transparency slider or use the transparency box, Power-Point automatically previews the transparency effect on the slide.

5. **When you're satisfied with the color and transparency you've chosen, click Close (to dismiss the Format Background dialog box and apply your new background to the currently selected slides) or Apply to All (to dismiss the Format Background dialog box and apply your new background to every slide in your presentation).**

Adding a Gradient Effect

A solid colored background, like the ones you learned to apply in the previous section, sometimes do the trick. But some folks think a *gradient* effect (Figure 4-9) looks a bit more sophisticated. Instead of a single color, gradients blend multiple bands of color for mild to wild effects. All of the basic background options that PowerPoint suggests (Figure 4-7) include gradients, but you can apply your own custom gradient effect quickly and easily.

To apply a gradient effect to your background:

1. **Choose Design → Background → Background Styles.**

   A gallery of background color options appears, complete with cool gradient effects.

2. **In the gallery, choose Format Background.**

   The Format Background dialog box appears.

3. **On the Fill tab, turn on the radio box next to "Gradient fill."**

   PowerPoint applies a basic fill to your slide, and the gradient-related options you see in Figure 4-10 appear.

4. **Click the down arrow next to "Preset colors."**

   A gallery of preset gradient options appears (Figure 4-11).

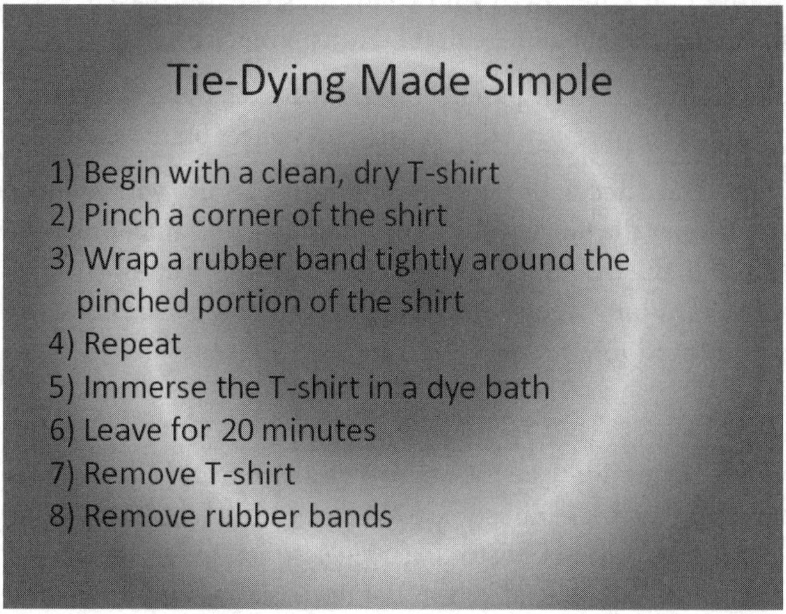

Tie-Dying Made Simple

1) Begin with a clean, dry T-shirt
2) Pinch a corner of the shirt
3) Wrap a rubber band tightly around the
    pinched portion of the shirt
4) Repeat
5) Immerse the T-shirt in a dye bath
6) Leave for 20 minutes
7) Remove T-shirt
8) Remove rubber bands

Figure 4-9. No doubt about it: Whether on a big-screen projector or decent-sized computer monitor, gradient backgrounds look more sophisticated than solid-color backgrounds. Subtle colors and a hint of transparency tone down the gradient so your audience can focus on your content.

5. **Click to choose one of the gradient presets.**

   If you like, you can customize the preset you selected by adding one of the following options:

   ▶ **Hide background objects.** Tells PowerPoint not to display background graphics on top of your gradient (assuming you've added background graphics to your slides). See page 278 for details.

   ▶ **Type.** Lets you choose from among Linear (straight bands), Radial (bulls-eye bands), Rectangular (rectangular bands), Path (rectangular bulls-eye bands), or "Shade from title." Shade from title tells PowerPoint to display the gradient radiating from the title area outward; otherwise, the gradient radiates from the bottom right corner of the slide.

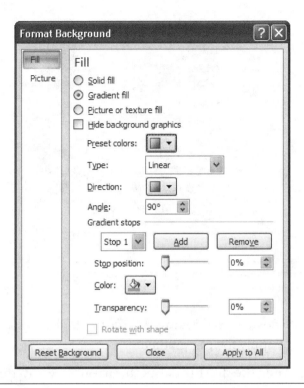

Figure 4-10. PowerPoint gives you a dizzying array of options you can apply to create customized gradient effects.

- ▶ **Direction.** Available only if you choose a type of Linear, Radial, or Rectangle, this option lets you choose from thumbnails showing gradient bands running in different directions (straight across, up at an angle, and so on).

- ▶ **Angle.** Available only if you choose the Linear gradient, this option lets you choose the angle at which the bands appear (45 percent is diagonal; 90 percent is straight across).

- ▶ **Gradient stops.** Click Add to tell PowerPoint to display an additional gradient band (10's the max). To delete one of the gradient bands you begin with, choose one from the drop-down box and then click Remove.

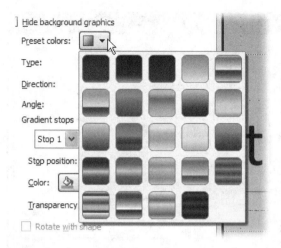

Figure 4-11. This black-and-white screenshot doesn't do justice to the color-drenched gradient presets, or precreated gradient effects, that PowerPoint offers.

▶ **Color.** Click the down arrow next to this option to display a color picker and choose a color to apply to your gradient.

▶ **Stop position.** Drag the slider (or click the arrows) next to this option to tell PowerPoint where to begin your gradient's color bands.

▶ **Transparency.** Drag the slider (or click the arrows) next to this option to fade your gradient, from 100 percent (see-through) to 0 percent (completely opaque).

▶ **Rotate with shape.** Normally, choosing this option tells PowerPoint to rotate the gradient bands along with the shape—but when you apply a gradient background effect to a slide, PowerPoint deactivates (grays out) this radio box.

When you're satisfied with your gradient effect, choose Close to apply it to the currently selected slide or Apply to All to apply it to all of the slides in your presentation.

Reapplying Themes, Colors, and Fonts

It's great having the freedom to apply your own custom colors, fonts, and effects—until you make so many changes that your presentation looks like something your three-year-old might have created. Luckily, if that happens, you can reapply Power-Point's professionally designed themes, color schemes or fonts to your presentation, which clears most of your changes and lets you start over from scratch. Reapplying themes is also a great way to try out new looks.

WARNING

Because many themes feature different fonts, your text may appear misaligned after you reapply a theme or font. To avoid having to flip through slides and fix misaligned text, apply the theme you want before you've filled all 600 of your intricately laid-out slides with text.

Reapplying a Theme

Themes contain information that tells PowerPoint what fonts, colors, images, and layouts to apply to your presentation. You can reapply a theme after you've added content to your slides, but be aware that depending on the theme you choose to reapply, you may have to go back through your slides and eyeball them to make sure they look okay. (Different fonts and sizes can make a presentation that looked great in one theme look terrible in another.)

To reapply a theme:

1. **If you want to reapply a theme to one or more slides—but not *all* the slides in your presentation—select the slides you want to change.**

   Page 142 shows you how to select multiple slides.

2. **In the Design → Themes group, right-click the theme you want to reapply.**

   A shortcut menu appears.

TIP

Thanks to real estate constraints, the Design tab shows only a handful of themes. To see all of the themes you can apply to your slideshow, click the down arrow next to the displayed themes. Mousing over a theme tells PowerPoint to preview the theme in real time on your slide.

3. **From the shortcut menu, choose one of the following:**

   ▶ **Apply to All Slides.** Applies the theme to every slide in your presentation.

   ▶ **Apply to Selected Slides.** Applies the theme only to those slides you've selected.

   PowerPoint reapplies the selected theme.

WARNING
> Warning: A reapplied theme does *not* always overwrite the custom background you've added to your presentation. To delete a background effect you've applied to a slide, click the Reset Background button in the Format Background dialog box (Figure 4-10).

Reapplying a Color Scheme

Professionally designed themes—including the ones that come with PowerPoint—typically come with multiple color combinations, or *schemes*. These color schemes tell PowerPoint which colors to use for heading text, regular text, hyperlinks, slide backgrounds, and more. All of these colors were chosen by the theme designers to look good together, so choosing one of the theme-sanctioned color schemes ensures you of a reasonably attractive result.

If you decide halfway through creating a presentation that you'd like it to appear in different colors, or if you've experimented with changing font colors (page 95) and want to put your presentation back to the way it was, then you can do so by reapplying a color scheme.

To reapply a color scheme:

1. **Choose Design → Themes → Colors.**

   A gallery of color schemes similar to the one you see in Figure 4-12 appears.

2. **Click to choose one of the color schemes.**

   The gallery disappears. On your slide, PowerPoint changes the color of your background and text based on the color scheme you chose.

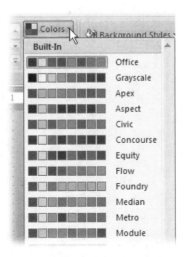

Figure 4-12. The color schemes you see listed in the gallery depend both on the theme you apply to your presentation. (The scroll bar indicates there are a few more color schemes to choose from.)

Reapplying a Font

There are two reasons you may want to reapply a font to your presentation:

▶ You've done a bit of experimenting with fonts, changing the text on the first couple of slides to one font, the text on the next couple of slides to a different font, and so on. Now you're unhappy with the helter-skelter results and want to reapply a single, consistent font.

▶ You've assembled your presentation from several other presentations—either ones you've done yourself, or ones you've cadged from the office stockpile—and now you want to unify all these disparate-looking slides by applying a consistent font.

To reapply a font to all of the text in your slideshow, go to Design → Themes → Fonts. Then, in the Fonts gallery, simply click to choose the font you want to reapply.

EDITING YOUR SLIDESHOW

5

- ▶ Viewing Multiple Slides
- ▶ Adding, Deleting, and Moving Slides
- ▶ Inserting Slides from Other Slideshows
- ▶ Editing Slide and Layout Masters
- ▶ Adding Headers and Footers

If you want to give a great presentation, then you have to practice. But if you're like most folks, every time you fire up PowerPoint, clear your throat, and start rehearsing, you find a few places in your slideshow that need tweaking. For example, you may realize that you've duplicated information on a couple of slides. Or maybe you discover that you've forgotten to cover a critical point, or decide that a small graphic on each slide would reinforce your message. Or, worst of all, you realize that the way you've organized your content is all wrong.

I've Got Good News and Bad News...

Most presentations fit into one of three broad categories, and thinking about which category your message falls into helps you organize your content effectively: *good news*, *bad news*, and *here's some stuff you should know*.

* **Good news.** The classic example of a good news presentation is the sales pitch, where the good news is that your widget will bring health, wealth, and increased productivity to every customer smart enough to buy it.

  If you're giving a good news presentation, then consider placing your main point—the benefit your audience can expect—both at the beginning and end of your presentation. Always finish a good news presentation by telling your audience specifically what they need to do, to receive the benefit—for example, call a certain number to place an order.

* **Bad news.** Layoffs, budget cuts, and a new freeway displacing a neighborhood's homes are all examples of bad news presentations.

To prepare your audience for bad news, state the problem first in the most sober terms possible. "Our company's losing so much money we're nearly out of business," for example. Spend the middle of your presentation elaborating on the problem and describing possible alternatives, and then place your main point—the bad news you want your audience to accept—at the end of your presentation. Always finish a bad news presentation by reminding your audience how they can salvage some benefit from the bad news you're laying on them. ("The company is offering a generous severance package and help finding a new job," for example.)

* **Here's some stuff you should know.** This type of presentation isn't likely to engender a strong reaction in your audience, either good or bad. "Human Resources just changed the process for switching HMOs," for example. For neutral, informative topics like these, you need only place your main point at the beginning of your presentation.

In this chapter, you'll see how to make all these changes and more. You'll learn to reorder your slides as easily as you shuffle a pack of cards. You can add, delete, move, duplicate, and renumber slides, and even copy slides from other slideshows. You'll also see how to control the overall look and feel of your presentation by editing its behind-the-scenes slide masters.

Viewing Multiple Slides

When you're adding text and graphics to an individual slide, as described in Chapter 1, you're concerned with just one slide at a time—the slide you're working on. Not so when you want to edit your slideshow as a whole. In that case, you need a way to spread all your slides out in front of you (virtually speaking) so you can see what you've got and then decide which slides you want to delete, duplicate, move, and so on.

PowerPoint gives you two handy ways to see most (if not all) of your slides at once: the Slides pane that appears in Normal view (Figure 5-1), and Slide Sorter view (Figure 5-2).

Slides Pane

PowerPoint assumes you want to see the Slides pane (Figure 5-1) until you tell it otherwise. The Slides pane is mighty handy: When you right-click individual slides in the Slides pane, you can delete them, duplicate them, move them, and so on, as described in the following pages.

To get rid of the Slides pane, click the X in the upper-right corner. To bring it back again, click the Normal icon or choose View → Normal. If you don't see a bunch of thumbnails, check to make sure you've selected the Slides tab.

Slide Sorter View

For situations where you only need to see three or four slides at a time, the Slides pane is the way to go. But if you need to work with more slides at a time—for example, if you need to move slides 1–5 to the end of a 25-slide presentation—then you need to switch to Slide Sorter view (Figure 5-2).

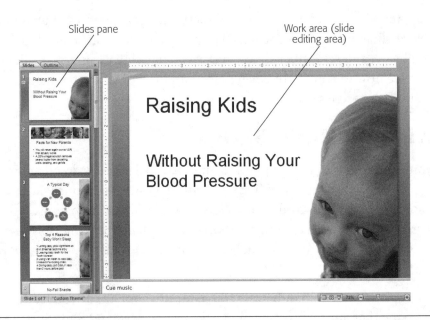

Slides pane

Work area (slide editing area)

Figure 5-1. When you click to select a slide in the Slides pane, PowerPoint displays the editable version of the slide in the work area. The number of slides you see in the Slides pane depends on how many slides are in your presentation, and how big you've made the Slides pane. Make it skinny, for example, and you'll see a lot more slides—but then PowerPoint has to make them really tiny to fit them all in. Drag the right edge of Slides pane to resize it.

To switch from one-slide-at-a-time Normal view to Slide Sorter view, either click the Slide Sorter icon or select View → Presentation Views → Slide Sorter.

— TIP

> Double-clicking a slide in Slide Sorter view pops you back to Normal view with the slide you double-clicked front and center, ready for you to edit.

Adding, Deleting, and Moving Slides

The best way to begin creating a PowerPoint presentation is to start with an outline, either a hand-sketched one or one created in a word processor (such as Microsoft Word). That way your material is pretty much organized before you begin putting your slides together (Figure 5-3).

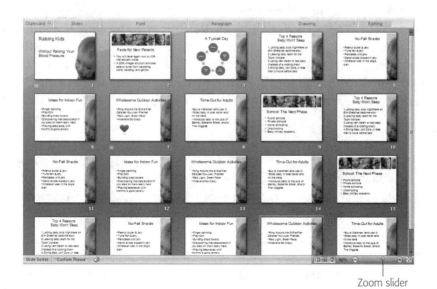

Zoom slider

Figure 5-2. An expanded version of the Slides pane in Slide Sorter view lets you see and work with about 20 slides at once (or more if you zoom out). When you have more than that, scroll bars appear in Slide Sorter view so you can scroll around and see them all.

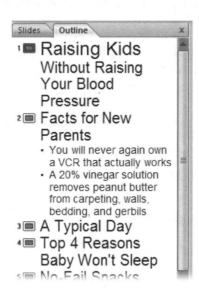

Figure 5-3. When you display your slideshow in Outline view, you see each slide's title and subtitle text—perfect for double-checking overall content. You can cut or delete slides from Outline view just as easily as you can from the Slides pane or Slide Sorter view.

Nobody gets everything right the first time, though. Even if you follow this wise design practice, you'll find yourself adding, deleting, and moving the individual slides that make up your slideshow as you rehearse your presentation. After all, you want your slideshow to be tight and well organized so you can concentrate on your message without worrying about repeating yourself, leaping from one unrelated topic to another, or leaving out main points altogether.

Adding Blank Slides

You can easily add a blank slide to your slideshow. (You can also bring in a slide from another slideshow, as shown on page 144.) When you create a new blank slide, PowerPoint lets you choose one of several popular layouts. For example, you can create a title slide or a slide containing two columns of text.

> **NOTE**
>
> Each of the layout options that PowerPoint offers corresponds to a *slide master,* which serves as a template for creating predesigned slides.

To add a slide to your slideshow:

1. **In the Slides pane, click to select the slide *after* which you want to add a new slide.**

   When you want to add a slide at the very beginning of your slideshow, add it after your first slide. Then move it to first position, as described on page 142.

2. **Go to Home → Slides and click the down arrow next to New Slide.**

   A layout gallery similar to the one in Figure 5-4 appears.

3. **Click to choose one of the canned layouts. (You can always change the layout of the slide later if it's not exactly what you want.)**

   PowerPoint creates a new blank slide based on your layout choice and displays the slide in your workspace, ready for you to edit.

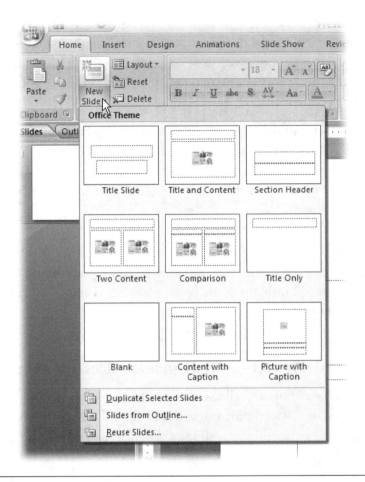

Figure 5-4. The basic slide layouts PowerPoint lets you choose from look similar to the ones you see here, but the details (like the graphics and the positioning of the title text) depend on the slide masters attached to your presentation. You can learn all about slide masters on page 147.

___ **NOTE** ___

PowerPoint gives you two additional, super-quick ways to add a slide. You can either click Home → Slides → New Slide (instead of the down-arrow next to New Slide), or—in either the Normal view's Slides pane or Slide Sorter view—you can right-click a slide and then, from the context menu that appears, choose New Slide. These methods don't let you choose a new layout, though; both simply create a basic Title and Content slide. To change to a different layout, right-click the newly added slide and choose Layout.

Deleting Slides

As you might expect, deleting a slide neatly excises it from your slideshow. After you delete a slide, it's gone; the only way to get it back is to click Undo, and *that* only works if you click Undo soon after you delete the slide. (PowerPoint only "undoes" so many actions per work session, as explained on page 66.)

If you're sure you want to delete the slide, then in the Slides pane that appears in Normal view, click to select the slide and then either click Home → Delete, or press the Delete key. Alternatively, in the Slides pane (or in Slide Sorter view), right-click the slide you want to delete and then choose Delete Slide from the shortcut menu that appears.

Moving Slides

Rearranging slides in PowerPoint has the same effect as rearranging transparencies—but because you shuffle them using your mouse, you can't accidentally drop them all over the floor.

To move one or more slides from one position in your slideshow to another:

1. **In Slide Sorter view, click to select the slide (or slides) you want to move.**

   To select multiple contiguous slides, click the first slide, then Shift-click the last slide. When you do, PowerPoint automatically highlights all the slides in between. To select multiple noncontiguous slides, Ctrl-click each slide separately.

2. **Drag your selection.**

   As you move your mouse, PowerPoint displays a line between slides (see Figure 5-5) to let you know where it will place your selection when you let go of your mouse.

> **TIP**
>
> If you can't drag your selection, check to make sure you've let go of the Ctrl and Shift keys. If you forget and keep one of them pressed down, then PowerPoint won't let you drag your selection.

3. **When the line appears where you want to put your selection, let go of your mouse.**

   PowerPoint removes your selection from its original position and inserts it into your slideshow at the point where you dropped it.

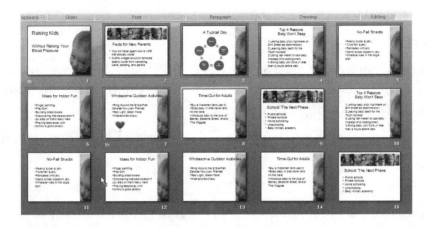

Figure 5-5. You can move slides in the Slides pane or Outline view, too, but it's easier in Slide Sorter view since you can see more slides. You can move slides before your first slide, after your last slide, or anywhere in between.

Duplicating Slides

If you do much work with PowerPoint, then you'll probably run into a situation eventually where you want to create two similar slides through duplicating. For example, maybe the last slide in your show reiterates what was on the first slide. Duplicating is also a handy way to experiment with the formatting or content of one slide and keep a good copy in case your editing efforts go haywire. In situations like these, you'll find it easier to duplicate a slide and then tweak the duplicate than to create two similar slides from scratch.

You can duplicate slides in the Slides pane, Outline view, or Slide Sorter view. To do so, select the slide (or slides) you want to duplicate, and then choose Home → Slides → New Slide → Duplicate Selected Slides. You can also right-click your selection and then select Duplicate Slide from the shortcut menu. PowerPoint duplicates the selected slide (or slides) and places the duplicate immediately after the selection.

Another (slower) way to duplicate slides is to copy and paste them, as described next.

Cutting, Copying, and Pasting Slides

PowerPoint's cut, copy, and paste commands are an alternative way to move and duplicate slides. There's nothing new to memorize, since these commands work exactly the same way as the cut, copy, and paste commands in other programs. You may also prefer the precision of clicking-and-picking to dragging slides around using your mouse.

To cut slides:

1. **In Normal, Outline, or Slide Sorter view, select the slide (or slides) you want to cut. Right-click the selection and then choose Cut from the shortcut menu (or click the selection and then press Ctrl+X).**

    The selection disappears. If you're in Slide Sorter view, a blinking vertical line appears in the spot where the selection used to be.

To copy slides:

1. **In either Normal or Slide Sorter view, select the slide (or slides) you want to copy. Right-click the selection and then choose Copy from the shortcut menu (or click the selection and then press Ctrl+C).**

To paste slides that you've cut or copied:

1. **Still in Normal or Slide Sorter view, click between the two slides where you want to paste your cut or copied slides.**

    A blinking line appears where you click.

2. **Press Ctrl+V or choose Home → Paste.**

    PowerPoint pastes in the most recently cut or copied slides and renumbers all of the slides in your slideshow.

Inserting Slides from Other Slideshows

If you create a lot of PowerPoint slideshows, then you'll be happy to know there's an easy way to grab slides from one slideshow and put them into another. Taking slides from other PowerPoint slideshows is useful not just for reusing chunks of slideshows that you've put together yourself, but also for borrowing from presentations that other folks have created.

Make the ^&$*@! Clipboard Go Away

Every time you cut, copy, or paste stuff on your slides, you're using the Office Clipboard—a fact that you may be unaware of until it slaps you in the face.

If you do a lot of cutting, copying, and pasting, then PowerPoint takes it upon itself to display the Clipboard pane, unceremoniously bumping your Slides pane out of the way and shrinking your workspace, which can be unnerving.

You'll find the Clipboard pane useful if, for example, you want to paste a line of text you copied two minutes ago into a new slide. You can grab the text and plunk it onto a slide even if you've cut and pasted other things in the meantime.

But most of the time, you'd probably rather have the screen space back. You can temporarily dismiss the clipboard by clicking the X in the upper-right corner, but it'll just pop up again.

To get the Clipboard to leave you alone until you summon it, head to the bottom of the Clipboard pane and click Options. Then, in the pop-up menu, turn off the checkbox next to Show Office Clipboard Automatically. Should you want to bring the Clipboard back into view, go to the Home tab, and then click the Clipboard dialog box launcher.

Of course, you can always open both slideshows, hunt around in slideshow #2 for the slides you want to copy, copy them, and then paste them into slideshow #1, exactly as described on page 144. But there's an easier approach—the Reuse Slides command.

To insert a slide from another slideshow:

1. **Open the slideshow into which you want to insert a slide from another slide-show.**

2. **In the Slides pane in Normal view, click to select the slide you want the new slide to appear** *after.*

   If you skip this step, then PowerPoint assumes you want to add a new slide after the first slide of your main slideshow.

3. **Choose Home → New Slide → Reuse Slides.**

   The Reuse Slides pane appears (Figure 5-6). Slideshow files you've previously borrowed from appear in a drop-down list.

Figure 5-6. The Reuse Slides pane gives you several ways to choose the slideshow you want to borrow slides from.

4. **From the "Insert slide from" drop-down menu, choose the slideshow you want to borrow from.**

   Alternatively, you can head to the bottom of the Reuse Slides pane, right under where it says Open, and click the name of the recently opened PowerPoint file you want to borrow from.

   ___ **TIP** _____

   You can click Browse → Browse File (or click the "Open a PowerPoint File" link) to look for PowerPoint files on your computer, using an Open dialog box like the one in Figure 1-9.

   _____

   In the Reuse Slides pane, a Slide Sorter view of the selected slideshow appears (Figure 5-7).

5. **Click the slide you want to add to your slideshow.**

   PowerPoint adds the slide to your slideshow *after* the currently selected slide.

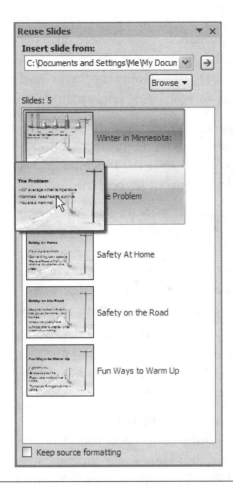

Figure 5-7. The preview section of the Reuse Slides pane shows you thumbnails of each slide in the other slideshow. If it's a huge slideshow, then scroll bars appear in the preview section so you can scroll down and see all of the slides. Each time you mouse over a slide, PowerPoint expands it so you can see it better. Click the expanded version of a slide to add it to your main slideshow.

Editing Slide and Layout Masters

Slide masters and layout masters determine the initial look of every single slide in your slideshow. For example, if you place one background image, three text place-holders, and a date-and-time footer on a slide master, then every slide in your slide-show will contain the same background image, the same three text placeholders positioned in the same spots, and the same date-and-time footer.

In fact, you've been using slide masters without even knowing it. Whenever you choose a theme for your presentation, you're actually applying a set of slide masters. A *theme* (page 36) is nothing more than a collection of masters. More specifically, a theme includes a *slide master* and a handful of *layout masters* packaged in a special file format (*.thmx*) so that you can easily apply them to different presentations.

The purpose of slide masters is to help you create an attractive, cohesive-looking slideshow: Make a change once, and it appears on dozens of slides instantly. And because PowerPoint lets you override the slide master by editing individual slides directly, you're not locked into an all-or-nothing look.

But if you want to tweak a theme or create your own—in other words, if you want to add the same color scheme, formatting, or object (graphic, text, background, and so on) to multiple slides—then you need to learn to how masters work. Fortunately, editing PowerPoint's masters is just as easy as editing any other slide. The only difference is that you're not editing an individual slide—you're setting up a sort of blueprint that you can then apply to any number of slides.

PowerPoint has a few different types of masters, which makes sense because the different presentation elements—slides, notes, handouts—require slightly different kinds of formatting. To understand masters in PowerPoint, all you need to know is what each one does:

▶ **Slide master.** A *slide master* is a visual blueprint of how you want to format all the slides in your slideshow. Add a blue background and your company logo to your slide master, for example, and every single slide in your slideshow will have a blue background and that logo. Although most of the time one slide master per slideshow will do you just fine, you can create additional slide masters if you like.

▶ **Layout master.** A *layout master* expands on the slide master to let you tell PowerPoint how you want specific types of slides to look. In other words, you can apply different formatting to Title slides, Title and Text slides, Title and Content slides, Comparison slides, and so on. For example, say you have a slide master similar to the one described in the previous paragraph. If you put an italicized header on the Title and Content layout master, then that header (in addition to the blue background and logo) automatically appears on every slide you format using the Title and Content layout. Then you're free to use, say, a bold header (not italicized) on Title slides, since that's a different layout.

The Right Way to Add Graphics to Slide Masters

Slide masters and layouts give you a lot of power. Make a change once, and PowerPoint applies it to every slide on your slideshow—whether it's a scrap of text, a graphic, or a color and formatting effect.

But before you go crazy applying textured backgrounds and logos, you need to think about these two important design considerations:

* **Always leave blank spots for your titles and subtitles.** Ever notice how, on most CD and book covers that contain graphics, the designers leave a blank spot for the title? They do this for one very simple reason: Generally speaking, text looks awful—if not downright unreadable—when you plaster it over a busy background.

* **Apply the same look and feel (but not necessarily the same images and formatting) to all your slides.** Your title page is a good place to go a bit wild with backgrounds, textures, colors, and fonts. But for the meat of your presentation—your text and content slides—you want your audience to focus on your message, not your skill with Clip Art.

PowerPoint automatically attaches one slide master and several layout masters to every presentation you create. To edit them, you have to switch into Slide Master view. You use the same steps whether you're editing a slide master or one of the layout masters:

1. **Create a new presentation (or open an existing one). Select View → Presentation Views → Slide Master.**

   PowerPoint displays the slide master in your workspace, ready for editing (Figure 5-8). The Master Slide tab appears and, on the left side of the screen where the Slides pane usually sits, you see instead the Thumbnail view of the slide master and the layout masters.

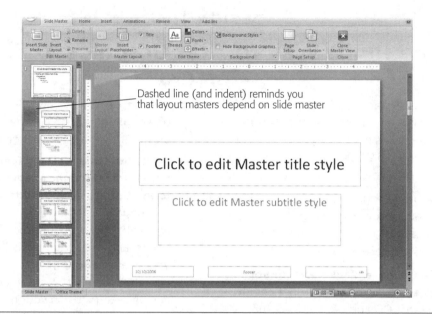

Dashed line (and indent) reminds you
that layout masters depend on slide master

Click to edit Master title style

Click to edit Master subtitle style

Figure 5-8. You can tell you're looking at a slide master (as opposed to an individual slide) by the Slide Master tab and by the dashed lines you see in the Thumbnail view. These dashed lines remind you that the layout masters all depend on the slide master. In other words, PowerPoint applies any changes you make to the slide master to all of the other layouts in the theme.

2. **Mouse over the thumbnails on the left side of the screen to see a description of each layout. Then click to choose the slide master or layout you want to edit.**

   ▶ **[Name of Theme] Slide Master.** All of the changes you make to this grand-daddy slide master affect each of the slides in your slideshow. The changes you make to this slide master affect all of the associated layout masters, too.

   ▶ **[Name of Content] Layout.** These masters are your layout masters. Edits you make to them affect only those slides that have that particular layout applied to them. Your choices include Title Slide, Title and Content (a title plus some text), Section Header, Two Content (two-column), Comparison (another two-column option, this time with column headings), Title Only, Blank, Content with Caption, and Picture with Caption.

   After you make your choice, PowerPoint displays the selected slide master or layout master in the workspace.

__ NOTE _____

When you want to add text to a slide master (because, for example, you want to add the same quote or slogan to each of your slides), you need to insert a new text placeholder. Typing text inside an existing text placeholder doesn't affect what you see on your slides when you run your slideshow. Instead, it appears only when you're editing your slides.

3. **Edit the slide master or layout master.**

   Everything you can add to a regular slide—text, special effects, background colors, and so on—you can add to a slide master or layout master. On the Slide Master tab, you see options for changing the theme, theme-related fonts, effects, colors, and background of your slide master or layout master. You can also click the Home tab or Mini Toolbar (to format text) or the Insert tab (to insert text boxes and other objects). Figure 5-9 shows you an example of editing the Title and Text Content layout master.

4. **When you're finished editing the master, click Close Master View.**

   PowerPoint scoots you back to the slide editing workspace, where you see that PowerPoint has automatically updated all of the slides that correspond to the slide master or layout master you just changed (Figure 5-10).

Applying Multiple Slide Masters

PowerPoint lets you apply multiple slide masters to your slideshow. You don't want to go crazy and apply a different slide master to every single slide because that would counteract the whole time-saving point of slide masters. Still, in some situations—like when you want to format the sections of a long presentation differently—the ability to apply multiple slide masters comes in handy.

To apply a new slide master to one or more slides:

1. **In the Slide pane, select the slides to which you want to apply a new slide master. Go to Design → Themes and click the down arrow next to the thumbnails.**

   The Themes gallery appears. Mousing over each theme shows you a live preview, right there on your slide.

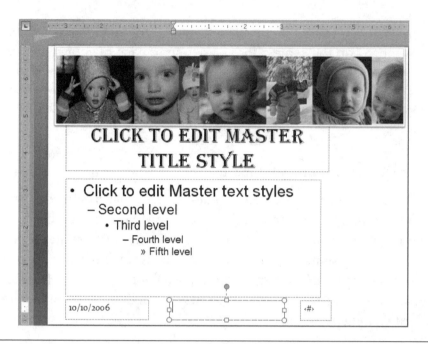

Figure 5-9. The Title and Text Content Master has been edited to change the font of the title and to include a graphic. You can change the formatting of the text placeholders that PowerPoint gives you, but you can't change the text itself. (Well, you can, but PowerPoint won't apply the changed text to your slides.) To add text to a slide master or layout master, you need to add your own text box and then type in your text.

2. **In the Themes gallery, right-click the theme you want to apply to your slides and, from the shortcut menu, choose how you want to apply the theme. Your choices are:**

   ▶ **Apply to selected slides.** Applies the selected theme only to the slides you've highlighted in the Slides pane.

   ▶ **Apply to matching slide.** Applies the selected theme only to those slides that share a layout with the slides you've selected.

   ▶ **Apply to all slides.** Applies the selected theme to all of the slides in your slideshow.

   PowerPoint reformats your slideshow based on your selection.

Figure 5-10. This slide was created using the Title and Text layout, so it reflects the changes made in the Title and Text Content Master, as shown in Figure 5-9. The title is in a funky font and a graphic strip appears across the top of the slide.

3. **Repeat steps 1–2 once for each slide master you want to apply to your slide-show.**

— TIP —

If you change your mind immediately after applying a slide master, then press Ctrl+Z or click Undo to tell PowerPoint to reverse your change.

Adding Headers and Footers

You can add any recurring text to the top or bottom of every slide in your slide-show, every handout, and every page of your speaker notes. PowerPoint gives you an efficient way to add recurring information to your presentation: built-in header and footer placeholders. And here's the best part: Simply by turning on a checkbox, you can choose to hide or show your headers or footers when you go to print your presentation.

Adding Footers to Your Slides

PowerPoint lets you add headers to your *handouts* using the Header and Footer dialog box, but you can't add headers to your *slides* this way. If you want to add a header to your slides, add it to the slide master, as described on page 147.

To add footers to your slides using the Header and Footer dialog box:

1. **In the Slides pane (Normal view), select the slides to which you want to apply a footer.**

   You can skip this step if you want all of the slides in your slideshow (or all of your slides *except* your title slide) to have a footer.

2. **Choose Text → Insert → Header & Footer.**

   The Header and Footer dialog box shown in Figure 5-11 appears.

3. **On the Slide tab, choose what you want to appear on your slides.**

4. **Your options include:**

   ▶ **Date and time.** Turning on the checkbox next to this option lets you choose the current date and time, which PowerPoint can either update automatically (turn on the "Update automatically" radio box) or not (turn on the radio box next to Fixed). Choosing "Update automatically" also lets you specify the format in which you want the date and time to appear, the language, and the calendar type.

   ▶ **Slide number.** Turn on the checkbox next to this option to tell PowerPoint to add automatically generated numbers to your slides.

   ▶ **Footer.** Turning on the checkbox next to this option activates a text box into which you can type the text you want to appear at the bottom of your slides.

   As you choose options, PowerPoint automatically highlights the corresponding footer placeholder in the Preview section of the Header and Footer dialog box (see Figure 5-11).

5. **If you don't want your date, slide number, or text box footer to appear on your title slide, then turn on the checkbox next to "Don't show on title slide."**

6. **If you want to apply your date, slide number, and text box footer only to those slides you selected in step 1 above, then click Apply. Otherwise, click Apply All to tell PowerPoint you want the information to appear on every slide in your slideshow (except, possibly, your title slide; see step 4).**

The Header and Footer dialog box disappears, and PowerPoint applies your footer options to your slides.

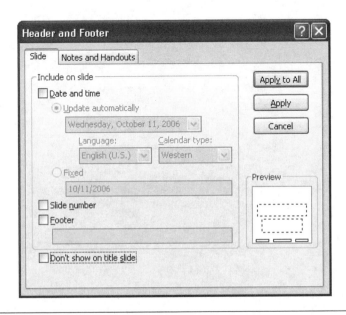

Figure 5-11. *After you tell PowerPoint to add the date and time, custom footer text, or automatically generated page numbers using the Header and Footer dialog box shown here, you can tweak the appearance of your header or footer content in Slide Master view (page 149).*

Adding Headers and Footers to Notes Pages and Handouts

The Header and Footer dialog box lets you apply a date- and timestamp, automatically generated page numbers, and the same header and footer text to your notes pages and handout pages.

Choose Home → Insert → Header & Footer, and then click the Notes and Headers tab to select it. Your options are identical to the ones described on page 154 with the addition of a Header checkbox, which lets you type in the text you want to appear in the upper-left corner of your notes and handout pages. When you're done choosing what you want to appear in your header and footer, click Apply to All.

The Header and Footer dialog box disappears, and PowerPoint applies your footer options to your notes and handout pages.

ADDING CHARTS, DIAGRAMS, AND TABLES

▶ Creating Charts

▶ Creating Diagrams

▶ Creating Tables

MAKING YOUR POINT VISUALLY is almost always more effective than slapping up a bunch of bullet points or a column full of numbers. That's why PowerPoint lets you create awesome charts, diagrams, and tables. Many new PowerPointers avoid these tools out of intimidation. That's a shame, because a good bar chart, Venn diagram, or data table can communicate more information than a dozen slides full of bullet points—with far fewer droopy eyelids.

Microsoft has seriously upgraded PowerPoint 2007's charting, diagramming, and table-creation tools. There's a new graphics engine, dozens of new diagram types, and galleries of professionally designed pick-and-click styles. You can even preview the styles live on your charts, diagrams, and tables before applying them. In short, you've got no excuse for leaving eye-popping, effective visuals out of your presentation. This chapter gets you making great-looking charts, diagrams, and tables *fast*.

> **TIP**
>
> PowerPoint's new tools are really Microsoft Office's new tools. In other words, the way you create charts, diagrams, and tables in Word and Excel is pretty darn similar to the way you create them in PowerPoint, and the result is identical-looking visuals.

Creating Charts

You can talk numbers until you're blue in the face, but when you *really* want to get your audience's attention—and get your point across in the shortest time possible—you need a chart.

Sometimes referred to as a *graph*, a *chart* is nothing more than a visual representation of a bunch of numbers. The ubiquitous pie chart (Figure 6-1) breaks up a circular area into easy-to-understand, color-coded wedges, each of which represents a numerical quantity. PowerPoint 2007 lets you add punch to your presentations with the same bar charts, line charts, scatter graphs, and so on that PowerPoint 2003 offered. Only now they're better looking, since Microsoft Excel has replaced Power-Point 2003's Microsoft Graph program.

Go Easy on the Extras

This chapter shows you the quickest, most powerful ways to customize your visuals, and the Appendix shows you how to get help with the more arcane customization options PowerPoint offers.

But before you roll up your sleeves and customize every single tiny detail of your charts, diagrams, and tables, consider that the goal of every presentation is the same: to communicate something to an audience. In most cases, your audience couldn't care less if you beveled your table column headings to point up instead of down, or chose pink over salmon for your diagram's background. Your audience is after *meaning*. So always keep these question in mind: *Why* are you showing them this particular chart or diagram? *Why* have you chosen to highlight the second row of the table and not the third?

If you've presented solid data in the clearest, most dramatic way possible and you have a little time left over, by all means add that bevel effect. Otherwise, save yourself some work (and your audience some eye-rolling) and leave it out.

NOTE

You don't need to have Excel installed on your computer to create charts. If PowerPoint 2007 finds Excel on your PC, it uses Excel. Otherwise, it falls back on the built-in graphics program, Microsoft Graph. See the box on page 166 for the full scoop.

Creating a chart in PowerPoint is a straightforward process. You tell the program which type of chart you want to create (pie chart, bar chart, and so on), you type a few rows of data into an Excel (or Graph) spreadsheet, and then you apply a predesigned Chart Style and Chart Layout. Bingo—instant chart. And if you've never seen a chart built with an Office 2007 program, you'll be amazed how good it looks.

Choosing a Chart Type

PowerPoint's charts look great, but they're not all suited to every type of information. Do you know which one to choose? The chart type you pick affects how Power-Point interprets your information, which affects your audience's conclusions. So

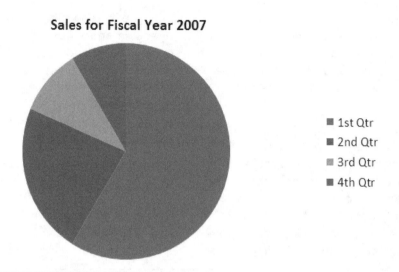

Acme Widgets, Inc.

Sales for Fiscal Year 2007

- 1st Qtr
- 2nd Qtr
- 3rd Qtr
- 4th Qtr

Figure 6-1. *Charting is an art unto itself, as all liars and statisticians are well aware. PowerPoint doesn't care whether the numbers you chart are accurate or whether your chart makes your conclusions dangerously misleading—it leaves those judgments up to you.*

choose a chart type based on what you're trying to communicate, not on what PowerPoint lets you do.

Charting is both art and science, and it's far too complex to tackle in a book about PowerPoint. Consider the following descriptions in deciding which type of chart to create:

▶ **Bar chart.** One of the most popular types of charts, the bar chart depicts numbers—like dollars, products sold, or the number of times something happened—using big, thick, hard-to-miss rectangles. Bar charts show numbers in the context of time. They can show how many field goals each high school's football team scored over the last five seasons. Bar charts can be *stacked*, which means Power-Point stacks all of the data from all of the categories into one bar per event; or they can be *clustered*, which means that each data category gets its own bar for each event.

- **Column chart.** A column chart's the same as a bar chart, but lying on its side (with x- and y-axis labels flipped to match). Fancy types of column charts include *cylinder*, *cone*, and *pyramid*.

- **Line chart.** Line charts show noncumulative data horizontally, over time, so you can track performance. Consider a line chart if, for example, you're trying to show the progression of your company's quarter-by-quarter performance over the past fiscal year, compared with your two closest competitors' performances over that same period of time. Similar to bar charts, line charts track numbers in relation to time. But unlike bar charts, which clump the data for specific events (like field-goal totals for those five football seasons), line charts show a continuous intersection of activity. Thus, if it's events you're interested in comparing, then use a bar chart; when it's a continuous progression of up-and-down movement, use a line chart.

- **Pie chart.** Because pie charts show percentage values as slices of a circle, this type of chart makes sense only if you have a single column of numbers that add up to 100. For example, you can use a pie chart if you're trying to show how much of every dollar raised for your charity goes to overhead, to individual programs, and so on.

- **Scatter chart.** Use a scatter chart when you're working with data that neither occurs at regular intervals nor belongs to a series. Sometimes referred to as *XY charts* or *scatter graphs*, scatter charts show information as points distributed around an x-y axis—think darts thrown at a dartboard. The dots give a quick visual showing the relationship between the data represented by the x and y axes. You might use a scatter chart to plot the relationship between the prices of ovens and how long the ovens last. Scatter charts are popular with scientists.

- **Area, bubble, doughnut, stock, surface, and radar charts.** Theoretically, you can graph any data you want any way you want, and in this spirit PowerPoint offers the doughnut, stock, radar, and other specialty graphs. For example, a radar graph is useful for comparing the aggregate values of a bunch of data series. Say you want to compare the vitamin levels of three different brands of orange juice. Creating a radar chart lets your audience see at a glance which brand of juice contains the most Vitamin C, Vitamin D, Vitamin A—*and* which is the most nutritious overall.

Remember, though, the more complicated a graph is, the harder it is for your audience to understand it—even if you're there in person to explain it. And complexity totally defeats the purpose of a graph. Most of the time you should stick with the bar, column, line, and pie charts.

Figures 6-2 and 6-3 show you the different configuration your numbers and headings need to work with the different kinds of charts PowerPoint lets you create.

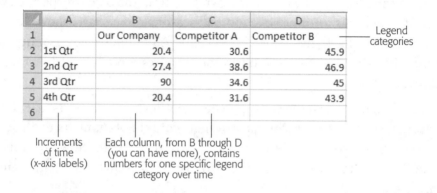

Figure 6-2. The mocked-up data PowerPoint starts you off with would be a lot more useful if the program gave you a clue of how to interpret each cell. Here's how your data needs to appear for the Bar, Column, and Line charts (the ones that, along with Pie charts, you're most likely to use).

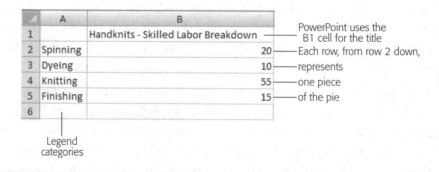

Figure 6-3. Because pie charts can deal with only one category of numbers (in chart-speak, one data series), you need to arrange your figures as shown here for PowerPoint to graph your pie chart correctly. Also double-check your data range as described in the box on page 167, since PowerPoint doesn't always extrapolate correctly.

Creating a Chart

To create a chart, first tell PowerPoint what type of chart you want, and then feed it some data. The steps that follow explain how.

___ NOTE ___

Creating a chart is pretty simple, as you'll see in the following steps. But if you're new to Excel or spreadsheets in general, it's useful to walk through the process visually. A screencast at *www.missingmanuals.com* shows you how to create a chart in PowerPoint, complete with accompanying narration that explains each step.

1. **Go to Insert → Illustrations → Chart (Figure 6-4).**

Figure 6-4. If you've applied a Title and Content or Two Content layout to the slide you're adding your chart to, you'll see two versions of the Chart icon: one on the Insert ribbon (as shown here) and one in the center of your slide. Clicking the Chart icon in either location displays the Create Chart dialog box shown in Figure 6-5.

   The Insert Chart dialog box (Figure 6-5) appears.

2. **Choose the kind of chart you want to add to your slide, and then click OK.**

   To find one you like, zip to the left side of the Insert Chart dialog box (Figure 6-5) and click a category (such as Bar, Area, or Doughnut), which whisks you straight to the section you're interested in. Or, if you prefer, you can use the scroll bar to browse leisurely through all the chart options.

___ NOTE ___

You can also double-click a chart type to add it to your slide.

Once you click OK, PowerPoint shrinks to half size and scoots over to make room for Excel, which appears on the right side of your screen complete with placeholder data displayed in an Excel spreadsheet titled "Chart in Microsoft

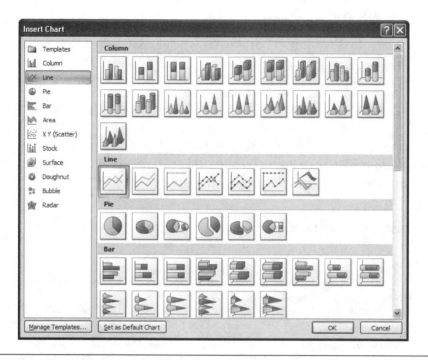

Figure 6-5. The Insert Chart dialog box offers dozens of different types of charts. PowerPoint doesn't support live previews for charts the way it does for just about everything else, but it does display short descriptions as you mouse over each chart icon.

Office PowerPoint." In PowerPoint, the Chart Tools | Design, Chart Tools | Layout, and Chart Tools | Format tabs appear (Figure 6-6).

3. **Replace the mocked-up data you see in Excel with the real data you want to chart.**

    To do so, you can:

    ▶ Click in each cell and type your own numbers and headings.

    ▶ If you've already got a spreadsheet containing the numbers you want to chart, you can copy the cells from that spreadsheet and paste them into the spreadsheet PowerPoint gives you. (For quick tips on pasting from Excel, see the box on page 170.)

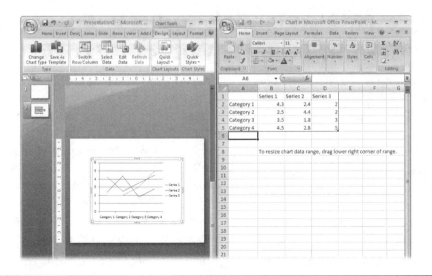

Figure 6-6. Excel starts you off with a column or two of mocked-up data—one piece of information per spreadsheet cell—so that you can get a feel for what your chart will look like. To expand the tiny chart preview PowerPoint displays on your slide, in PowerPoint either click Zoom a few times or drag the Zoom slider.

As you add, change, and delete data in the Excel spreadsheet, Excel's data range outline automatically changes to encompass your new data columns and headings, and your PowerPoint chart updates automatically to reflect your changes.

4. **When you're finished adding data, check to make sure the data range bounding box surrounds your entire data range, including your column and row headings.**

If it doesn't, drag the lower right corner of the data range bounding box so it covers all your cells (but no additional blank rows or columns).

5. **Click anywhere on your PowerPoint slide.**

PowerPoint whisks you back to slide-editing mode and updates your chart with the data you just gave it.

Creating Charts Without Excel

PowerPoint uses Excel to do all its charting now. But I don't have Excel, just PowerPoint. Does that mean I can't do charts?

Microsoft Office comes with both programs, so lots of people who use Office have both PowerPoint and Excel installed on their computers. But not everyone who installs Office chooses to install both programs—and some folks choose to buy just PowerPoint, not the entire Office suite.

If you *do* have both PowerPoint and Excel installed on your computer, creating a chart in PowerPoint automatically kicks Excel into gear, as shown in this chapter.

But if you *don't* have Excel installed, you can still create charts. Here's why: when PowerPoint can't find Excel, it automatically launches Microsoft Graph, the same charting and drawing program that came with PowerPoint 2003. Microsoft Graph doesn't offer the same bells and whistles that Excel does—which is why Microsoft replaced it with Excel in PowerPoint 2007—but you *can* use it to do the same basic things. For example, you can click in Microsoft Graph data cells to type in your own numbers and column headings, just the way you can in Excel.

This book focuses on creating charts in *PowerPoint* (and not Excel), so all of the instructions work the same for you as they do for someone who has Excel installed—even if what you see on your screen looks slightly different from the figures in this book. But if you run into a snag, then click the Microsoft Graph spreadsheet and choose Help → Microsoft Graph Help.

TIP

If your spreadsheet accidentally disappears (perhaps you clicked the X in the upper-right corner by mistake), you can get it back again by selecting your chart and then choosing Chart Tools | Design → Data → Edit Data.

Customizing Charts with Prebuilt Layouts and Styles

PowerPoint 2007 gives you the option of choosing both a canned Chart Layout and a canned Chart Style scheme. You simply pick one of PowerPoint's professionally

Trying Data On for Size

PowerPoint lets you pinpoint the perfect chart by "trying out" different sets of data. This is useful if you want to experiment to find out which of several sets of data translates to the most dramatic chart.

Here's how it works:

1. Create a chart as described on page 163.

2. Choose Chart Tools | Design → Data → Select Data to display your spreadsheet (if it isin't visible already) and to display the Select Data Source dialog box.

3. In your spreadsheet, create another complete set of data; then click the new data range and drag to outline your newly created columns and rows. Notice that PowerPoint automatically adjusts the Select Data Source dialog box to reflect your changes.

4. In the Select Data Source dialog box, click OK to tell PowerPoint to update your chart using your new data.

5. Repeat steps 3 and 4 for as many sets of data as you have. After you've decided to stick with one, don't bother deleting the others from your spreadsheet. Leave them there in case you change your mind.

---

designed Chart Layout schemes, some of which show the legend on the side of the chart, some at the bottom, and so on. Then you pick one Chart Style scheme, which sets the colors, data point markers, and a background for your chart.

Applying prebuilt Chart Layouts

Since you're going to be working on your chart's appearance, give yourself a nice big view. If PowerPoint isn't maximized on your computer screen, click the Maximize button in the upper-right corner of the window to maximize it. Then follow these steps:

1. **On your slide, click your chart to select it.**

   PowerPoint displays the Chart Tools contextual tab.

2. **Go to Chart Tools | Design tab.**

   You see tools for formatting your chart's looks (Figure 6-7).

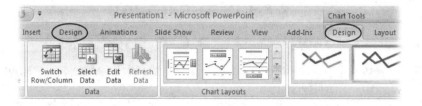

Figure 6-7. Confusingly, when you select a chart, two Design tabs appear: the regular Design tab, and the Chart Tools | Design contextual tab, which appears above the ribbon. PowerPoint also highlights the contextual tab to make it stand out a bit. The Chart Tools | Design tab is specifically for working with your chart.

3. **Click the Chart Layout gallery to expand it (Figure 6-8). Then click to choose the layout you want to apply to your chart.**

   PowerPoint redisplays your chart based on the layout you chose.

Figure 6-8. The Chart Layout gallery varies depending on the type of chart you choose. Layouts define where chart elements such as titles, legends, and data and axis labels appear. This gallery shows the layouts that PowerPoint can apply to Line charts.

Applying prebuilt Chart Styles

The Chart Style schemes that come with PowerPoint give you a quick way to choose the color of your chart's data elements, as well as your chart's background. Because all of the colors in the Chart Style schemes are professionally designed to coordinate with each other, your chart looks good no matter which one you choose—and no matter how many data elements you're charting.

To apply a Chart Style:

1. **On your slide, click your chart to select it. Then go to Chart Tools | Design tab.**

   Tools for formatting your chart's appearance show up on the ribbon.

2. **Click to expand the Chart Styles gallery (Figure 6-9). From the Chart Styles gallery, click to choose the style you want to apply to your chart.**

   PowerPoint redisplays your chart based on the style you chose.

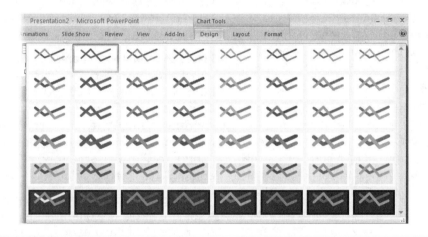

Figure 6-9. The Chart Styles gallery gives you a super-easy way to apply an attractive color scheme (including background colors and gradients) to your chart—here, a line chart. You can tweak the colors if you like, of course (see page 95).

Customizing chart titles

If you customize nothing else about your chart, you need to customize your title. That's because even though every chart needs a title, PowerPoint doesn't automatically assign one. You'll want to decide where to display your title, too.

Excel: The Least You Need to Know

If you really want to get down and dirty with Excel, you need a good reference on the subject. (One to try is *Excel 2007: The Missing Manual,* by Matthew MacDonald.) But when all you want to do is to put together a decent-looking chart in PowerPoint and then get on with your life, you'll do all right if you know how to:

Copy and paste cell data from an existing spreadsheet. You've already got a spreadsheet containing the data you want to chart, and you don't want to retype it into the spreadsheet Power-Point provides. Copy and paste the data. Here's how:

1. In the Excel spreadsheet PowerPoint opened (the one titled "Chart in Microsoft Office PowerPoint"), choose Office button → Open and open a new spreadsheet (the spreadsheet containing the data you want to chart).

2. In the newly opened spreadsheet, drag to select the data you want to copy, and then choose Home → Copy (or press Ctrl+C) to copy it.

3. In the "Chart in Microsoft Office PowerPoint" sheet, click in cell A1, and then choose Home → Paste or press Ctrl+V to paste the data.

Delete the contents of cells. To clear out the contents of cells you don't want to chart (and don't want to see), drag to select the cells; then right-click the selection and choose Clear Contents from the shortcut menu

Widen columns. If you type text into two side-by-side cells, you may not be able to read all the text in the first cell. To widen the first cell's column, click the edge of the column header and drag to widen the entire column.

Insert and delete rows and columns. To insert a row or column, right-click the cell after which you want to add a row or column and then choose Insert from the shortcut menu. When the Insert dialog box opens, turn on the radio box next to "Entire row" (to insert a row) or "Entire column" (to insert a column).

To add data to your chart, you may have to delete a row or column. Right-click the row or column heading (the actual letter or number of the row or column, as opposed to a cell in the row or column) and then choose Delete from the short-cut menu.

Creating Diagrams

Microsoft really upped the ante when it comes to using diagrams in your presentations. PowerPoint 2007 lets you create more types of diagrams than earlier versions of the program, they look snazzier, and they're easier to create and update. In some cases, when you tweak one section of a diagram, PowerPoint automatically redraws the rest of it to match.

In this section, you'll see two ways to create a diagram: by choosing a diagram type and filling in the text, or by converting an existing text list into a diagram. Then you'll learn to add a quick, professional-looking style to your diagram.

FREQUENTLY ASKED QUESTION

When to Diagram

Now *you tell me about diagrams! I've just typed a list of all one hundred employees in my company on a PowerPoint slide. I see now the names would work better in an organizational chart. Is it too late?*

Well, if you were using PowerPoint 2003, the answer would be yes. If you wanted to add a certain type of diagram to a slide—an organizational chart, for example—you had to add it to your slide first, and then fill in the employees' names later. In fact, you can still do it that way in PowerPoint 2007, if you want.

But you may run into a situation where you're adding text to a slide and *then* realize that a diagram would make more sense. Say you realize you've just typed a list that would be much more effective as a chevron diagram—one that shows a series of steps, for example, or that shows some other type of relationship. Power-Point 2007 lets you experiment by turning that list into a diagram with the click of a button. See Figure 6-10 for an example. For instructions, flip to page 174.

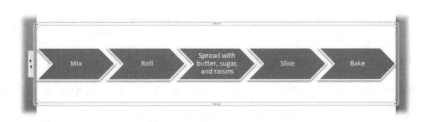

Figure 6-10. This horizontal chevron diagram is just one of dozens of different diagrams that you can add to your PowerPoint slides. Because your audience needs to read your diagrams easily, no matter which diagram type you choose, you'll want to keep the individual steps to no more than a handful.

Adding Diagrams to Slides

Adding a diagram to a slide is simple. All you need to do is select a diagram type and click a button, as the following steps show.

1. **Select the slide to which you want to add a diagram. Go to Insert → Illustrations → SmartArt.**

   If you used a layout such as Title and Content, Comparison, or Content with Caption, then you can click the Insert SmartArt Graphic icon in the center of your slide. Either way, the Choose a SmartArt Graphic dialog box you see in Figure 6-11 appears.

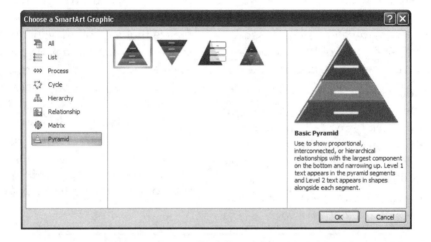

Figure 6-11. PowerPoint 2007 offers a lot more diagrams than earlier versions of the program. If you're not familiar with one of the more exotic diagrams, click it. When you do, PowerPoint displays a helpful description on the right side of the Choose a SmartArt Graphic dialog box.

2. **Click one of the diagram categories you see on the left side of the dialog box.**

   Diagram types related to that category appear in the middle of the dialog box.

3. **Double-click a diagram type to add it to your slide.**

   Instead of double-clicking, you can click a diagram type (to see a helpful description) and then, when you're satisfied you want to add it to your slide, click OK.

PowerPoint displays the SmartArt Tools | Design and Format contextual tabs (Figure 6-12), and the selected chart appears on your slide, complete with a diagram text edit pane (see Figure 6-13 for an example).

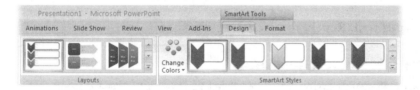

Figure 6-12. The SmartArt Tools | Design contextual tab displays different options than the standard Design tab, so try not to confuse the two. How to tell the difference: The SmartArt Tools | Design tab appears only when you've selected a diagram, and PowerPoint draws your attention to it with a warm colored glow.

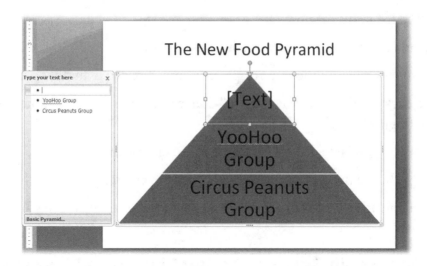

Figure 6-13. When PowerPoint adds a diagram to your slide, it surrounds it with a frame you can click to expand or reposition the diagram. Clicking the [Text] placeholder lets you type your own text for the various shapes that make up your diagram. Or, if you prefer, you can click in the box that Power-Point displays to the left of the diagram and type your text in there.

4. **On your slide, add text to the diagram shapes by clicking in one of the place-holder text boxes.**

   PowerPoint highlights the diagram shape you clicked and activates the cursor so that you can begin typing.

NOTE

You can also click in the diagram's text edit pane as shown in Figure 6-13. If you're a fast typist and have several items to type, this method is for you.

5. **Type your text. Repeat for each diagram shape.**

Turning Lists into Diagrams

If you find yourself creating a bulleted or numbered list (see Chapter 3) and realize it would be more effective as a diagram, you're in luck. PowerPoint 2007 lets you convert a list directly to a diagram. With the click of a button, you can even try out different diagram types until you find one that presents your list in the most compelling format.

To convert a list into a diagram:

1. **First, add a bulleted or numbered list on your slide.**

   You can type right on the slide, or paste in some text from another program.

2. **Right-click the list and then choose "Convert to SmartArt" from the shortcut menu (Figure 6-14).**

   PowerPoint displays a list of diagram types to choose from.

3. **Click to choose the type of diagram you want to create.**

   PowerPoint adds the selected diagram to your slide, pre-filled with your list data (Figure 6-15).

Applying Prebuilt Styles and Color Themes to Diagrams

Applying a predesigned look-and-feel to your diagram lets you turn out an attractive diagram in no time flat. To counter the accusations of cookie cutter slides lobbed at earlier versions of the program, PowerPoint 2007 offers a wide range of predesigned SmartArt Styles, which you can dress up with an optional color theme. For a couple of clicks, you get a great-looking diagram that's unlikely to look like the ones Bob in Accounting churns out.

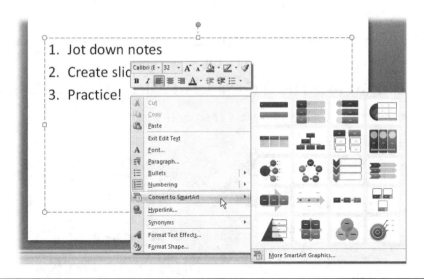

Figure 6-14. When you convert a list into a diagram, PowerPoint offers you a modest handful of different diagram types. If you don't see one you like, click More Conversion Options to see the full complement of diagram types.

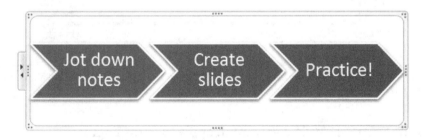

Figure 6-15. Click the frame PowerPoint displays around a diagram, and you can resize the diagram as a whole by dragging the sides or corners. Clicking the individual elements lets you modify the shapes independently. To edit diagram text, click either of the arrows on the left side of the frame to display the diagram text edit pane.

To apply a SmartArt Style and optional color theme to your diagram:

1. **Click to select the diagram you want to format.**

   The SmartArt Tools contextual tab appears.

2. **Click the SmartArt Tools | Design tab.**

The SmartArt Tools/Design tab (flip back to Figure 6-12) appears. Next, you'll apply a SmartArt Style to your diagram.

3. **Go to SmartArt Tools | Design → SmartArt Styles and click the down-arrow.**

The SmartArt Styles gallery appears (Figure 6-16).

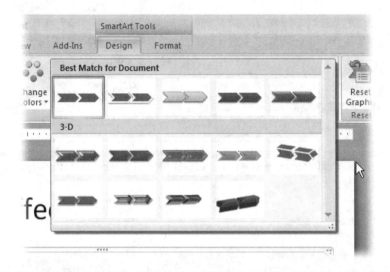

Figure 6-16. The gallery options you see depend on the diagram type you choose. You can apply these styles, which include cool 3-D options, to a chevron diagram.

4. **Click the SmartArt Style you want to apply to your diagram.**

PowerPoint redisplays your diagram based on your selection.

5. **To choose a color theme for your diagram, go to SmartArt Tools | Design → SmartArt Styles → Change Colors.**

The Primary Theme Colors gallery appears (Figure 6-17).

6. **Click to select a color theme.**

PowerPoint redisplays your diagram based on the color theme you selected.

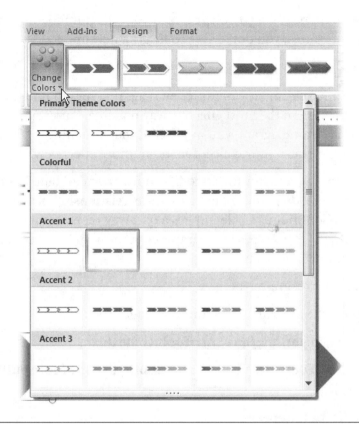

Figure 6-17. Even though the color themes PowerPoint suggests all look different, they coordinate with the overall theme you chose for your slideshow (page 36). As you mouse over each theme, PowerPoint shows you a live preview on your slide.

Tweaking Diagrams

PowerPoint lets you change most elements of your diagram. For example, you can add titles, switch to a different type of diagram, or change the text in an existing diagram. You can also select your diagram to return to the SmartArt Tools contextual tab to adjust its design and color.

Adding titles

Oddly, when you create a diagram, PowerPoint doesn't start you out with a title placeholder. Instead, you have to insert and position your own text box, which you can see how to do on page 40. (If you've added your diagram to a slide that already contains a title, of course, you don't have to insert a new one.)

Switching to a different type of diagram

If you like, you can experiment with different diagram types to find one that presents your information in the most effective way possible. For example, if you've created a Basic Chevron diagram, you might find that switching to a Closed Chevron diagram demonstrates your conceptual point more effectively.

Just make sure the diagram you switch to fits your particular data. For example, a Multidirectional Cycle diagram implies a two-way relationship between diagram elements, while a Continuous Cycle implies a one-way repeating relationship. Because these two different types of diagrams communicate two very different messages, they're not interchangeable.

To switch to another diagram type:

1. **Click to select the diagram you want to change.**

   PowerPoint highlights the SmartArt Tools contextual tab.

2. **Go to SmartArt Tools | Design → Layouts and click the More button (the down-arrow).**

3. **A gallery of layouts appears.**

   If what you want doesn't appear, select More Layouts to show the "Choose a SmartArt Graphic" dialog box, which shows you the complete set of diagrams you can create in PowerPoint.

   ___ NOTE _____

   To summon the "Choose a SmartArt Graphic" dialog box you can also right-click your diagram and then, from the menu that appears, choose Change Layout.

   _____

4. **Click a diagram type to select it, and then click OK.**

   PowerPoint redisplays your diagram based on the new type you just selected.

Changing diagram text

As your practice and hone your presentation, you'll probably find you need to change the text that appears in one or more diagram shapes. You can edit diagram text simply by clicking the text and typing, just as you edit the text in any text box—but there's an easier way. Displaying the diagram text edit pane (Figure 6-18) lets you see and edit all of the text in your diagram easily, without having to click from shape to shape.

To edit diagram text using the diagram text edit pane:

1. **If a text edit pane similar to the one you see in Figure 6-18 isn't already visible, right-click your diagram and then, from the context menu that appears, choose Show Text Pane.**

   The text edit pane appears.

2. **In the text edit pane, click the text you want to edit and begin typing.**

   PowerPoint automatically redisplays your diagram to reflect your changes.

Figure 6-18. Another way to display the text edit pane is to click one of the two arrows that appear on the left side of the diagram frame (shown back in Figure 6-15). Pressing Enter adds more elements to your diagram. To close the pane, click the X in the upper-right corner.

Creating Tables

Since ancient times, people have organized information into tables—rows and columns containing a number or bit of text in each cell. By now, you'd think working with tables would be a no-brainer.

It's not. Adding a table to your slideshow is easier in PowerPoint 2007 than it was in earlier versions of the program and the results are more impressive looking. But thanks to the overwhelming number of choices PowerPoint 2007 gives you, the process of adding a table can cause more headaches then ever. You start with four ways to create a table, plus you have dozens of ways to tweak every imaginable table element, from the lines that separate your columns to the shading that appears in your rows.

But nothing lets your audience compare figures better than a table. So eventually, you must create one. This section shows you the easiest way to create a table. Then, you'll see how to add the basics: data, a title, column headings, and so on.

Creating a Basic Table

PowerPoint gives you four different ways to create a table: by mousing over a grid, by typing your table dimensions into the Insert Table box, by drawing the table's outline on a slide, or by inserting an Excel table. Most of the time, you want to use one of the first two options, which are the quickest and easiest. (You can read about the other two methods in the boxes on pages 181 and 183.)

Whichever approach you choose, after you've created your table, you need to fill it with data and add a title and column headings. The following sections walk you through the entire process.

Creating rows and columns

To create a table, you start by telling PowerPoint how many rows and columns you want your table to have. PowerPoint gives you a gloriously easy way to do so—mousing over a grid to define the size and shape of your table.

Here's how:

1. **Select the slide where you want to place your table. Go to Insert → Tables → Table.**

    Up pops a menu similar to the one shown in Figure 6-19.

2. **Move your mouse over the grid to select your desired configuration of rows and columns.**

    PowerPoint highlights the cells your cursor passes over, and displays your proposed table dimensions at the top of the menu. In Figure 6-19, for example, the top of the menu reads "4x3 Table," corresponding to the four-column-by-three-

Drawing Tables

On page 180, you see two ways to create a basic table: by mousing over a grid, or by typing in the number of columns and rows you want. These two table creation options are all most folks will ever need.

But suppose you're trying to work your table around other slide content and can't guess precisely how many rows and columns you need to create a table that *just* fits the space you have. PowerPoint's got your back: It lets you draw the outline of a table the size you want it, and then carve it up into rows and columns later.

1. If you like, go to the Table Tools | Design → Draw Borders group and click Pen Style, Pen Weight, and Pen Color to customize the table border you're about to draw. You can choose a border style of solid, dashed, or dotted; a border thickness; and a border color, respectively.

2. Choose Insert → Tables → Table → Draw Table.

3. Mouse over your slide. As you do, your cursor turns into a tiny pencil.

4. Drag to draw the outline of your table. As you drag, you create a dotted outline. When you let go of your mouse, PowerPoint replaces the dotted outline with a proper table frame.

5. Press Esc to turn off drawing.

6. Choose Table Tools | Layout → Merge → Split Cells Layout.

7. In the Split Cells dialog box that appears, type in the number of columns and rows you want your table to have; then click OK.

8. PowerPoint carves up your table based on the number of columns and rows you specified.

---

row grid that's highlighted. On your slide, PowerPoint previews your table, which grows and shrinks as you highlight more and less of the grid. (The table preview shows the rows only, not the columns.)

3. **When your cursor reaches the bottom right cell of the table you want to create, click that cell.**

PowerPoint adds a table to your slide containing the number of rows and columns you specified, and displays the Table Tools tab (see Figure 6-20).

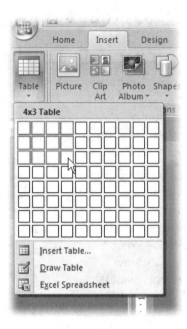

Figure 6-19. Mousing over a grid, as shown here, is the easiest way to tell PowerPoint how many columns and how many rows you want your table to have. But if you want to create a table that's larger than 10 columns by 8 rows, or if you're more comfortable typing than using a mouse, then use one of the three options at the bottom of the menu for creating a table.

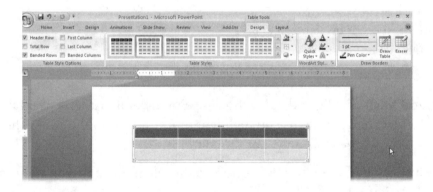

Figure 6-20. Behold the basic table, complete with a header row (the darker-colored row) across the top. Unless you tell it different, PowerPoint lightly tints, or bands, every other row to make it easier for your audience to read your table. You see how to change both of these formatting effects starting on page 186.

Instead of using your mouse to tell PowerPoint how many columns and rows you want your table to have, you can go to Insert → Tables → Table → Insert Table to display the Insert Table dialog box (Figure 6-21) and type the number of columns and rows you want. When you finish, click OK to dismiss the dialog box and add your newly created table to your slide.

Figure 6-21. To add a table to a slide, select Insert → Tables → Table → Insert Table. The Insert Table dialog box also pops up when you're working on a slide to which you've applied a content layout, and you click the table icon displayed in the center of the slide.

POWER USERS' CLINIC

Inserting an Excel Table

PowerPoint has some nifty table tools, but nothing like Excel's sophisticated spreadsheet formulas. If you need to use calculations or scientific notation in your table, you can borrow these features from Excel. Just tell PowerPoint where you want to insert the table, pop into Excel, whip out your table, and then pop back to PowerPoint, where you find your newly created Excel table displayed on your slide. Here's the step-by-step:

1. Choose Insert → Tables → Table → Excel Spreadsheet. Excel's ribbon replaces PowerPoint's, and a blank Excel spreadsheet appears on your slide (Figure 6-22).

2. Create your table using the Excel tools.

3. Choose File → Close. Excel's ribbon disappears.

4. In the "Do you want to save the changes you made to your presentation?" dialog box that pops up, click Yes.

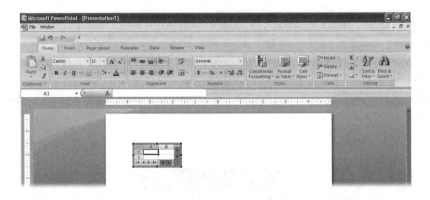

Figure 6-22. It's a little disconcerting when Excel's ribbon takes over, but that's what happens when you insert an Excel table. The benefit, of course, is that you can use the power of Excel to create a whiz-bang table directly on your PowerPoint slide.

Selecting cells, rows, and columns

Before you can add data to a cell or format a cell, row, or column, you first have to select that cell, row, or column. To select a cell, simply click in the cell. To select multiple cells, click in one cell, and then drag your cursor to select additional cells. PowerPoint highlights cells as you mouse over them to let you know which cells you're selecting.

— **TIP** —

Another way to select multiple cells is to click in one cell, and then Shift-click in another. Doing so tells PowerPoint to select all the cells in between.

To select a column or a row:

1. **Mouse above the column you want to select (or to the left of the row you want to select).**

   Your cursor turns into a thick down-arrow (see Figure 6-23).

2. **Click just above the column (or to the left of the row) you want to select.**

   You can also click a cell in the column or row you want to select, and then click Table Tools | Layout → Table → Select → Select Column or Table Tools | Layout → Table → Select → Select Row.

   PowerPoint tints the column (or row) to let you know you've selected it.

Figure 6-23. As you mouse just above a column, wait for your cursor to change to a small arrow. When it does, click to select the column. Here you can see the tinting that PowerPoint uses to let you know you've successfully selected a column.

Selecting entire tables

PowerPoint makes a distinction between selecting all the cells in a table, and selecting the table itself. You select all the rows and columns in a table if you want to delete or format the contents of all the cells. You select the table itself if you want to resize, reposition, or delete the table, or if you want to change the font of your table text by applying a table style (see page 187).

The previous section shows you how to select all the cells in a table. To select the table itself, click any cell in table you want to select. Then choose Table Tools | Layout → Table → Select → Select Table. You can also drag your cursor around your table to select it. (Or, if you prefer, right-click any cell in your table and then, from the context menu that appears, choose Select Table.)

Whichever way you go about it way, after you successfully select a table, PowerPoint highlights the table frame and turns your cursor into a four-headed arrow.

___ **WARNING** _____

> Clicking in a cell highlights the table frame, too, which can mistakenly lead you to think you've selected the table. But if you want to, say, delete or apply an effect (such as color) to your table as a whole, then you need to select the table as described above: simply clicking in a cell doesn't cut it.

Adding data

After you've added a table to your slide, you need to fill the cells with data. To do so, click in any cell and begin typing. To move to the next cell, press Tab or click in the next cell.

Adding a title

PowerPoint doesn't offer you any special way to add a title to your table. Instead, you simply add a text box, type in the title text you want, and then position the text box over your table. Chapter 1 shows you how to add and position text boxes.

Adding column headings

You add a column heading the same way that you add any other bit of data to a table cell—by clicking in the cell and then typing. But because most folks want to draw special attention to column headings, PowerPoint gives you a quick way to highlight them.

Here's how it works. When you create a table, PowerPoint highlights the first row (Figure 6-23) for you. But if the first row of your table doesn't appear highlighted—perhaps your co-workers has been fiddling with your presentation file—you can recover the highlighted effect by going to Table Tools → Design → Table Style Options and, in the Table Style Options group, turning on the Header checkbox.

PowerPoint tints the first row of your table an attractive color based on your table's style. It also automatically switches the color of the text in the first row to a contrasting color. See Figure 6-23 for an example. (Want to change these row highlights? See the next page.)

Tweaking Tables

Adding a basic table to your slide may be all you need. But once you type more than a couple rows' data, odds are good you'll need to insert a row here or resize a column there. Also, once you've got your table data typed in the way you want it, you may decide to spice up your table with a bit of formatting. You might want to change the color of your table so that it coordinates with your company's logo, or draw a big, thick border around a section of your table to draw attention to it.

PowerPoint lets you change virtually every element of your table, from the width of your rows and columns to the background color of each cell. This section shows you the most useful ways to work with table data and modify your table's appearance.

Applying prebuilt styles

The basic table you create in PowerPoint is just that—basic. To spice it up with a predefined collection of formatting effects including color, shading, and borders:

1. **Click any cell in your table. Then go to Table Tools | Design → Table Styles. In the Table Styles group, mouse over the style options.**

   As you mouse over each option, PowerPoint displays a live preview on your slide.

   To see a gallery of additional style options, click the down arrow in the Table Styles group.

2. **Click the style option you want to apply to your table.**

   PowerPoint redisplays your table based on the style you chose.

Highlighting rows and columns

Say you're showing your boss or your teacher an important table. You know she's going to have only a few minutes to examine it, so to emphasize the important numbers, you take a yellow pen and highlight them. PowerPoint lets you do something similar in the tables you add to your slides: you can highlight specific columns or rows (such as the totals row) or tell PowerPoint to lightly tint every other column or row for readability.

If you've had a chance to check out Figure 6-23, you've already seen how Power-Point applies header rows and banded rows to your table. In addition to tinting the first row of your table and lightly tinting every other row, you can tell PowerPoint to add a totals row, highlight the data in the first or last column, or band columns (instead of rows). Here's how:

▸ Click any cell in your table to select the table. Then choose your options from the Table Tools | Design tab → Table Style Options group.

   You can choose from the following:

   —**Header Row.** Tints the first row of the table and adjusts text color accordingly.

   —**Total Row.** Draws a thicker line above the last row of data and bolds the last row of data.

—**Banded Rows.** Lightly tints every other row.

—**First Column.** Bolds all the data in the first column.

—**Last Column.** Bolds all the data in the last column.

—**Banded Columns.** Lightly tints every other column.

PowerPoint redisplays your table based on your choice. Figure 6-24 shows you an example.

Skeins sold	Wool	Cotton	Silk
Jan-March	5,000	3,000	2,523
Apr-June	5,250	3,500	3,110
July-Sep	6,500	4,200	4,239
Oct-Dec	7,333	6,430	5,274
Total Yearly Sales	24,203	17,250	15,280

Figure 6-24. Turning on Total Row tells PowerPoint to add a thicker line, and bold the data and color the background in the last row of the table.

Inserting and deleting rows and columns

You've typed in twenty cells' worth of data when you realize you accidentally skipped a row. No sweat: simply insert a new blank row and type the skipped numbers.

To insert a row or a column, right-click one of the cells in your table and then, from the context menu that appears, choose Insert → Insert Above or Insert → Insert Below (to insert a row to the above or below your currently selected cell, respectively) or Insert → Insert Left or Insert → Insert Right (to insert a column to the left or right of your currently selected cell, respectively).

To delete a row or column, right-click any cell in the row or column you want to delete and then, from the context menu that appears, choose Delete Rows or Delete Columns. To delete multiple rows or columns, select them first; then right-click.

Changing the width of a row or column

Each table that you create begins with standard, consistently sized rows and columns. But depending on the content that you add to your cells, you may want to increase or decrease the width of a row or column. For example, if you type a column heading wider than the column width, PowerPoint assumes you want to break it up into two lines. If you don't agree, you can widen the column.

To adjust the width of a row or column:

1. **Click anywhere in your table.**

2. **Mouse over the cell border of the row or column you want to adjust.**

   Your cursor turns into the double-headed arrow cursor shown in Figure 6-25.

3. **Click the cell border and drag to adjust the row (or column) width.**

   __ NOTE _____

   If you'd prefer to type numbers for the width and height of your rows or columns, you can. Just select the rows or columns you want to work with, then choose Table Tools | Layout → Table Size → Width or Table Tools | Layout → Table Size → Height and click the arrows to increase or decrease row (or column) size. As you adjust the numbers, PowerPoint automatically redraws your table.

Aligning data inside cells

Unless you tell it otherwise, PowerPoint assumes you want the text and numbers you type into your table cells to be top- and left-aligned. But you're free to change that to anything else you like. For example, text often looks nice when centered. Numbers are usually easier to read when right aligned.

Because most folks find vertical alignment options (top, center, and bottom) most useful, those are the options easiest to get to. But by using the Cell Text Layout dialog box described below, you can align your data eight ways to Sunday.

Skeins sold	Wool	Cotton
Jan-March	5,000	3,000
Apr-June	5,250	3,500
July-Sep	6,500	4,200
Oct-Dec	7,333	6,430
Total Yearly Sales	24,203	17,250

Figure 6-25. Simply drag to adjust the width of a column, as shown here, or a row. You know you're exactly over a column border when you see the double-headed arrow.

To realign data:

1. **Select the cells whose contents you want to realign.**

2. **Go to Table Tools | Layout → Alignment and choose Align Top, Center Vertically, or Align Bottom.**

   PowerPoint redraws your table using the alignment you selected.

3. **If vertical alignment isn't what you want, click Table Tools | Layout → Alignment → Cell Margins → Custom Margins.**

   The Cell Text Layout dialog box appears.

4. **In the Cell Text Layout dialog box, click the Internal Margins options to align your text the way you want it to appear.**

   PowerPoint redraws your table using the alignment options you selected.

To align the text in your data cells horizontally, follow the same steps, but adjust the internal left and right margins.

Merging (and splitting) cells

Depending on the data you're trying to present, you may want to merge cells (erase the border between cells) or split cells (add a border between cells). Merging cells is especially useful for creating a heading inside your table, as shown in Figure 6-26 (top). You want to consider splitting cells when you find yourself cramming more than one or two words, phrases, or sentences in a single cell (Figure 6-26, bottom).

Pros & Cons of Adding Visuals to a PowerPoint Presentation	
Table	Pro: Your teacher (boss) expects a table. Con: You don't have any relevant data (or any idea where to find some).
Chart	Pro: A process chart will get across your ideas succinctly and powerfully. Con: You've already got a chart you created in UNIX using X's and O's that you want to use.

Pros & Cons of Adding Visuals to a PowerPoint Presentation	
Table	Pro: Your teacher (boss) expects a table.
	Con: You don't have any relevant data (or any idea where to find some.
Chart	Pro: A process chart will get across your ideas succinctly and powerfully.
	Con: You've already got a chart you created in UNIX using X's and O's that you want to use.

Figure 6-26. Top: The text in this table is okay, but its placement isn't particularly stellar.

Bottom: Here you see the same table, with two minor adjustments: the two cells in the top row were merged, and the two cells in the right column were each split. The result (after a bit of the cell alignment magic described on page 189) is attractive and professional looking.

To merge a cell, select the cells you want to merge and click Table Tools | Layout → Merge → Merge Cells. You can also right-click a selection and choose Merge Cells.

To split a cell, select the cell you want to split and then click Table Tools | Layout → Merge → Split Cells (or right-click the selected cell and choose Split Cells). In the Split Cells dialog box that appears, type in the number of columns and number of rows you want your newly split cell to have. When you finish, click OK.

Resizing Tables

PowerPoint gives you two options for resizing your table:

▶ **Drag to resize.** Dragging is the easiest approach, and it's the way to go if eyeballing the resulting size of your table is good enough. To resize your table by dragging, mouse over the dots you see on the corners and at the sides of your table frame (Figure 6-26). When your cursor in the right place, it turns into a two-headed arrow. As soon as you see the two-headed arrow, drag to resize your table.

▶ **Specify numbers for table width and height.** If you need to create a table of a very specific size—you want to match your table to a background image or a table on another slide, for example—you want to go this route. First, go to Table Tools | Layout → Table Size. Then use the Width and Height boxes to increase or decrease the current dimensions. (You can either click the arrows to dial up or down, or type a number in directly.)

Repositioning Tables

You move a table around on your slide similar to the way you move pictures, charts, and other objects—by dragging. Simply mouse over your table's frame until you see a four-headed arrow, and then drag to reposition your table.

Deleting Tables

You'll probably be surprised to learn that you *don't* delete a table the way you delete just about everything else in PowerPoint—by right-clicking it and then choosing Home → Delete. (Doing so deletes the slide on which the table appears.)

Instead, you need to select the table (page 185) and then press Delete.

You can also cut the table by selecting it and then choosing Home → Cut. (Technically speaking, cutting isn't the same things as deleting, but it's close enough. See page 60 for details.)

PART TWO: DELIVERING SLIDESHOWS

DELIVERING PRESENTATIONS

7

▶ Setting Up a Slideshow

▶ Slideshows for Multiple Audiences

▶ Presenting Your Slideshow

▶ Creating PowerPoint Shows

▶ Emailing Your Presentation

▶ Packaging Presentations for CD

▶ Optimizing Presentations

IN THE OLD DAYS, GIVING A POWERPOINT PRESENTATION almost always meant connecting your laptop to a computer projector. You'd stand in front of a live audience and use a remote control to click through each slide while you explained each of your points in detail. You can still give a "stand and deliver" presentation, but today you can also:

▶ Package your presentation for delivery on CD. This option is ideal for interactive, audience-paced presentations like tutorials or continuously running kiosk presentations.

▶ Email the presentation to your audience.

This chapter covers both of these presentation delivery options. It also shows you how to optimize your PowerPoint presentation file to make running it and passing it around easier.

___ **NOTE** _____

You can also convert your presentation to a Web page, complete with clickable links that viewers can use to navigate your slideshow and even jump to other documents or Web sites. For more on these and other advanced features, see *PowerPoint 2007: The Missing Manual* (O'Reilly).

_____

Setting Up a Slideshow

After you've put together your slideshow—created slides, added text and graphics, and so on—you have to give PowerPoint a few instructions on how it should display the slideshow when it's show time. Say you're creating a slideshow that you want to run continuously on a kiosk, with no human intervention. You might want to tell to linger a few seconds longer on certain slides than on others. Or imagine that you have two monitors hooked up to your computer: one set into the wall of a conference room, and one on a laptop placed strategically where only you can see it. You can have PowerPoint display the slideshow on the wall monitor, and the speaker notes on the laptop.

Using the Slide Show tab (Figure 7-1), you can set these options and more. The following sections show you how.

Figure 7-1. The Slide Show tab offers a grab-bag of options you can set to tell PowerPoint how you want your slideshow to appear when it runs on a computer.

Choosing a Slideshow Mode

The first thing to do when you're setting up your slideshow is to decide which mode you want your slideshow to run in: full-screen, browser, or kiosk. Your choice affects the way folks can interact with your slideshow while it's running, as well as which other options you can set.

Full-screen mode

Full-screen mode (Figure 7-2) is the way to go if you'll be the one giving your presentation. As the name implies, in full-screen mode slideshows take up the entire screen. Depending on the PowerPoint options you've set, ghosted controls appear in the lower-left corner of a full-screen slideshow. Other ways you can interact with a full-screen slideshow running include keyboard shortcuts and a right-click menu (page 210).

The program assumes you want full-screen mode unless you tell it different. But if you (or a coworker) has set your slideshow to another mode and you want to set it back, here's how:

1. **Choose Slide Show → Set Up → Set Up Slide Show.**

   The Set Up Show dialog box (Figure 7-3) appears.

2. **Turn on the radio button next to "Presented by a speaker (full screen)."**

Browser mode

When you set up a slideshow to run in browser mode, your slides don't take over the entire screen; instead, they appear in a self-contained window (see Figure 7-4). A specialized right-click menu appears (page 211), offering choices that folks running your presentation might find handy—printing your slides, for example. Designed to

Top 4 Reasons
Baby Won't Sleep

1. Letting baby pick *Nightmare on Elm Street* as bedtime story
2. Leaving baby teeth for the Tooth Monster
3. Using Van Halen to rock baby (instead of a rocking chair)
4. Giving baby *Jolt Cola Jr.* less than 2 hours before bed

Figure 7-2. Full-screen mode is the way to go if you plan to run your slideshow yourself, because it gives you the most options for interacting with your slideshow. Pressing Esc ends the presentation.

be relatively easy for non-PowerPoint folks to figure out how to run, browser mode is an option for slideshows you're planning to distribute by CD or email.

To set up your slideshow to run in browser mode:

1. **Choose Slide Show → Set Up → Set Up Slide Show.**

    The Set Up Show dialog box appears.

2. **Turn on the radio button next to "Browsed by an individual (window)."**

3. **For your audience's sake, also make sure the Show Scrollbar checkbox, which now becomes available, is turned on.**

    If you leave this option turned off, your audience won't see an obvious way to scroll through your slides. They must either know to right-click (which displays a menu of options) or sit there frustrated.

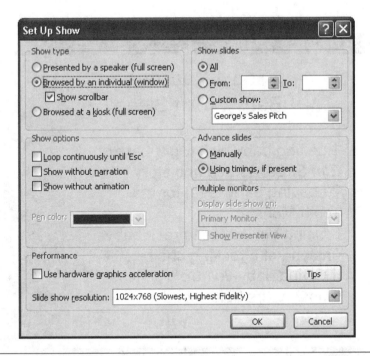

Figure 7-3. The Set Up Show dialog box lets you set useful but relatively seldom-used options that wouldn't fit on the Slide Show tab.

Kiosk mode

If you're planning to let your slideshow run unattended, kiosk mode is what you want. In kiosk mode, there are no ghosted controls or right-click menus—which means there's nothing built-in that your audience can click to start your slideshow, stop it, hop from one slide to the next, or otherwise interact with your slides. After all, since there won't be a presenter, you don't want to include presenter controls and risk someone wandering by and fiddling with them.

But what no presenter controls also means is that if you set up your slideshow to run in kiosk mode, you must set automatic timings (page 202) so your slideshow plays automatically all the way through before looping around again.

To set up your slideshow to run in kiosk mode:

1. **Choose Slide Show → Set Up → Set Up Slide Show.**

    The Set Up Show dialog box appears.

Figure 7-4. In browser mode, no PowerPoint experience is necessary. To scroll from slide to slide, your audience uses familiar scroll bars. To close the slideshow, they click the familiar X in the upper-right corner of the browser window.

2. **Turn on the radio button next to "Browsed at a kiosk (full screen)."**

   Typically, you'll save kiosk-mode slideshows as self-running PowerPoint shows (page 212).

TIP

Pressing Esc stops a slideshow running in kiosk mode, so if you're setting up a kiosk slideshow to run automatically and want to prevent folks from inadvertently stopping it in its tracks the second you turn your back, make sure you hide the keyboard.

Hiding Individual Slides

First, make sure your slideshow includes all the slides you want to show—and none that you don't. To eliminate a slide from a particular slideshow, you don't have to delete it from the presentation—you can choose to hide it temporarily. That way, you can always take it out of hiding when you want to use it again.

Say you're giving a presentation to management. One of your slides is quite high-tech—a complicated chart and some head-busting equations. Since this level of detail may confuse your audience, you can hide that slide. If someone in your audience happens to ask a pertinent question during the presentation, you can display the slide manually, as described in the table on page 210. The same slide may be appropriate for the engineers you're giving the same presentation to later in the week, so you can bring it out of hiding for that show.

> **NOTE**
>
> Because hiding a slide doesn't delete it, don't rely on hiding to conceal sensitive or proprietary information. There's always a chance that you (or someone else running your slideshow) could unhide it accidentally. Instead, either delete the slide or create a custom slideshow (page 206).

To hide a slide:

1. **In the Slides pane in Normal view, select the slide (or slides) you want to hide.**

    If you don't see thumbnails of your slides on the left side of your screen, choose View → Presentation Views → Normal to restore the Slides pane.

2. **Click Slide Show → Set Up → Hide Slide.**

    In the Slides pane, the number of your newly hidden slide appears with a line through it (Figure 7-5).

3. **The next time your presentation runs, PowerPoint skips the hidden slide(s).**

Setting Up a Speaker Notes Screen

Pros use teleprompters for a reason: they work. When your brain goes blank and you forget an important point, having an electronic cheat sheet that only you can see can save your presentation (and your reputation as a confident, extemporaneous speaker). PowerPoint offers the next best thing to a teleprompter: It lets you run your slideshow on one monitor, and your speaker notes on another. While your audience is looking at your slides or at you, you can sneak a peek at your notes. And because you're not fumbling with 3×5 cards, no one will be the wiser.

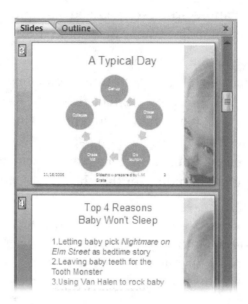

Figure 7-5. Hide Slide is a toggle option, so clicking Hide Slide while you've got a visible slide selected hides the slide. Clicking it while you've got a hidden slide selected unhides the slide. You can also hide slides from Slide Sorter view.

To set up a presenter view, first connect two different monitors to the computer you intend to run your presentation on. (A laptop computer counts as one monitor.) Once the monitors are plugged in, open the presentation you want to set up as a presenter view. Then go to Slide Show → Monitors and turn on the checkbox next to Use Presenter View.

Click the down-arrow next to Show Presentation On (which has now become available), and then, from the list that appears, choose the monitor on which you want your *slideshow* to appear. Your speaker notes appear on the monitor you're using to follow these steps.

Setting Up Automatic Timing

You've got two choices when it comes to clicking through your slides at showtime: you can click through each slide manually, or you can set up an automatic slideshow by telling PowerPoint when to go from one slide to the next. An automatic slideshow is useful if, for example, you're delivering your presentation on a kiosk, or if you have exactly 40 minutes to give your presentation and need PowerPoint to keep you on track. Also, if you've done a presentation many times, you may be able to give your spiel and let PowerPoint change the slides automatically, at just the right moment.

The key to setting up an automatic slideshow is to rehearse your presentation. You run through it just as you would in front of a live audience, while PowerPoint's virtual stopwatch keeps track of how many seconds you spend on each slide. Then, if you're satisfied with the pacing, you tell PowerPoint to keep those timings.

___ TIP ___

Instead of painstakingly rehearsing your presentation, you can assign each slide, say, a minute and a half (or any amount of time you choose). In the Slides pane, select a slide. Then select Animations → Transition to This Slide, turn on the "Automatically after" checkbox, and type the amount of time you want the currently selected slide to remain onscreen. (Make sure you turn off On Mouse Click.) Repeat for the remaining slides in your slideshow. Alternatively, for each slide you can type the amount of slide time you want in the Rehearsal dialog box (Figure 7-6).

To rehearse your presentation and set timings:

1. **Click Slide Show → Set Up → Rehearse Timings.**

   PowerPoint begins a full-screen version of your slideshow and displays the Rehearsal toolbar (Figure 7-6).

Figure 7-6. Rehearsing your timing not only helps you cement in your mind what you're going to say and how you're going to say it, it also lets you know whether you have enough slides to fill your allotted speaking time (or too many).

2. **Step through your presentation as you normally would, speaking aloud and gesturing to a pretend audience.**

   Hopping around slides in your slideshow affects your rehearsal timings. For example, clicking Repeat to back up to an earlier slide stops the overall slideshow clock, which doesn't start up again until you return to (or pass) the slide you were on when you clicked Repeat.

Typing the number of a particular slide and then pressing Enter to hop directly to that slide resets the current slide clock even if you've already timed that slide; meanwhile, the overall slideshow clock keeps on ticking away.

If the phone rings, the dog barks, your boss steps in, or you're otherwise interrupted, head to the Rehearsal toolbar and click Pause to stop the clock. Then, after you've handled the interruption, click Pause again to resume your rehearsal where you left off.

3. **When you get to the last slide, take as long as you need to wrap up your presentation, and then press Esc.**

   PowerPoint kicks up the dialog box you see in Figure 7-7.

Figure 7-7. If you're not sure you're happy with the pace at which you just rehearsed your presentation, choose Yes anyway. You can always rehearse again later—and when you do, PowerPoint will discard these timings and use your new timings.

— TIP

You can also press Esc at any time to abort the rehearsal.

4. **Choose Yes if you want PowerPoint to flip through the slides at the pace you just rehearsed the next time you run your slideshow. Choose No if you want to flip through your slides manually, or if you've discovered during your rehearsal that you need to add or delete slides, rearrange your slideshow, or come up with a lot more banter.**

   If you chose Yes, PowerPoint displays the Slide Sorter view showing your timings. (If you chose No, PowerPoint simply returns you to Normal view.)

5. **On the Slide Show tab, make sure Use Rehearsed Timings checkbox is turned on.**

The next time you start your slideshow, PowerPoint uses your rehearsed timings to click through your slides automatically.

Looping Continuously

Whether you choose to click through each slide yourself or use automatic timings (page 202) to tell PowerPoint how fast to move through each slide, you usually want to stop the slideshow after the last slide. But for those times when you *do* want your slideshow to loop continuously (to begin the slideshow over again the instant it finishes), you can do that by clicking Slide Show → Set Up → Set Up Slide Show to open the Set Up Show dialog box. Then, in the Show Options section, turn on the "Loop continuously until 'Esc'" checkbox. When you take down the show at the end of the day, just press the Esc key to stop the show and regain control of your laptop.

> **NOTE**
>
> If you set up your slideshow to run in kiosk mode (page 199), you don't have to tell PowerPoint to loop continuously—it assumes that's what you want. In fact, PowerPoint deactivates the "Loop continuously until 'Esc'" option.

Slideshows for Multiple Audiences

If you give a lot of presentations, you've probably found yourself creating one big comprehensive presentation on a particular topic, and then adjusting it for different audiences. For example, say you want to give slightly different variations of the same sales pitch to small-business owners, government acquisitions teams, and purchasing departments in large corporations. Say, too, that you want a ten-minute version of your presentation that skims the highlights for those times when all your potential clients will give you is ten minutes of their time. But you also want thirty-minute and hour-long versions that cover the technical features of your product.

You could reinvent the wheel by copying slides from one slideshow into another, reorganizing them, and saving the newly copied slides as a separate slideshow. But PowerPoint gives you an easier way to accomplish the same result. By creating a *custom slideshow*, you tell PowerPoint which subset of slides in your comprehensive presentation you want to designate as a new version. You even get to change the order the slides appear. Then you give your new version a meaningful name, like *small_business* or *ten_minute*, to remind you what situations to use it for.

Because you don't actually duplicate slides or files when you create a custom slideshow, you don't have to worry about carting around multiple PowerPoint files (or keeping them all updated and in synch).

> **NOTE**
>
> Unfortunately, you can't mix-and-match slides from different slideshows in the same custom slideshow. To create a new slideshow from a bunch of different slideshows, you need to copy-and-paste individual slides (page 144).

Creating a Custom Slideshow

The term *custom slideshow* is a little misleading. When you create a custom slideshow, you're not actually creating a new PowerPoint file; what you're creating is a new version of the original slideshow in the form of a named list of slides. The slides themselves stay right where they are, in the original slideshow, which is exactly what makes custom slideshows so useful. Since they're essentially nothing but lists of slides, no matter how many times the slides themselves change, your custom slideshows always stay automatically up-to-date.

> **NOTE**
>
> Additional ways to adjust the way your slideshow runs include hiding slides (page 200) and looping your slideshow continuously (page 205).

To create a custom slideshow:

1. **Select Slide Show → Start Slide Show → Custom Slide Show.**

   If you've created custom slideshows in this presentation before, their names appear here, along with the Custom Shows option. (If you haven't, only the Custom Shows option appears.)

2. **Select Custom Shows.**

   A Custom Shows dialog box similar to Figure 7-8 pops up.

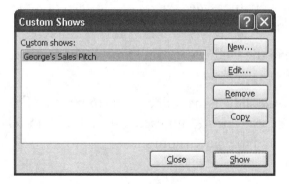

Figure 7-8. If you haven't previously created any custom shows in this presentation file, you won't see any listed here, and all of the options except New appear grayed-out. To create a new custom show, click New.

3. **In the Custom Shows dialog box, click New.**

   The Define Custom Show dialog box appears (Figure 7-9).

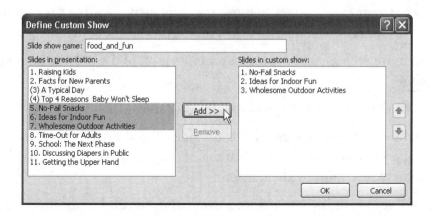

Figure 7-9. PowerPoint lists each slide in your comprehensive slideshow along the left side of the Define Custom Show dialog box, ready for you to pick and choose which slides you want to add to your custom version. PowerPoint designates hidden slides with parentheses as you can see here on Slide 3.

4. **In the "Slide show name" box, type a name for your new custom slideshow.**

   Pick a short name that reminds you of either the content of the slideshow you're putting together, or the length (for example, *thirty_minute*). (In Figure 7-9, the custom slideshow's name is *food_and_fun.*) Instead of underlines between words, you can use spaces if you like.

5. **On the left side of the Define Custom Show dialog box, select the slide you want to add. Then click Add.**

   PowerPoint lists the slide in the "Slides in custom show" box on the right side of the dialog box. Repeat this step for each slide in the comprehensive slideshow that you want to add to your custom show.

   ___ TIP _____

   To select multiple contiguous slides, click the first slide, and then Shift+click the last slide to select that slide plus all slides in between. To select multiple noncontiguous slides, click the first slide, then Ctrl+click each additional slide.

   _____

6. **If you like, you can change the order of the slides in your custom slideshow: in the "Slides in custom show" list, click the slide you want to reorder. Then press the Up or Down arrow to move the slide up or down in the custom show's organization (it doesn't affect their order in the actual presentation).**

   As you move each slide, PowerPoint renumbers all of the slides in your custom slideshow.

7. **When you're satisfied with your custom slideshow, click OK.**

   The Define Custom Show dialog box disappears, and the Custom Shows dialog box reappears with your new custom slideshow listed. You can test your custom slideshow at this point by clicking Show.

8. **Click Close to dismiss the Custom Show dialog box and return to normal editing mode.**

Editing a Custom Slideshow

Because a custom slideshow is nothing but a list of slides, you can't edit a custom slideshow's slide content directly. (To do that, you need to edit the content of the original slideshow's slides.) But you *can* add, delete, and reorder the slides that make up your custom slideshow.

To edit a custom slideshow:

1. **Go to Slide Show → Start Slide Show → Custom Slide Show → Custom Shows.**

   A list of custom shows appears.

2. **Click to select the name of the show you want to edit, and then choose one of the following options:**

   ▶ **Edit.** Lets you rename the custom show, and add, remove, and reorder slides.

   ▶ **Remove.** Deletes the custom slideshow.

   ▶ **Copy.** Copies the custom slideshow (good for creating additional versions that aren't too different from one you've selected).

3. **When you've finished editing your custom slideshow, click Close to dismiss the Custom Show dialog box and return to normal editing mode.**

FREQUENTLY ASKED QUESTION

The Poor Man's Custom Slideshow

All I want to do is show the first half of my slides. Do I have to go to all the trouble of setting up a custom slideshow just to do that?

If all you want to do is show the first half of your slideshow, the last half, or any other contiguous set of slides (for example, slides 4 through 22) in order, Power-Point gives you a much quicker and easier option than creating a custom slideshow. Here's what you do:

1. Select Slide Show → Set Up → Set Up Slide Show.

2. In the Set Up Show dialog box that appears, head to the Show Slides section, turn on the From radio button, and then choose slide numbers in the From and To boxes.

3. Click OK to dismiss the Set Up Show dialog box. The next time you run your slideshow, PowerPoint will show only the specified slides.

Presenting Your Slideshow

The control you have when it comes time to present your slideshow depends on how you've chosen to set up your slideshow: as full-screen, browser, or kiosk mode (see page 197).

▶ **Full-screen mode.** Right-clicking your mouse while you're running a slideshow in full-screen mode kicks up a context menu that lets you choose how to present your slideshow, as you can see in Figure 7-10. But most folks find it quicker (and less distracting to the audience) to use the keyboard shortcuts described in Table 7-1. In addition, when you run a slideshow in full-screen mode, you see the ghosted controls shown back in Figure 7-2, and you can control your presentation with a remove control.

Table 7-1. Key Strokes for Navigating Your Slideshow

To Do This	Press This
Go forward one slide	Enter, Space, Page Down, N, click, right-arrow, down-arrow
Back up one slide	Backspace, Page Up, P, left-arrow, up-arrow
Jump directly to a specific slide, even if it's hidden (page 200)	Type the slide number and then press Enter, or right-click the slide and, from the menu that appears, click the title of the slide you want to go to
Scroll back and forth through slides quickly	Roll the wheel on your mouse
Black out the presentation	B or . (period)
White out the presentation	W or , (comma)
End the slideshow	Esc or Ctrl+Break
Hide the cursor (pointer)	= (A to show pointer again)
Start drawing (annotating) electronically on a slide using your mouse or a graphics pen	Ctrl+P, then drag mouse (or stylus) to draw
Stop drawing and turn pen back into arrow pointer	Ctrl+A
Erase all the ink annotations on a slide	E
Pause a slideshow that's running automatically	S (Press S again or + to restart it)

Figure 7-10. Anything you can do with keyboard shortcuts, you can do with the context menu shown here. Trouble is, your audience has to sit through the menu selections, which may not do much for their concentration.

TIP

Even if you're not normally a keyboard shortcut fan, you may want to familiarize yourself with Table 7-1. That way, if you're in the middle of giving a presentation and you suddenly notice your slides racing by, for example, you'll know why (and what to do about it).

▶ **Browser mode.** If you set up your slideshow to run in browser mode *and* told PowerPoint to show scroll bars (page 198), you can use the scroll bars in the browser window to scroll from slide to slide. Right-clicking shows a different context menu (shown in Figure 7-11) than the one that appears for full-screen presentations. Finally, only a few keyboard shortcuts work for browser-mode slideshows: Go forward one slide, Back up one slide, and End the slideshow (see Table 7-1).

▶ **Kiosk mode.** If you set up your slideshow to run in kiosk mode (page 198), no ghosted controls appear, and no right-click menu appears, either. What's more, none of the keyboard shortcuts shown in Table 7-1 work. Instead, you need to set up automatic timings (page 202) so that the slideshow runs through your slides automatically so that folks who stop by the kiosk can navigate your slideshow.

Figure 7-11. Right-clicking a slideshow set up to run in browser mode displays a different menu than the one that appears when you right-click a slideshow set up to run in full-screen mode.

Creating PowerPoint Shows

A *PowerPoint show* is a version of your slideshow saved in a special format (.ppsx, .ppsm, or .pps) that folks who don't have PowerPoint installed on their computers can run. Instead, when you distribute a PowerPoint show—by burning it to CD, for example, by emailing it—all your recipients need to run your show is a copy of the *PowerPoint viewer*. The PowerPoint viewers is a freely downloadable Microsoft program that lets viewers run and print slideshows, but not edit them.

The difference between a slideshow saved as a PowerPoint show and the same slideshow saved as a PowerPoint presentation file is simply this: opening the show in PowerPoint or in the PowerPoint viewer runs it in slideshow mode; opening the presentation file in PowerPoint runs it in editing mode. Both shows and presentation files can be edited in PowerPoint.

> **NOTE**
>
> When you package your slideshow for CD, PowerPoint automatically throws in a copy of the free PowerPoint viewer so the recipient of your CD doesn't have to hunt one down herself. To run a slideshow that's on a CD, simply insert the disc into a computer's CD drive. Windows launches PowerPoint (or the PowerPoint viewer), and the show starts playing automatically.

To create a PowerPoint show:

1. **Choose Office button → Save As.**

    The Save As dialog box appears.

2. From the "Save as type" drop-down menu, choose "PowerPoint Show (*.ppsx)".

3. In the "File name" box, type the filename you want your file to have. In the "Save in" box, type the folder where you want to save your file. When you're done, click Save.

    PowerPoint saves your show using the filename and folder you specified, and the Save As dialog box disappears.

Emailing Your Presentation

Thanks to PowerPoint 2007's new, more compact file formats, emailing presentation files is easier on your audience than ever. Emailing a presentation is especially easy if you have Outlook installed on your computer. You never have to leave the comfort of PowerPoint.

NOTE

If you don't have Outlook installed on your computer, you need to email your presentation the old-fashioned way. In your email program, create a new email message. Then fill in your recipients' email addresses, attach your presentation file (for example, *myPresentation.pptx*), and then send the email.

To email a presentation, make sure you've saved your presentation, and then choose Office button → Send → Email. Microsoft Outlook opens a blank email message with your presentation automatically attached. Customize the email message, type your recipients' email addresses, and click Send to send the message.

Packaging Presentations for CD

File-wise, creating a PowerPoint presentation can get messy fast. You've got your presentation file itself, of course, but depending on which elements and effects you've added to your slides, your presentation file may depend on additional files containing fonts, audio and clips, images, linked content, and so on. And if you've ever tried to make a quick copy of a presentation (for example, on your way out the door to catch a plane) you know how frustratingly hard this theoretically easy task is to pull off in reality.

Fortunately, PowerPoint can automate the process. When you package your presentation for CD, you tell PowerPoint to gather up all of the files you need to run your slideshow (complete with a copy of the PowerPoint viewer, if you like, to make sure they have everything they need to run the slideshow) and stick them in a single folder, which you can then store on your computer or, if you happen to have a CD burner connected to your computer, copy directly to disk.

— NOTE

> You can save more than one presentation to a CD (or to a named file). If you do, PowerPoint lets you specify what order you want your presentations to run in (see step 5 on page 216).

If you've created additional files such as supporting documentation, electronic brochures, or text scripts, you can tell PowerPoint to add them to the package, too. Supporting documentation helps offset the fact that your audience (and not you) will be running the slideshow. For example, if your slideshow is a tutorial, you can include self-tests, answer keys, instructional drawings, a bibliography, or anything else you want students to be able to refer to after they've worked through the tutorial.

To package a presentation for CD:

1. **Office button → Publish → Package for CD.**

    A Package for CD dialog box similar to Figure 7-12 appears.

2. **In the Name the CD box, type the name you want to give your CD (or, if you're not planning to burn a CD, the name you want to give your presentation's file folder).**

    Your audience will see this name, so make sure it's both meaningful and appropriate.

3. **If you have supporting files you'd like to add to your CD (or to your folder), click Add Files. In the "File name" box, type the name of the file you want to add (or browse your computer to find the file). Then click Add.**

    The Add Files dialog box disappears, and PowerPoint adds the file to the list of things to burn to your CD.

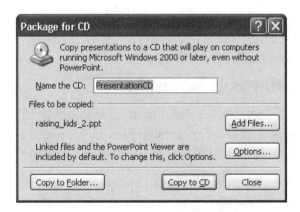

Figure 7-12. The Package for CD option is a bit of a misnomer. Yes, you can use it to gather up all your presentation-related files and burn them to a CD—but you can also use it to organize the files in a single folder, an option you may find useful if you're hooked up to a network. Clicking Options displays the dialog box in Figure 7-13.

Figure 7-13. Here's where you customize the way your audience runs your packaged presentation.

4. **To tell PowerPoint how you want your audience to run your packaged presentation, click Options.**

   The Options dialog box opens (Figure 7-13).

5. **Turn on the Viewer Package radio button.**

   This popular option tells PowerPoint to include a copy of the PowerPoint viewer in your package, as well as an executable file that launches the viewer preloaded with your presentation as soon as your audience inserts the CD.

   If you choose this option, PowerPoint also lets you click the down arrow next to "Select how presentations will play in the viewer" and choose one of the following: "Play all presentations automatically in the specified order," "Play only the first presentation automatically," "Let the user select which presentation to view," or "Don't play the CD automatically."

   When you've finished setting options, click OK to close the Options dialog box.

6. **In the Package for CD dialog box, choose one of the following:**

   ▶ **Copy to CD.** Choose this option if you want to copy your presentation files to a CD. Obviously, this option doesn't work unless you have a CD burner attached to your computer.

   ▶ **Copy to Folder.** Choose this option if you want to copy your presentation files to a named folder on your own computer, or to a computer on your network.

   PowerPoint pops up a dialog box that lets you type in a name for your folder, as well as where on your computer (or network) you want to store it.

7. **Click Close.**

   PowerPoint saves your presentation to disk or to your computer.

Optimizing Presentations

Optimization in PowerPoint means *keeping file size as small as possible*. If you plan to display your presentation on a laptop or email it to each of your department heads for sign-off, you should pare down the size of your PowerPoint file by applying the strategies outlined in the following sections.

Choose Insert over Dragging or Pasting

PowerPoint gives you a variety of ways to add pictures, spreadsheets, and other objects to your slides. But the tidiest approach is the Insert tab. Using the Insert options to add an object to a slide can save you big bytes over adding that same object by dragging or cutting and pasting it from another program.

Recycle Your Images

In PowerPoint as in life, reusing makes good sense: for the file size cost of a single image, you can display the image dozens of times—or more. To get the benefit of recycling, add images to your slide master (page 147) instead of adding them to individual slides. Reusing the same graphic on multiple slides doesn't just keep file size to a minimum, it also makes good sense design-wise.

Get Rid of Invisible Stuff

If you edit your slides a lot—adding and deleting objects, for example, or changing your objects' color or transparency—you could end up with objects on your slides that don't actually appear, either because you've accidentally hidden then behind a larger object, because you've made them transparent or the same color as your slide's background, or because you turned off their visibility in the Selection and Visibility pane. Even if they don't appear, though, they're going to add to your file size. To check for—and get rid of—invisible objects:

1. **Select Home → Editing → Select → Selection Pane.**

   The Selection and Visibility pane (Figure 7-14) appears.

2. **In the Selection and Visibility pane, check the object listing.**

   Look for objects whose listings are missing an eyeball icon, meaning they're on your slide but not visible to see if you spot anything you don't expect. For example, you may find an image you thought you'd deleted.

3. **If you still don't spot anything amiss—it's hard to spot something that's not there, after all—click Show All.**

   All the objects you added to your slide appear on your slide.

4. **If you do spot an object that you don't want on your slide, in the Selection pane, click the object name.**

   PowerPoint selects that object on your slide.

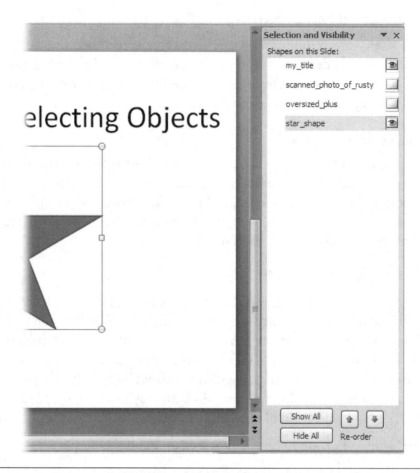

Figure 7-14. Drilling down to the Selection and Visibility pane is a pain, but it's worth it. Click to toggle the eyeball icon on and off. If it's visible, the object is visible; if it's not, neither is the object. Clicking the name of an object selects the object on your slide.

5. **Press Delete.**

   PowerPoint deletes the object from your slide.

When you save your file, PowerPoint deducts the size of your deleted object from your overall file size.

___ **TIP** _____

When you're checking for hidden objects, don't forget to check your slide, notes, and handout masters as well as your slides.

Compress Your Images

When you crop or shrink an image in PowerPoint, the program saves the cropped digital scraps (or large version) just in case you want to change your mind and restore your image to its original dimensions later. That's great while you're still editing your slides, but when you've got them the way you want them, you need to tell PowerPoint to delete those file-size-bloating extra scraps and unused versions.

1. **On your slide, click to select the image you want to compress. (If you want to compress all of the images in your slideshow, you can click any image.)**

   The Picture Tools | Format tab appears (Figure 7-15).

Figure 7-15. The Picture Tools | Format tab appears automatically any time you click an image on a slide; click it to see the options shown here. You can use the options you find on this tab to crop, resize, or add effects to your image. When you've got it the way you want it, you can compress it to optimize your PowerPoint file size.

2. **Click Compress Pictures.**

   The Compress Pictures dialog box (Figure 7-16) appears.

Figure 7-16. In the Compress Pictures box, clicking Options displays the Compression Settings dialog box in Figure 7-17.

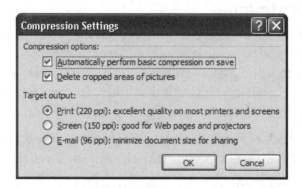

Figure 7-17. Out of the box, PowerPoint assumes you want it to compress your pictures and discard any cropped-off scraps. But you can choose just how radically you want PowerPoint to be when compressing your file. Choosing E-mail as your target output squeezes your file as small as it can possibly go.

3. **If you like, you can turn on the checkbox next to "Apply to selected picture only" to tell PowerPoint to compress the picture you selected in step 1 (but none of the other images in your presentation).**

   For maximum file optimization, you want to leave this checkbox turned off.

4. **Tell PowerPoint how you want it to compress your file. To do so, click Options.**

   The Compression settings dialog box shown in Figure 7-17 appears. In most cases, the options that PowerPoint picks for you work just fine. The only time you really need to mess with them is if you intend to deliver your presentation on a computer or send it by email, in which case you can trim extra bytes by choosing the Screen or E-mail options described in the next step.

   If you like, you can turn on (or off) the checkbox next to one of the following compression options:

   ▶ **Automatically perform basic compression on save** tells PowerPoint to use the compression settings you change in this dialog box automatically, every time you save your presentation.

   ▶ **Delete cropped areas of pictures** discards the slivers of any images you've cropped.

5. **Tell PowerPoint what quality/compression balance it should shoot for by choosing one of the following target output options:**

   ▶ **Print** (highest quality but lowest compression; choose this option if you plan to print your presentation).

   ▶ **Screen** (best balance between quality and compression, useful if you plan to deliver your presentation over the Web or on a computer projector, or if you intend to package it on CD).

   ▶ **E-mail** (lowest quality but highest compression; choose if you plan to e-mail your presentation, either for peer review or to deliver it to your audience).

6. **Click OK.**

   The Compression settings dialog box disappears.

7. **In the Compress Picture dialog box, click OK.**

   The Compress Picture dialog box disappears. The next time you save your presentation file, PowerPoint pares down your file based on your selections.

Don't Embed Fonts (But If You Have To, Do So Wisely)

One way to format the text on your slides is to apply fonts, or typefaces, to your text, which you see how to do on page 89. But unlike other formatting elements, such as colors and images, the fonts you choose aren't automatically added to your PowerPoint file. Instead, PowerPoint assumes it will be able to find the fonts when you run your slideshow, installed on whatever computer you happen to be running your presentation on. If it can't, it automatically substitutes one of the fonts it *can* find.

That's the way PowerPoint works out of the box. And most of the time, this approach works just fine. Unless you choose a wild, wacky font you found on some boutique Web site, PowerPoint will probably be able to display your slide text perfectly. After all, most computers these days come complete with the same bunch of standard fonts.

But folks who feel a bit uneasy about letting PowerPoint choose which font to display—after all, the wrong font can mess up the slide layout you spent so much time on—can choose to *embed* their fonts instead. The thing is, when you embed a font, you explicitly tell PowerPoint to add all the information necessary to display the alphabet in that font. You get control, but at the cost of a bulked-up PowerPoint file. Bottom line: if you're trying to keep your file size to a minimum, don't embed fonts.

If you absolutely *have* to embed a font—for example, say you work for a publisher and the purpose of your presentation is to discuss different languages, fonts, and formatting styles—you can tell PowerPoint to embed just that portion of the font that you've actually used in your slideshow. So, for example, instead of having to add display instructions for everything from A–Z, both uppercase and lowercase, you can get away with adding just the handful of letters that make up your slide text.

To embed just enough of a font to display your slideshow correctly formatted:

1. **Choose Office button → PowerPoint Options.**

   The PowerPoint Options dialog box opens (Figure 7-18).

2. **On the left side of the PowerPoint Options dialog box, click Save.**

   Save-related options appear.

3. **Head down to the bottom of the dialog box and turn on the "Embed fonts in the file" checkbox.**

4. **Choose "Embed only the characters used in the presentation (best for reducing file size)," and then click OK.**

   The next time you save your presentation file, PowerPoint embeds (adds) font information directly into the file, but only the bare minimum it needs to display the text that's currently on your slides.

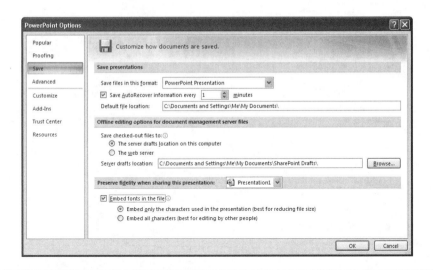

Figure 7-18. Embedding fonts swells the size of your file, and frankly, for most presentations your audience will be just as happy (if not happier) with Times New Roman as it would have been with FroofyLookAtMe. One caveat: choose "Embed all characters" if you're going to be passing your presentation around for feedback so your colleagues will be able to add additional text without goofing up the formatting.

___ **NOTE** ___

PowerPoint won't let you embed all fonts (for example, you can't embed PostScript fonts).

PRINTING PRESENTATIONS

8

- ▶ Printing Slides (One Slide per Page)
- ▶ Handouts (Multiple Slides per Page)
- ▶ Overhead Transparencies
- ▶ Speaker Notes
- ▶ Presentation Outline

MOST OF THE TIME, you'll deliver your PowerPoint presentations electronically, on a computer or digital projector. So with all these high-tech bits-and-bytes options, why on earth would you print your slides?

Here are three cool things you can do with printed slides:

▶ **Create a foolproof, fail-safe backup.** Printouts may not look as glamorous as full-color, widescreen slideshows, but they're invaluable when you have a technology meltdown. So when you reach your client's office with three minutes to spare and discover that your preschooler poured maple syrup into your laptop when you weren't looking, you at least have hard copies to work from.

▶ **Run off quick-and-dirty handouts.** For really useful audience handouts, you'll probably want to create separate supporting materials, as described on page 233. But to give your boss a quick outline of your presentation, printouts are the way to go.

▶ **Deliver your presentation in low-tech but effective ways like overhead transparencies.** You can't always control your presentation environment. For example, if you're in a location where an old overhead projector is all that's available, you can turn your presentation into overheads.

In addition to printing your slides, for some presentations you may want to print related materials like speaker notes for moral support behind the podium; a presentation outline, for double-checking that you've included all your important points; and even tent cards, for making your audience feel welcome. Another reason you might want to print a slide is because you've created a layout meant to be printed, such as an award certificate or a calendar. (See page 147 for the scoop on using Microsoft's own slide designs to create these and more printable layouts.)

Printing Slides (One Slide per Page)

The most straightforward to way to print your presentation is to print each individual slide on a separate piece of paper. You can keep paper printouts in a file, bring them with you to the presentation as a failsafe, or use them to practice your spiel or proof your slides (some errors are easier to spot in plain black and white).

When you commit your slides to paper, you have a few extra decisions to make. For example, onscreen slides don't usually have a footer with a page number and date, but that kind of information is mighty handy on a hard copy. You can also choose exactly which slides to print, whether to print in black and white or color, and more. The following tutorial walks you through all your options.

— TIP

A super-fast way to print one slide per page is to select Office button → Print → Quick Print. But because choosing this option tells Power-Point to begin printing immediately—without giving you a chance to inspect or change your print settings—you probably don't want to use it unless you've printed your presentation at least once following the steps in this section.

To print your slides:

1. **Choose Office button → Print → Print Preview.**

   The Print Preview tab (Figure 8-1) appears, along with a preview of your first slide. As you mouse over the preview, your cursor turns into a magnifying glass bearing either a plus sign (+), which tells PowerPoint to zoom in when you click, or a minus sign (-), which tells PowerPoint to zoom out when you click.

Figure 8-1. Out of the box, PowerPoint assumes you want to print your presentation one slide per page, so that's what you get if you click the printer icon. But because printing a presentation is a time-consuming proposition, you'll want to set a few options before you actually tell PowerPoint to start printing.

2. **Make sure the word Slides appears in the Print What box.**

   If it doesn't, click the drop-down arrow next to Print What and, from the list of options that appears, choose Slides.

3. **Click Options → Header and Footer.**

The Header and Footer dialog box (Figure 8-2) appears.

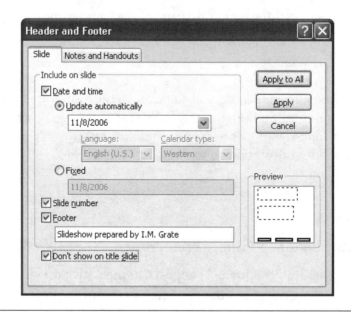

Figure 8-2. As you turn on the checkboxes next to Date and Time, Slide Number, or Footer, Power-Point adjusts the thumbnail in the Preview section to let you know where it intends to put each footer element: left, center, or right. Here, the checkboxes next to all three elements are turned on, so all three footer elements in the Preview area appear black. Turning off an element grays out its position in the Preview.

4. **Check to make sure the Slide tab is selected; if it isn't, click to select it.**

This tab lets you set a host of printing options:

▶ If you want to add a date, timestamp, or both to your footer, then turn on the checkbox next to Date and Time. Then choose either Update automatically (to tell PowerPoint to adjust the date or time so that it always matches today's, in which case you need to choose a date-and-time format from the drop-down list shown in Figure 8-2) or Fixed (in which case you need to type the fixed text you want PowerPoint to add to your footer).

▶ If you want to add a consecutively numbered page number (beginning with 1) to the footer that appears on each page of your printout, then turn on the checkbox next to Slide number.

▶ If you want to add text to your footer, turn on the Footer checkbox and then, in the text box, type in the text you want to appear at the bottom of each page of your printout.

▶ If you don't want your footer to appear on the first page of your presentation (most folks don't, because the first page usually contains the title of their presentation and nothing more), then turn on the checkbox next to "Don't show on title slide."

After you've chosen your settings, click Apply to All to tell PowerPoint to add your footer to each page of your document.

5. **To choose whether to print in color, grayscale (like the illustrations in this book), or plain black and white, click Options → Color/Grayscale.**

   From the list that appears, choose one of the following: Color, Grayscale, or Pure Black and White. As you click, you can see each option in the Preview pane. Choose Color when you need color printouts to show in public (this option uses a lot of ink). Choose Grayscale if you don't have a color printer, but want your printed slides to look as much as possible like they do in PowerPoint. Choose

Pure Black and White only if your presentation doesn't contain a lot of graphics and you want to print it out as quickly as possible. (See box on page 232 for more on the differences between Grayscale and Pure Black and White.)

6. **Choose one or more of the following options, which determine how the slide appears on the page:**

   ▶ **Options → Scale to Fit Paper.** Tells PowerPoint to stretch the content of your slide, leaving the tiniest of margins on all sides.

   ▶ **Options → Frame Slides.** Tells PowerPoint to draw a thin black line around the content of each slide.

   ▶ **Options → Print Hidden Slides.** Tells PowerPoint to print any slides you've previously earmarked as hidden (page 200). PowerPoint doesn't activate this option if your slideshow doesn't contain any hidden slides.

7. **Click Next Page and Previous Page to scroll through the preview of your presentation and make sure everything looks good.**

   Alternatively, you can use the scroll bars that appear in the Preview area to scroll through each slide. You want to make sure your slideshow looks good—right down to the headers, footers, and margins—*before* you've spent half an hour (and half an ink cartridge) printing it.

8. **If you spot a problem, then click Close Print Preview.**

   The Print Preview tab disappears, and you return to the main ribbon. Make any changes you want, and then choose Office button → Print → Print Preview. Repeat steps 2 through 8 until you're satisfied with how your presentation looks in preview mode.

9. **When you're ready to print, click the Print icon.**

   The Print dialog box you see in Figure 8-3 appears.

10. **Tell PowerPoint which pages you want to print by choosing one of the following options:**

    ▶ **All.** Prints every page of your presentation. PowerPoint assumes you want this option, unless you tell it differently.

    ▶ **Current slide.** Prints only the currently selected slide.

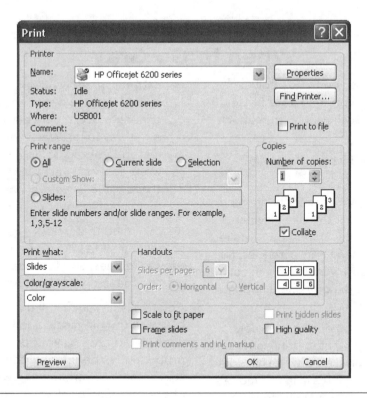

Figure 8-3. Most of the options you see here are options you've already set in the Print Preview ribbon. (When you set them in the Print Preview ribbon, PowerPoint carries them over to this dialog box.) Two options that you do want to set (or double-check) here: which pages you want to print, and how many copies you want to print.

▶ **Selection.** Prints a range of selected slides. PowerPoint doesn't activate this option until you select multiple slides in the Slides pane (see page 137).

▶ **Custom show.** Prints a named subset of your slideshow called a custom show. To see how to create a custom show, flip back to page 206.

▶ **Slides.** Lets you specify a print range, which may be contiguous (1–12) or non-contiguous (1, 2, 5, 6).

11. **Tell PowerPoint how many copies of your presentation you want to print in the "Number of copies" box.**

If you want just one copy, then you can skip this step: PowerPoint assumes you want to print one copy unless you tell it differently.

When to Go Gray

PowerPoint gives you three choices when it comes to printing your presentation: color, grayscale, and in pure black and white.

Here's when (and why) you would choose each:

* **Color.** If you have a color printer and you don't expect to make black-and-white copies of your printout—you're printing overhead transparencies, for example—you'll want to print in color. This option is the only one that prints slide backgrounds.

* **Grayscale.** If you don't have a color printer, or just want to print some inexpensive black-and-white handouts, then choose Grayscale. In this mode, PowerPoint prints graphic portions of your slides that it won't print in pure black and white. The quality of the images is like the black-and-white photographs in a newspaper.

* **Pure black and white.** If you don't have a color printer, your presentation doesn't contain a lot of graphics (fills, patterns, shadows, backgrounds, and so on), and you want to speed up the printing process, pure black and white is the way to go. When you print using this option, graphic fills and patterns won't appear in your printouts, and any shadow effects you've applied to non-text objects appear pitch black.

Keep in mind that unless you print in color, your slide backgrounds, background images, and text shadow effects *won't* appear in your printouts.

And finally, if you're still trying to decide between the grayscale and black-and-white, head back to your presentation proper and experiment with the many subtle shading variations PowerPoint offers, and *then* print your slides. Go to View → Color/Grayscale and choose either Grayscale or Pure Black and White. Doing so pops up either the Grayscale or Black and White tab, where you can select (and preview) several shading options.

---

12. Click OK to print your presentation.

The Print dialog box disappears, and PowerPoint sends your presentation to the printer. At the bottom of the PowerPoint interface you see the print status (Figure 8-4). If you notice that your presentation isn't printing the way you want it, click the X icon to cancel printing.

Print: Page 1 of 20   Printing Page 8   ⊗

Figure 8-4. After you click Print, a status bar appears to let you know PowerPoint's busy gearing up to print—which is a really a good thing, because printing a PowerPoint presentation of any length typically takes so long that, without feedback from the status bar, you might wonder if something was wrong.

Handouts (Multiple Slides per Page)

In PowerPoint-ese, a *handout* is a printout designed to accompany your presentation. There are two major differences between printing handouts and printing slides: You can only print slides one per page, but you can print handouts anywhere from *one to nine* slides per page. Also, when you print handouts (even one slide per page), PowerPoint automatically adds a basic header and footer and leaves good-sized margins for note taking.

Theoretically, your audience can jot down notes on their handouts during your presentation and be left with useful information they can refer to days or weeks afterward. The problem with this theory is that most slides make terrible handouts—for two reasons:

▶ **Good slides are brief; good handouts aren't.** To be effective, the text on your slides needs to be brief, concise, and compelling. For example, short sentences that either ask questions or make controversial statements (which you, of course, answer or explain during your presentation). The same text on a handout, on the other hand, is only going to confuse the audience a week later.

▶ **Good slides are colorful; good handouts aren't.** Light-colored text on a nice dark background with a couple of tasteful graphics thrown in for good measure looks great onscreen. The same slide printed in black and white isn't going to look good at all—in fact, the background won't even print. And it goes without saying that any animated effects, sound clips, and interactive links that you've added to your slides aren't going to translate to printed form.

Printer Problems

If you've printed a presentation from your computer using an earlier version of PowerPoint, then chances are you won't have any problems printing in Power-Point 2007. But if this is your first time using PowerPoint 2007, you might run into a couple of snags. Here's what to look for:

* **You're trying to print to the wrong printer.** If you've ever had more than one printer hooked up to your computer, PowerPoint may be trying to print to the wrong one—even one that's no longer hooked up to your computer. To choose the right printer, in the Print dialog box, click the down arrow next to Name and then, from the drop-down menu that appears, choose the right printer. (If you don't see the name of the printer you're trying to print to, see the next point.)

* **PowerPoint doesn't know about your printer.** If you've hooked up a new printer recently, PowerPoint might not be aware of it. If you don't see the

name of your printer in the Name drop-down box, click Find Printer and follow the instructions that appear.

* **You've set options in your printing software that PowerPoint can't override.** Most printers let you set options, such as print quality, that PowerPoint can't override. To see these options, click Properties. (The dialog box that appears—and the printer options you can and can't override—depend on your printer's particular make and model.)

* **You've set options in the PowerPoint Options dialog box that override the options you set in the Print dialog box.** Choosing Office button → PowerPoint Options and clicking Advanced lets you set printing options (such as whether you want to print slides or handouts, color or grayscale) that PowerPoint uses to print your presentation no matter what you've set in the Print dialog box.

The best handouts provide detailed, lengthy, or dense background information that supports your slides—testimonials, reports, charts, graphics, and so on. Thus, creating really useful handouts is a lot harder than simply selecting a print option and then clicking Print. You have to double your efforts by creating handout material from scratch, most likely in another program like Microsoft Word. PowerPoint lets you jump-start this process by selecting Office button → Publish → Create Handouts in Microsoft Office Word. Whether the results are worth the extra effort, only you—the presenter—can say.

On the other hand, when you're in a hurry, PowerPoint's quick-and-dirty version of handouts may be better than none at all.

TIP

One use for PowerPoint handouts that's often overlooked is as a practice aid. With multiple-slides-to-a-page handouts in front of you, you can easily practice your presentation on an airplane, on a bus, or even in a staff meeting—no laptop necessary.

To print handouts:

1. **Choose Office button → Print → Print Preview.**

   The Print Preview ribbon appears.

2. **In the "Print what" box, choose one of the following: Handouts (1 slide per page), Handouts (2 slides per page), and so on, all the way up to Handouts (9 slides per page).**

   A preview of your handout's configuration appears in the Preview area. Figure 8-5 shows an example.

3. **You can switch the orientation of your handout pages from Landscape to Portrait (or vice versa) by heading to the Print Preview tab and clicking Options → Portrait or Options → Landscape.**

   If you've chosen to print six slides per page or more, then you can tell PowerPoint whether you want it to arrange the slides in horizontal rows or vertical columns. To do so, click Options → Printing Order and then choose either Horizontal or Vertical.

4. **You can change any of several other print settings explained beginning on page 227. When you're ready to print, click the Print icon.**

   The Print dialog box appears.

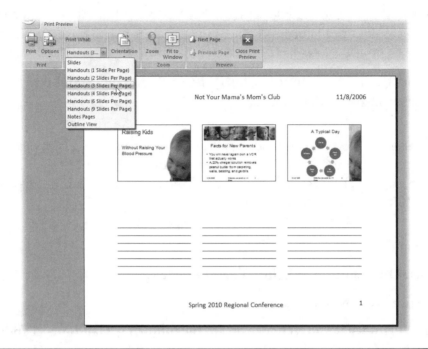

Figure 8-5. The good thing about choosing to print three pages per slide is that PowerPoint gives you lines for note taking. (You get extra room on the page with other options, but no lines.) Notice that PowerPoint assumes you want your handouts to include page numbers. You can delete the page numbers by selecting Options → Header and Footer, clicking the Slide tab, and turning off the radio button next to Slide number.

5. **Tell PowerPoint how many copies of your handout you want to print, and then click OK.**

   The Print dialog box disappears, and PowerPoint sends your presentation to the printer.

Overhead Transparencies

Overhead transparencies, also known as *foils* or just plain *overheads*, are see-through sheets of plastic you slap onto an overhead projector. In the old, pre-PowerPoint days, overheads (and chalkboards) were the only means folks had to deliver presentations. But even today, with PowerPoint 2007 at your disposal, you may have occasion to print your presentation onto overheads.

For example, imagine you're on a plane, headed for the most important presentation of your entire career. You're settling into a taxi when you discover you left your laptop in the airport terminal. When you get to the conference center, there's not enough time to get your office to email a copy of the presentation and then wrestle it onto an unfamiliar computer. If the conference center has an overhead projector (most do) and you've got a stack of overheads in your briefcase, you're golden.

Printing out overheads isn't a lot of extra work. It involves the same steps you take to create a regular printout, with the following exceptions:

▶ **Replace the paper in your printer with a stack of overhead transparencies, available at any office supply store.** (You don't need a special printer or special ink.)

▶ **Consider printing your presentation on paper first to make sure it looks exactly the way you want it to.** It's often easier to spot goofs on paper printouts than onscreen.

▶ **If your slides have colored backgrounds, consider printing grayscale or black-and-white (page 232) versions.** Doing so leaves white space you'll appreciate if you tend to draw or jot notes on your transparencies while you're presenting.

▶ **If you're the one feeding the printer, watch it like a hawk. Transparencies tend to shift, slide, and stick together.** Printing your presentation in two or three batches makes it easier for you to catch missing and misprinted overheads.

Speaker Notes

Speaker notes, as you may recall from page 50, are notes you can attach to any slide of your presentation to remind yourself of things you want to say but don't want your audience to read, like "Remember to tell the joke about the priest, the rabbi, and the lawyer before you start this slide" or "Haul out the flip chart when you get to bullet #2."

Chapter 7 shows how you can set up an extra computer screen to display your speaker notes while you're running your presentation from your main computer (page 201). But in most cases, simply printing your speaker notes and keeping them with you while you give your presentation is sufficient.

To print speaker notes:

1. **Choose Office button → Print → Print Preview.**

   The Print Preview ribbon appears.

2. **From the Print What drop-down menu, choose Notes Pages.**

   The Notes pages you've attached to your slides appear in the Preview area (Figure 8-6).

_ TIP

If you'd like to add a header or footer before you print, check out page 153.

---

3. **To double-check your speaker notes, click Next Page and Previous Page (or use the scroll bars that appear next to the Preview area to flip through your notes pages).**

4. **When you're satisfied, click Print.**

   The Print dialog box appears. For help in setting Print options, such as choosing which pages to print or how many copies to print, head to page 227.

5. **Click OK.**

   PowerPoint prints your speaker notes.

Presentation Outline

Printing an outline version of your presentation is useful for the same reason as examining your presentation in Outline view (page 47) is: It pares away all the formatting and lets you focus on the organization of your content, which is the heart of any good presentation. You might want to print an outline as a proofing tool, to help you double-check that you've included all the material you wanted to include. But you can also use a printed outline as a hard-copy backup of your presentation and even (in a pinch) as an audience handout.

To print an outline of your presentation, choose Office button → Print → Print Preview. From the "Print what" drop-down menu, choose Outline View (see Figure 8-7), and then follow the steps on page 226 to send your outline to the printer.

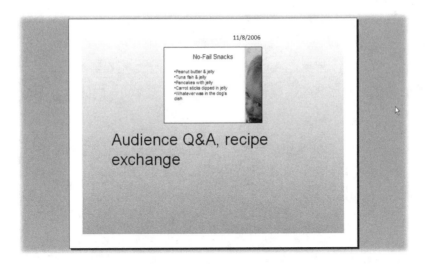

Figure 8-6. PowerPoint won't automatically print speaker notes attached to hidden slides, so if you've hidden any slides (page 200) but still want to see all of your speaker notes, make sure you turn on the radio box next to Print Hidden Slides in the Print dialog box shown in Figure 8-3.

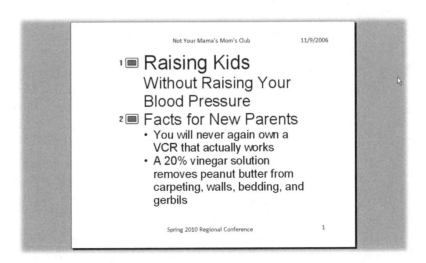

Figure 8-7. Instead of reading through all the text on each and every slide, try printing an outline of your spreadsheet to double-check that you've included all the important points you wanted to include in your presentation.

PART THREE: BEYOND BULLET POINTS—GRAPHICS AND TRANSITIONS

PUTTING IMAGES ON SLIDES

▶ Drawing on Slides

▶ Modifying Drawings

▶ Adding Pictures from Other Programs

▶ Modifying Pictures

POWERPOINT WOULD HAVE DISAPPEARED LONG AGO if all you could do with it was slap bullet points on a screen. Drawings, photographs, and other pictures add meaning, sophistication, and polish to your slideshow. They also serve as powerful visual cues to help your audience understand a point, or recall something you've previously said. They can also tie a slideshow together (when you use similar design elements on each slide), and even help with branding (think logo in the corner of every single slide).

It's not surprising, then, that PowerPoint lets you add all manner of visual elements to your slides. You can use everything from simple graphics you draw right on a slide, to photographs and images created in another program, to the free clip art that comes with PowerPoint. Once you've got the graphic on your slide, you can move it around and even modify its appearance.

> **NOTE**
>
> In addition to graphics, PowerPoint lets you add sound files to your slides-like music, sound effects, or your own voice-over narration. You can even put videos on slides. When you're ready to take on multimedia slides, consult a book like *PowerPoint 2007: The Missing Manual* (O'Reilly).

Drawing on Slides

The Internet's filled with photos and art you can use in presentations but sometimes you need a picture that's so specific you need to sketch it yourself. Imagine you're a defense attorney building a PowerPoint slideshow to present at trial, and you want to describe the route your client took from his desk to the bank vault. You can use stock images of desks, customers, and the bank vault, but you need to draw your own arrows to show your client's route.

Or say you're giving a presentation to management that explains why your department is over budget. You've created a chart (which you learned how to do in Chapter 6) that clearly shows the problem, but your audience (management, remember), needs things spelled out more clearly. You can use PowerPoint's drawing tools to place a big red circle around the negative total. And, right where the chart shows your department's performance taking a nosedive in October, draw a cartoon balloon with the words "Plant #2 burned down 10/15."

When to Use a Graphic

Whether it's clip art, a scanned photo, a picture you drew yourself, or any other artwork, the images you add to your slides need to do more than just take up space. They need contribute to the overall message you're conveying.

Here are a few tips for making sure images carry their weight:

* **Use images to reduce slide text.** Instead of describing stuff with words, think visually and see if you can make your point with a picture. For example, instead of listing the countries where your company does business, display a map of the world with your countries shown in bright yellow. Instead of spelling out in text that you've developed a new product or hired a new employee, consider using a picture of the product or employee.

* **Use images for emphasis.** To a chart or diagram, add text on a shape like an arrow, callout, or simple rectangle to indicate the point you're trying to make.

* **Use specific, relevant images.** Don't pepper your slideshow with stock graphics like clocks, generic machinery, or employees in business suits. They add neither interest nor meaning, and after the third or fourth one, your audience will wonder if the rest of your presentation is canned, too.

* **Use images sparingly.** Humans tend to value what's scarce. Cram a bunch of images onto every slide in your presentation, and your audience is going to start ignoring them. Add one or two, and they'll catch your audience's attention.

If you're artistically challenged, don't worry. There's very little you have to draw freehand in PowerPoint (although you can if you want to). PowerPoint 2007 gives you special tools for drawing lines, curves, and some 80-odd standard shapes including banners, stars, flowchart symbols, and arrows (Figure 9-1). You can also add built-in visual effects—like gradients, shadows, and reflections—to your drawings, and connect shapes with special lines called *connectors* that adjust themselves automatically when you reposition the shapes they're connected to.

___ **NOTE** _____

The kinds of things you can draw haven't changed in PowerPoint 2007, but the way you draw them has. The shape gallery in PowerPoint 2007 replaces the AutoShapes toolbar that appeared in PowerPoint 2003 and earlier versions of the program.

Drawing Lines and Shapes

Drawing in PowerPoint means choosing what you want to draw from a gallery of lines and shapes and then dragging them over your slide.

1. **Click Insert → Illustrations → Shapes.**

    PowerPoint displays the shape gallery (Figure 9-1).

2. **Click one of the line or shape options to select it and then move the mouse over your slide.**

    Your cursor turns into a giant + sign to let you know you can begin drawing.

3. **Click your slide where you want to begin drawing, and then drag your cursor. Let go of your mouse when your line or shape is the size you want it to be.**

    If you're drawing a curvy line, click where you want your line to curve, and then click again where you want your curved line to end. Keep clicking different parts of your slide to create a long curvy line. When you're finished drawing, press Esc.

    PowerPoint adds the line or shape to your slide (see Figure 9-2.) The Drawing Tools | Format tab appears. (Learn how to edit your newly created line or shape using the Drawing Tools | Format tab on page 252.)

Drawing Connectors

Connectors are special lines you draw between two shapes to connect them. The cool thing about connectors is that when you reposition one (or both) of the shapes, PowerPoint automatically adjusts the connecting line. Connectors are great for drawings like flow charts, where you frequently need to add and reposition shapes as you work.

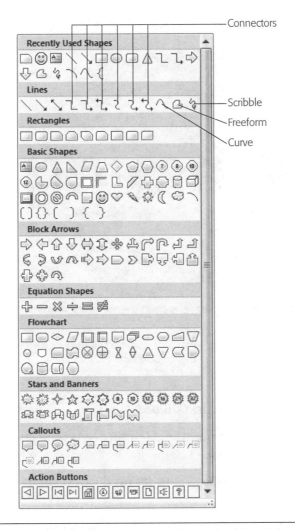

Connectors

Scribble

Freeform

Curve

Figure 9-1. Mousing over the options kicks up a handy description of each item you can draw. Without a description, it's pretty hard to tell the difference between the Curve and the Curved Connector options—and you need to tell the difference, because they behave quite differently after you add them to your slide.

To draw a connector:

1. **Create two shapes on your slide, and make sure one of them is selected.**

2. **Click Drawing Tools | Format → Illustrations → Shapes and choose a connector.**

Figure 9-2. PowerPoint's shape gallery lets you embellish your slides with everything from straight lines and curves to basic shapes, such as this circle/slash. Most of the time, lines and shapes aren't enough and you'll need to add text as shown here.

3. **Move your mouse over the first shape.**

   The cursor turns into a big plus sign, and tiny red connection squares appear around the edge of your shape (Figure 9-3).

4. **Click one of the red connection squares on the first shape and drag toward the second shape.**

   PowerPoint displays red connection squares around the edge of your second shape.

5. **When your cursor's over one of the red connection squares at the edge of your second shape, let go of the mouse button.**

   One red connector dot appears on each shape (Figure 9-4) to show where you've connected them.

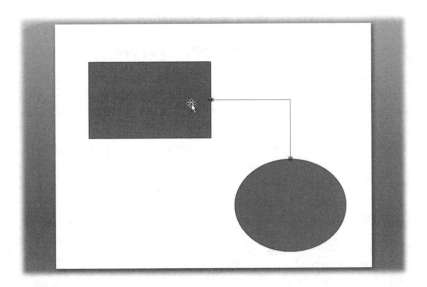

Figure 9-3. Small red squares around a shape mean you can connect that shape to something else on your slide using an automatically updating connector. This example shows one shape being connected to another shape, but PowerPoint lets you connect multiple shapes directly to each other, and to other connectors.

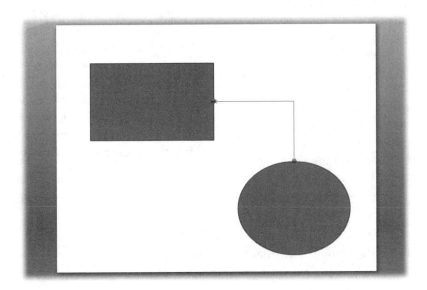

Figure 9-4. You know you've successfully connected two shapes when you see two red circles, one at each end of the connector. When you reposition a connected shape, PowerPoint automatically adjusts the connector so the connection doesn't break.

Tips for Faster Drawing

Using a computer program to draw anything more complicated than a quick callout or arrow can be tedious, no matter which program you're using—and PowerPoint is no exception. PowerPoint includes some shortcuts for faster, easier drawing, but it doesn't make them obvious.

So here they are, in no particular order:

* **Force perfection.** Pressing Shift while you draw a line or shape tells PowerPoint to force a line into a perfectly straight 45-degree angle, an oval into a perfect circle, a rectangle into a perfect square, and so on.

* **Draw more than one line or shape in a row (without having to reselect it over and over again).** After you finish drawing a line or shape, PowerPoint turns your cursor from a drawing instrument (+ sign) back into a regular point-and-click cursor (arrow). But to save some time, you can draw multiple lines or shapes without having to reclick the option every time: First, in the shape gallery, click the shape you want to draw. Then right-click that shape and choose Lock Drawing Mode. Now you can draw as many shapes as you like, one right after the other. Choose another shape (or any other ribbon option) to revert back to normal, one-at-a-time drawing mode.

* **Tweak shapes instead of redrawing them.** When you add a shape to your slide, one or more tiny yellow diamonds usually appear along the shape's outline. To distort the shape—to make the arrow shape just a little pointier, for example, or to turn the smiley face into a frowny face—click one of the diamonds and drag. (More on the distortion tool on page 262.)

* **Draw shapes from the center out (instead of from side to side).** Normally, when you add a shape to your slide and drag your cursor to resize it, PowerPoint draws the shape from left to right. But when you're trying to center your shapes along, say, a vertical line, press Ctrl as you drag. The Ctrl key tells PowerPoint to draw the shape starting at its center and extend equally on both sides.

You can tell PowerPoint to redraw, or *reroute*, an existing connector so it looks better. (Sometimes dragging the connected shapes around leaves the connector looking cramped or oddly bent.) To reroute a connector, select it and then, from the Drawing Tools | Format tab, choose Edit Shape → Reroute Connectors.

If you're still not happy with the way PowerPoint reroutes your connector, you can do it yourself. To move the connection from, say, the top of a shape to the bottom of the shape, click the connector and move it until the end of the connector snaps to the red connector square at the bottom of the shape.

Modifying Drawings

Just as you erase and redraw the sketches you make on paper, you can erase and redraw the drawings you add to your PowerPoint slides. This section shows you how to modify individual lines and shapes. The next section shows you how to layer, align, and group multiple lines and shapes.

Selecting Lines and Shapes

Before you can modify a shape or line, you first need to do one of the following:

▶ Select a single shape or line, mouse over it until your cursor changes from a normal, single-headed arrow into a four-headed arrow; then click.

▶ Select multiple shapes or lines, click the first shape or line to select it, and then hold down the Shift key as you click additional shapes and lines.

Applying Shape Styles

PowerPoint comes with a handful of Shape Style options that let you add professionally designed, theme-coordinated colors and effects (including glows and reflections) to your lines and shapes.

The great thing about Shape Styles is that they let you gussy up your drawings with one or two clicks. The downside is that you run the risk of producing a drawing that looks exactly like a million other drawings on a million other PowerPoint slides. (It's a modest risk because most folks use drawings infrequently and because you'll deliver such a compelling presentation that your audience won't notice.)

To format your drawings by applying a prebuilt Shape Style, first select the line or shape to which you'll apply your Shape Style. Go to Drawing Tools | Format → Shape

Styles and choose a Shape Style, or click More to see the entire gallery of styles (Figure 9-5) and then choose a Shape Style from the gallery.

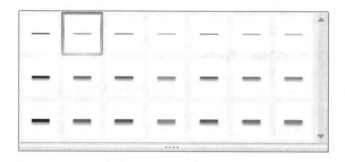

Figure 9-5. When you add a line to your slide, you see this style gallery. The style gallery varies depending on the shape you add to your slide, but the overall choices—a few different colors, a few different thicknesses, a few effects (like shadows and reflections)—are always the same. To preview a style, simply mouse over it.

Modifying Lines, Connectors, and Shape Outlines

You can change the lines and connectors you add to your slide by modifying their color, their weight (thick to thin), their type (dashes, dots, or solid), or by adding arrows to one or both ends. And because the outline of every shape you create in PowerPoint is a line, you can change those the same way.

Select the line, connector, or shape that has an outline you want to modify. Then click Drawing Tools | Format → Shape Styles → Shape Outline (Figure 9-6).

From the Shape Outline menu, choose one or more of the following:

▶ **Theme Colors.** Lets you make your line a theme-coordinating color.

▶ **Standard Colors.** Lets you turn your line one of several theme-breaking colors.

▶ **No Outline.** Removes an existing line or outline.

▶ **More Outline Colors.** Displays a palette of additional colors you can apply to your line.

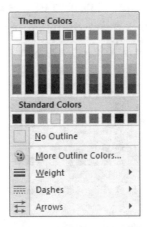

Figure 9-6. Because the outlines PowerPoint gives your shapes are nothing more than regular lines, use the menu shown here to modify shape outlines as well as lines and connectors. (Page 252 shows you how to modify the connecting points of a connector.)

▶ **Weight.** Displays a dialog box that lets you choose a thickness for your line, from skinny to fat.

▶ **Dashes.** Displays a dialog box that lets you choose from a collection of dashed and dotted (as well as solid) lines.

▶ **Arrows.** Displays a dialog box that lets you apply different kinds of arrowheads to one or both ends of your line.

— TIP —

To shorten or lengthen a straight line, mouse over one of the line's end points (your cursor turns into a double-headed arrow when you're in the right spot). Then drag to shorten or lengthen your line. (This trick also works for rotating lines, as described on page 255.)

Modifying the Inside of a Shape

Every shape you add to your slides consists of an outline (a *line*), and an inside (a *fill*). You can fill in a shape by changing its color, or by adding a picture (including built-in repeating pictures called *textures*) or a gradient.

Select the shape you want to modify. Then go to Drawing Tools | Format → Shape Styles → Shape Fill. From the menu shown in Figure 9-7, choose one or more of the options described in the list that follows.

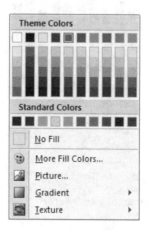

Figure 9-7. If none of the Shape Styles PowerPoint offers is exactly what you want, choose an option from this menu to customize your shapes by recoloring them or adding a picture or gradient effect.

▶ **Theme Colors.** Makes your shape a theme-coordinating color.

▶ **Standard Colors.** Turns your shape one of several theme-breaking colors.

▶ **No Fill.** Deletes the fill altogether.

▶ **More Fill Colors.** Displays a palette of additional colors you can apply to your line.

▶ **Picture.** Lets you paint your shape using any picture stored on your computer (Figure 9-8).

▶ **Gradient.** Lets you apply a light-to-dark pattern to your shape.

▶ **Texture.** Lets you add one of Microsoft's built-in, repeating pictures to your shape (think wallpaper).

Applying Special Effects

New in PowerPoint 2007 is the ability to add special effects like glows, reflections, shadows, and beveling to your shapes and lines with just a couple of mouse clicks.

Figure 9-8. Here, you see an example of the same shape filled with a picture, a gradient effect, and a built-in texture. All the shapes you create in PowerPoint have fills you can customize, even those (such as arcs) that don't appear to have them.

Technically, you can apply any special effect you like to lines as well as to shapes. But because lines tend to be skinny, they usually don't benefit much from 3-D effects.

Select the shape or line you want to apply a special effect to. Then, click Drawing Tools | Format → Shape Styles → Shape Effects. Mouse over an effect, like Preset (Figure 9-9) and then, from the gallery that appears, choose an option.

Rotating Drawings

You rotate lines and shapes the way you rotate and reposition every other type of object on your slides: by selecting them and then dragging the rotation handle.

Rotating lines

If you add a line to your slide and then decide you want to slant it a bit, no problem. PowerPoint gives you two different ways to rotate lines: dragging the end points, and using the Size and Position dialog box.

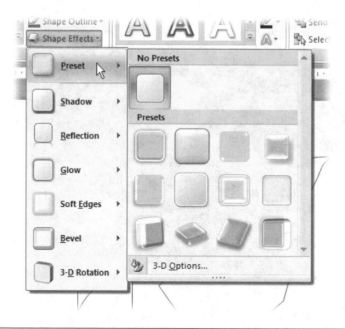

Figure 9-9. Mousing over an effect displays a gallery so that you can point-and-click your way to a good-looking shape.

On your slide, click to select the line you want to rotate. PowerPoint displays circular endpoints, one at each end of the line. Click one of the endpoints and drag to rotate the line. When you let go of your mouse, PowerPoint displays the rotated line (see Figure 9-10).

Figure 9-10. The easiest way to rotate a line is to click an endpoint and drag it in the direction you want your line to rotate, as shown here. For finer control, though, you'll want to use the Size and Position dialog box (Figure 9-11).

Rotating shapes

If you've got a steady hand, the quickest way to rotate a shape is to click the shape's rotation handle and drag. When you want to tell PowerPoint exactly how many degrees to rotate your shape, use the Size and Position dialog box shown in Figure 9-11 instead.

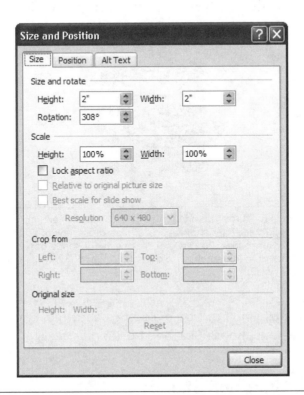

Figure 9-11. A holdover from PowerPoint 2003's Format AutoShapes dialog box, the Size and Position dialog box lets you rotate, resize (scale), reposition, and otherwise manipulate your lines and shapes by typing in specific numbers, such as the degrees of rotation you want to apply. To open it, go to Drawing Tools | Format → Size, and click the dialog box launcher. To rotate an object, go to the Size tab and then type a number of degrees in the Rotation box.

___ TIP ___

PowerPoint gives you a quick way to rotate a shape 90 degrees, as well as to flip shapes (rotate them vertically or horizontally). On the Drawing Tools | Format tab, click Arrange → Rotate and then choose one of Rotate Right 90º, Rotate Left 90º, Flip Vertical, or Flip Horizontal.

To rotate a shape by dragging, first select the shape you want to rotate. PowerPoint displays a selection box around the shape, along with a rotation handle (Figure 9-12).

When you mouse over the green rotation handle, PowerPoint changes your cursor into a curved arrow to let you know you're in the right spot. Click the rotation handle and drag to rotate your shape; when you're satisfied, click to finish the job.

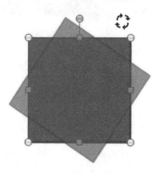

Figure 9-12. When your cursor turns into a curved arrow as shown here, click to begin rotating your shape; then start dragging. PowerPoint shows you a ghosted preview of your rotated shape as you drag. When you let go of your mouse, PowerPoint redraws your shape based on its new rotation. To restrict the rotation to 15-degree increments, hold the Shift key down while you drag.

— TIP ————————————————————————————————

To display the Size and Position dialog box shown in Figure 9-11, right-click any shape and choose Size and Position.

Repositioning Lines and Shapes

Similar to the way you rotate lines and shapes, you reposition them on your slide in one of two ways: by dragging them, or by using the Size and Position dialog box shown in Figure 9-11.

To reposition a line or shape by dragging, first select the line or shape you want to reposition. PowerPoint displays endpoints (line) or a selection box (shape). Move your mouse over the highlighted line or selection box. When your mouse is in the right place, your cursor turns into a four-headed arrow, and you can drag to reposition the selection.

Resizing Drawings

You automatically choose a size for your shapes and lines as you draw them, by dragging. But if you change your mind, you can easily resize them. To do so:

1. **On your slide, select the line or shape you want to resize.**

   PowerPoint displays endpoints (for the lines) and a selection box, complete with round and square resize handles (for the shapes).

2. **Click an endpoint or a resize handle and drag.**

   Your cursor changes from an arrow to a + symbol. As you drag, PowerPoint displays a semitransparent (*ghosted*) version of your line or shape (see Figure 9-13).

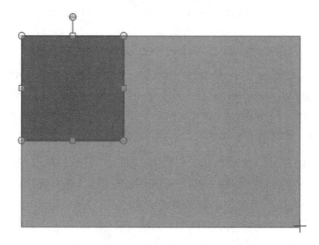

Figure 9-13. Dragging a square resize handle lets you distort your shape by stretching or shrinking just one aspect of the shape. Dragging a circular resize handle lets you enlarge or shrink your shape. (To enlarge or shrink the shape while keeping it in perfect proportion, press Shift while you drag.)

3. **When the ghosted line or shape is the size you want it, let go of the mouse button.**

   PowerPoint redraws your selection.

—— **NOTE** ——

   Another way to resize your drawings is with the Shape Height and Shape Width options on the Drawing Tools | Format tab. See Figure 9-14 for details.

Figure 9-14. If you know exactly how wide or tall you want your selected shape to appear on your slide, go to the Drawing Tools | Format tab, head to the Size section, and then click the Shape Height (top) or Shape Width (bottom) box to specify the height or width, respectively, to which you want to resize your shape. You can also type in a height or width (or both) directly.

Changing the Type of a Shape or Connector

Suppose you add a plain rectangle to your slide, add some text, and then you decide a fancier callout would look better. You're in luck: PowerPoint lets you experiment by changing any type of shape to another type of shape, and any type of connector to another type of connector—without losing formatting you've already applied.

To change a shape to a different type of shape, select it and then click Drawing Tools | Format → Insert Shapes → Edit Shape (Figure 9-15). On the menu that appears, mouse over the Change Shape menu option, and the Shape gallery appears. Click the shape you want to change your existing shape to.

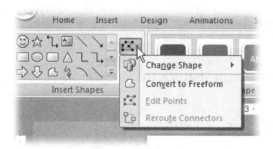

Figure 9-15. Because changing a shape into a line would automatically delete both the shape's fill and any text you'd added to the shape (lines don't have built-in text boxes), PowerPoint doesn't let you change a line into a shape or vice versa.

Changing a connector's type works a little differently: On your slide, right-click the connector you want to change. From the context menu that appears, choose

Connector Types and then one of the following (unchecked) options: Straight Connector, Elbow Connector, or Curved Connector.

Adding Text to Shapes

A rectangle or star isn't particularly compelling all by itself. But adding some text can send a powerful message. For example, say you've got a slide that shows a sales chart. On the chart you've drawn an arrow shape to point out a spike in company earnings. Adding a quickie text explanation to the arrow (*One-time State Contract*) provides your audience with instant clarity.

PowerPoint's shapes come with text boxes built in, so all you have to do to add text is select the shape and start typing. If you've just added the shape to your slide, chances are it's already selected. Just click in the text box and type away (Figure 9-16).

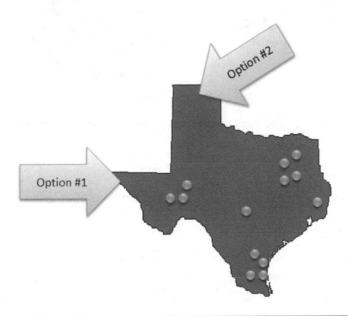

Figure 9-16. When you tilt a shape, the text you've added to it tilts, too. If that's not what you want, add an independent text box by heading to the Insert Shapes section of the Drawing Tools | Format tab, clicking the Text Box icon, and positioning your new text box how and where you like. (For details on inserting and positioning text boxes, check out page 40.)

You can format the text you just added by heading to the WordArt Quick Styles section of the Drawing Tools | Format tab and selecting one or more of the Text Fill, Text Outline, or Text Effects options. Chapter 3 walks you through the process of formatting text.

Reshaping and Distorting Shapes

PowerPoint displays little yellow diamond-shaped *distortion points* on some shapes (but not all). By clicking one or more distortion points and dragging, you can push, pull, and otherwise distort the basic shape into custom shapes (see Figure 9-17). Customizing a basic shape this way is usually easier than drawing your own custom shape.

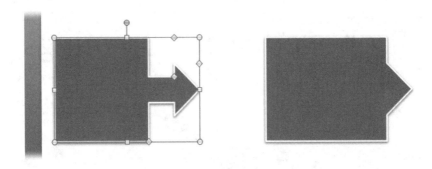

Figure 9-17. On the left, you see a basic shape; on the right, the same shape after dragging a distortion point (one of the little yellow diamonds).

For some shapes, PowerPoint strictly controls how much distortion you can apply. You can make the happy face into a frowny face, for example, but nothing in between.

Aligning Shapes and Lines

To help you lay out the different shapes and lines you add to your slides, PowerPoint lets you display helpful rulers and gridlines. It also lets you align multiple objects quickly. For example, you can line up a bunch of shapes on the left or right side of your slide simply by clicking a button.

To help you get the alignment right, you can have PowerPoint display rulers or gridlines (Figure 9-18). Choose View → Show/Hide → Ruler or View → Show/Hide → Gridlines. Another way to show these helpful tools: right-click a blank spot on a slide and choose Ruler or "Grids and Guides" from the shortcut menu.

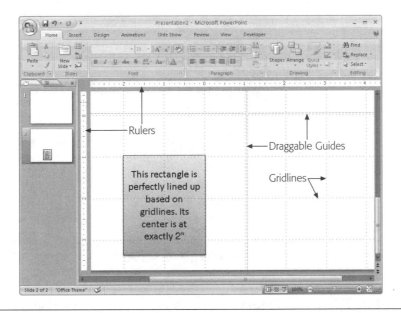

Figure 9-18. Displaying horizontal and vertical rulers and gridlines, as shown here, lets you layout your shapes exactly. Rulers and gridlines don't appear when you run your slideshow. Pressing Shift+F9 toggles grids on and off; to find out how to customize how far apart PowerPoint places the gridlines, turn to page 262.

NOTE

You can create additional guides by turning guides on (page 122), and then Ctrl-clicking a guide and dragging to create a new guide.

First select the lines or shapes you want to align. Then go to Home → Drawing → Arrange → Align to display the alignment menu shown in Figure 9-19.

Choose one or more of the following:

▶ **Align Left, Center, Right, Top, Middle, or Bottom.** Tells PowerPoint to line up your selected objects with respect to the slide (see Align to Slide below), or with respect the selected objects themselves (see Align to Selected Objects below). For example, choosing Align Left repositions your objects so that they're lined up on the left side of the slide (assuming you've also selected Align to Slide; see next).

▶ **Distribute Horizontally, Vertically.** Tells PowerPoint to spread out multiple objects so that they're equally distant from the sides and top-and-bottom of a slide, respectively.

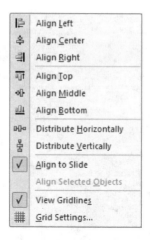

Figure 9-19. The number of options that PowerPoint activates (as opposed to grays out) depends on how many objects you've selected.

▸ **Align to Slide.** Tells PowerPoint to align left, center, right, top, middle, or bottom (see above) with respect to the edges of the slide.

▸ **Align Selected Objects.** Tells PowerPoint to align left, center, right, top, middle, or bottom (see above) with respect to the other objects you've selected.

▸ **Show Gridlines.** Tells PowerPoint to show gridlines.

▸ **Grid Settings.** Displays the Grid and Guides dialog box (Figure 9-20), which lets you customize the gridlines that appear (if you've told PowerPoint to show them as described above). The Grid and Guides dialog box also lets you tell PowerPoint to help you position objects so that they touch (*snap to*) gridlines or other objects on your slide.

___ **NOTE** _____

You can display the Grid and Guides dialog box shown in Figure 9-20 by right-clicking a slide and choosing Grid and Guides.

Adding Pictures from Other Programs

Instead of drawing your own image directly onto your slide, as described on page 246, you can insert a scanned photo, digital picture, professionally drawn sketch,

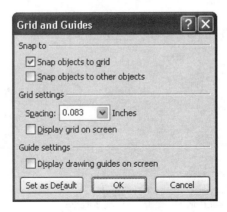

Figure 9-20. Because turning on snapping affects how PowerPoint lets you position objects when you're dragging them, most folks tend to either hate it or love it. Turning on the "Snap objects to grid" affects object positioning even when the gridlines aren't showing.

one of the stock images that come with Microsoft Office, or any other image you have stored on your computer.

The upside of using a canned picture, of course, is that it's easier than rolling your own. And depending on your artistic skills, the results could be more professional looking, too. The downside is that some folks are tempted to fill their presentations with generic images—dollar signs, handshakes, spinning globes, and so on—just because they have access to them. (See the box on page 270 for details.)

In this section, you see how to spice up your presentation with image files from your computer as well as from Microsoft Office's cache of free clip art. You also see how to create a super-quick slideshow consisting of nothing but captioned images called, appropriately enough, a photo album.

Inserting a Picture Stored on Your Computer

You can insert virtually any image file into your slideshow, from the common .jpg, .bmp, and .gif file formats to the less-well-known .cgm and .emz formats. The following steps walk you through the process:

1. **In the Slides tab in Normal view, select the slide to which you want to add an image.**

2. Click Insert.

The Insert tab shown in Figure 9-21 appears.

Figure 9-21. The Illustrations section of the Insert tab lets you add several different types of graphics to your slides: Picture, Clip Art, Photo Album, Shapes, SmartArt, and Charts, respectively.

___ **TIP** ___

> If you applied a content layout to your slide, then clicking the picture icon (Figure 9-22) displayed in the center of the slide automatically shows you the Insert Picture dialog box.

Figure 9-22. Content layouts, including Title and Content, Picture with Caption, and Comparison, come complete with clickable icons you can use to add pictures to your slide quickly, without having to click around on tabs.

3. From the Illustrations section of the Insert tabs, choose Picture.

The Insert Picture dialog box (Figure 9-23) appears.

4. Browse your computer for the file you want to add to your slide by clicking the "Look in" drop-down box, or the icons listed on the left side of the Insert Picture dialog box. When the name of your file appears in the center of the dialog box, click it to select it.

PowerPoint places the name of your file in the File name box.

5. **Click Insert.**

   PowerPoint inserts the selected file onto your slide, and the Picture Tools | Format tab appears. (You see how to use the Picture Tools | Format tab to modify pictures on page 269.)

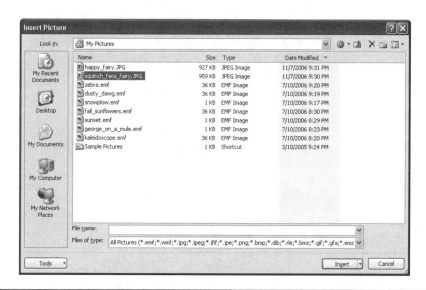

Figure 9-23. The Insert Picture dialog box is similar to just about every other dialog box PowerPoint uses to let you add non-PowerPoint files to a PowerPoint presentation. PowerPoint recognizes almost any imaginable type of image file, including the popular ones (JPEG, GIF, and TIFF), and many you've never heard of.

Adding Built-in Clip Art Drawings

When you install PowerPoint 2007 or any other Microsoft Office program, you automatically install a pile of free, built-in drawings you can add to your slideshows. Although some of the drawings are pretty cheesy, Microsoft maintains a large and growing online library of clip art drawings and photos (and animation and sound clips, too), some of which look downright sophisticated.

To add clip art to a slide:

1. **In the Slide tab in Normal view, select the slide you want to add clip art to. Then choose Insert → Illustrations → Clip Art.**

   The Clip Art pane you see in Figure 9-24 appears.

Figure 9-24. As you can see from these representative thumbnails, there's a reason clip art isn't called high art. Still, depending on the effect you're after, clip art can be perfectly serviceable. Check out the box on the next page for ideas.

2. **In the "Search for" box, type a description of the picture you'd like to add to your slide and click Go.**

   In the results area of the Clip Art pane, PowerPoint displays thumbnails of all the clip art pictures that match your search word or phrase.

   To see all the clip art images stored on your computer, don't type anything; just click Go.

3. **Click a thumbnail to add that drawing to your slide.**

   PowerPoint places a copy of the drawing in the center of your slide, on top of whatever else already happens to be there. You can also drag the thumbnail from the Clip Art pane to the precise spot on your slide where you want it.

Finding the Perfect Clip Art

Using the Clip Art panel to find just the right piece of clip art for your slideshow can be a challenge. Here are a few tips that should help:

* **Look in all the right places.** If a basic search (for *nature* or *industry*, for example) doesn't bring back any thumbnails, click the down-arrow next to "Search in" and make sure the checkboxes next to all of the possible collections (file folders) are turned on.

* **Filter out animation and sound clips.** When you're looking for clip art, it's frustrating to get a bunch of search results—only to find they're all sound clips. To confine your searches to images, click the down-arrow next to "Results should be" and make sure the checkboxes next to "Clip Art" and "Photographs" are turned *on* (and that the checkboxes next to "Movies" and" Sounds" are turned *off*).

* **Look online.** If you've searched for clip art and come up empty-handed, click the "Clip art on Office Online," which whisks you to Microsoft's growing online library of clip art.

* **Add your own images.** If you've got your own drawings, photographs, or other image files already stored on your computer, you can add them to the Clip Art Organizer (a fancy name for "file folder") so you can use them the next time you go looking for clip art. Here's how: Click the "Organize clips" link you find at the bottom of the Clip Art pane and then, from the dialog box that appears, choose File → Add Clips to Organizer.

Modifying Pictures

It's rare that you'll want to use an image file or piece of clip art as-is. If nothing else, you'll probably want to resize it or crop it to make it fit with the text and other elements on your slide. To be sure, PowerPoint isn't Photoshop, so don't expect editing miracles. In addition, your editing options are fewer when you use certain types of images (like photos) as compared to others (line-and-shape drawings you create in PowerPoint). Still, for most purposes you find PowerPoint's editing options more than adequate.

Using Clip Art Creatively

Clip art is convenient, but sometimes the problem is, well, it *looks* like clip art. If you want people to take your presentation seriously, you must avoid having your slides look like you plunked down the first cheesy stock image you found. PowerPoint doesn't enforce good graphic design principles, but if you follow these no-fail tips, you can turn cheese into *fromage*:

✳ **Keep it small.** Try to keep your clip art small and off to one side of the slide, leaving the bulk of the space for text, as shown in Figure 9-25 (top).

✳ **Make it transparent.** Applying a 75% or higher transparency effect to backgrounds, clip art, and even the basic shapes you add to your slides lets text shine through. (See Figure 9-25, bottom). If you use clip art, you need to avoid hard-to-read-text sitting on a busy background.

✳ **Not everything has to line up.** Sometimes, tilting an image just a little results in the rakish, attractive effect shown in Figure 9-26 (top).

✳ **Consider filled text boxes**. Applying a contrasting fill color to your text boxes doesn't just make text stand out; it also adds an appealing design element to your slides (Figure 9-26, top).

✳ **If all else fails, use contrasting text.** If you're using a strong, stylized image as a slide background, you can get away with pasting text on top—as long as you use a bold, contrasting font and color as shown in Figure 9-26 (bottom).

___ TIP ___

The way you select, resize, reposition, rotate, and align pictures is the same way you modify the shapes and lines you draw directly onto a slide (page 251). But some formatting is picture-specific, and that's the formatting this section acquaints you with: how to tweak a picture's brightness, apply special effects, and more.

Figure 9-25. Top: The easiest way to add clip art—by tucking it out of the way, as shown here—gives a conservative result.

Bottom: Transparency can be hard to pull off. Too transparent, and your audience may think there's a water stain on the overhead screen; not transparent enough, and they won't be able to read your text. Still, in the right situation and with the right degree of transparency, it can be effective.

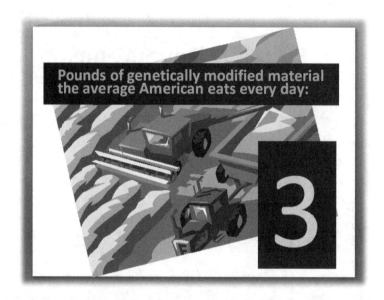

Figure 9-26. Top: In this example, a clip art image was enlarged, rotated, and overlaid with filled text boxes. The result is both readable and attention grabbing.

Bottom: This text-on-image technique works best when you're trying to get across a single point, although it can also be effective for the first and last slides in your presentation. Make sure the background image is relevant to your presentation and choose a strong, clean font.

Applying a Picture Style

PowerPoint makes it easy to apply a handful of attractive formatting options to your pictures. For example, you can add a picture frame, a shadow, and a rotated 3-D effect—with the click of a button.

To apply a Picture Style, select the picture you want to format. Then, on the Picture Tools | Format contextual tab, mouse over the thumbnail options in the Picture Styles section of the Picture Tools | Format tab (Figure 9-27). As you do, Power-Point shows you a preview of the formatting on your slide. Click the option you want to apply to your picture, and PowerPoint automatically redraws your picture based on your selection.

Figure 9-27. The thumbnails you see in the Picture Styles section of the Picture Tools | Format tab, shown here, are the most popular. But if you like, you can click More (note the pointer) to see the entire Picture Style gallery.

Recoloring Your Picture

Tinting, or recoloring, can turn an ordinary picture into an artful design element. You can give a colored picture an old-time look by tinting it sepia or give it a jazzy, sophisticated appearance by tinting it blue.

To recolor a picture, select the picture you want to tint. Choose Picture Tools | Format → Adjust → Recolor. Move your mouse over the color swatches in the gallery to preview each color on your slide. Click the color you want to apply to your picture, and PowerPoint redisplays your picture based on the color you selected.

Making Your Picture Transparent

Making a picture transparent lets the images or text you've placed behind it show through, similar to the example you see in Figure 9-25 (bottom). But it also lets you add a subtle watermark to your slides, such as a barely-there logo or the word Confidential.

To make a picture transparent:

1. **On your slide, select the picture you want to make transparent. Then choose Picture Tools | Format → Adjust → Recolor.**

   An option gallery appears.

2. **In the gallery, head to Color Modes and choose Washout.**

   PowerPoint applies a transparent effect to your picture.

Adjusting Brightness and Contrast

You can't do a whole lot to improve a picture after you've added it to your slide, but you *can* brighten and sharpen a muddy picture slightly. Don't expect miracles from the Brightness and Contrast options PowerPoint offers; they can't make a bad picture shot in too little light look good, just a bit better.

To adjust brightness and contrast:

1. **On your slide, click to select the picture you want to brighten. Choose Picture Tools | Format → Adjust → Brightness.**

   A menu of brightness options appears.

2. **Choose a positive brightness option to brighten the picture; choose a negative one to darken it.**

   The menu disappears, and PowerPoint applies your option to your picture.

3. **Choose Picture Tools | Format → Adjust → Contrast.**

   A menu of contrast options appears.

4. **Choose a positive contrast option to sharpen the picture; choose a negative one to equalize the light and dark portions of the picture.**

   The menu disappears, and PowerPoint applies your option to your picture.

Applying Special Effects

Sometimes, the difference between ho-hum and hot is as easy as applying a special effect—such as soft edges or a shadow—to your pictures. Figure 9-28 shows you an example.

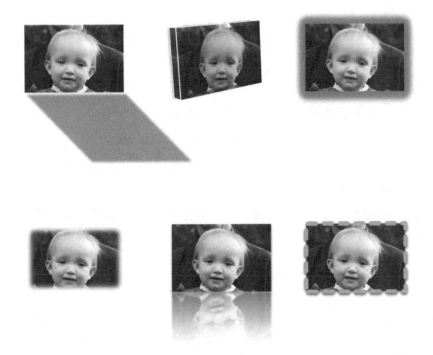

Figure 9-28. Here, you see the same picture with six different effects applied: a shadow, 3-D rotation, glow, soft edges, reflection, and a custom border. The picture is a scanned-in photo, but you can apply the same effects to clip art or any other picture. You can apply multiple effects to the same picture, too.

To apply a special effect to your picture:

1. **On your slide, click to select the picture you want to modify.**

    The Picture Tools | Format contextual tab appears.

2. **Click Picture Tools | Format → Picture Styles → Picture Effects.**

3. **From the gallery that appears, choose the option you want. You can use one of the following effects, or use them in combination:**

▶ **Preset.** Lets you apply one of the most popular 3-D rotation effects.

▶ **Shadow.** Lets you apply different shadows (left, right, in front, behind, and so on).

▶ **Reflection.** Lets you apply a reflection that mimics your picture sitting on a polished coffee table, turned this way or that.

▶ **Glow.** Lets you apply a thick, soft, colored border around your picture.

▶ **Soft Edges.** Lets you crop your picture using preset, softened borders.

▶ **Bevel.** Lets you turn ordinary shapes into 3-D buttons.

▶ **3-D Rotation.** Lets you apply a custom 3-D rotation effect, where you get to pick the angle of rotation and other particulars.

To create a custom border around your picture, click Picture Tools | Format → Picture Styles → Picture Border and use the Shape Outline, Dashes, and Weight options to tell PowerPoint what color you want your border, whether you want it dashed, dotted, or straight, and how thick you want it (page 253).

___ TIP ___

> If you apply a bunch of different effects to your picture and then change your mind, you may be able to get your original picture back quickly: clicking Picture Tools | Format → Adjust → Reset Picture tells PowerPoint to discard all of the formatting changes you made since you added the picture to your slide. (Unfortunately, Reset Picture doesn't always revert your picture to pristine condition. In that case, you can click Undo a few times or—worst case scenario—delete the picture from your slide and start over.)

Cropping Your Picture

Cropping a picture in PowerPoint is similar to taking a pair of scissors to a printed picture and snipping off the parts you don't want. Cropping is useful for discarding distracting background elements; it's also useful for reducing pictures to a serviceable size.

1. **Select the picture you want to crop. On the Picture Tools | Format tab, click Size → Crop.**

   Crop marks (Figure 9-29, left) appear at the sides and corners of your picture.

2. **Mouse over the crop mark nearest where you want to crop.**

   PowerPoint changes your cursor from an arrow to a crop mark.

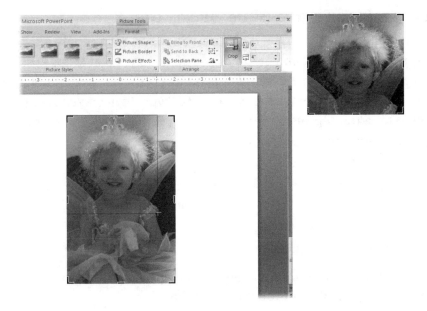

Figure 9-29. Left: Click a crop mark and drag to crop a picture.

Right: Cropping doesn't affect the uncropped portion of the picture; the result is the same as if you'd snipped off part of the picture.

3. **Click and drag a crop mark to tell PowerPoint how much to cut off.**

   As soon as you click, PowerPoint changes the crop-mark-cursor into a plus sign. After you let go of your mouse, PowerPoint redraws your picture without the cropped portion (Figure 9-29, right).

4. **Repeat steps 2 and 3 until you're satisfied with your picture.**

   When you're finished, click somewhere else on your side to turn the editing cursor back into the selection (arrow) cursor.

> Cropping reduces the visible size of a picture by snipping bits off the top, bottom, or sides. If what you want to do is shrink the whole picture, check out the instructions for resizing elements on page 258. To whack off the top and bottom in equal increments and blur the edges, check out the Soft Edges effect described on page 275.

Applying a Picture to a Slide Background

If you've got a subtle, well-designed picture, you may want to apply it to your slide's background so that the text and graphics you apply to your slide appear on top of it. Doing so provides visual interest; and depending on the background picture you choose, it can also reinforce the message you're trying to get across. Think sunset background for a travel presentation, or a background showing a photo of your development team for a slide describing milestones met.

NOTE

> For help in identifying a well-designed picture, check out the tips in the box on page 245. They work equally well for other types of pictures.

To designate a picture as a slide background:

1. **Right-click the slide you want to add a picture background to and then choose Format Background from the shortcut menu.**

    The Format Background dialog box appears.

    NOTE

    > If you want the background to appear on all the slides in your slide-show, you need to apply it to the slide master. See page 147 for details.

2. **On the left side of the Format Background dialog box, make sure Fill is selected; then, on the right side of the dialog box, turn on the radio box next to "Picture or texture Fill."**

    Additional options appear in the Format Background dialog box.

3. Under "Insert from," click File to use an image file stored on your computer as a background. (Or, if you prefer, click Clip Art to choose a clip art image.)

The Browse Image dialog box appears.

4. Browse your computer for the image file you want to apply to the background. When you find it, click to select it and then click Insert.

PowerPoint fills your slide's background with the selected image, stretching or squishing it as necessary to make it fit your slide. (If your image is tiny and you want to tell PowerPoint to repeat it over and over again to fill the slide instead of stretching it out of shape, turn on the "Tile picture as texture" checkbox in the Format Background dialog box.)

TIP

Because PowerPoint is so hugely popular, lots of companies offer backgrounds, multimedia clips, and themes specifically for you to use in your PowerPoint presentations. Prices vary widely, as does quality. Three companies you may want to look into: *www.powerfinish.com*, *www.powerpointart.com*, and *www.probackgroundart.com*.

SLIDE TRANSITIONS

10

▶ Slide Transitions

IF YOU'RE A MOVIE BUFF, you're familiar with scene transitions such as jump cuts, dissolves, and tasteful fades. Professional film directors know that how they move from one scene to the next has a huge impact on how audiences respond. Along with visual interest, transitions communicate subtle information about the scene to come. For example, when the audience sees a fade, it automatically assumes that the next scene begins in another time or place. PowerPoint isn't a movie-editing program, but it does let you control the transitions from one slide to the next.

Slide Transitions

When you start with a blank presentation, advancing from one slide to the next is a simple on-or-off proposition—a slide is either 100 percent visible, or 100 percent hidden. There's nothing wrong with simple, but by applying a *slide transition*—a named effect that makes slide content fade, drop, swirl, or gallop into view—you can convey a mood that supports your presentation (sobriety, sophistication, whimsy, and so on).

> **NOTE**
>
> Although PowerPoint lets you add slide transitions to individual slides, doing so can make your presentation look amateurish and disorganized. Instead, stick with the same slide transition to every slide. Doing so lets your audience focus on your content, not wondering which direction the next slide is going to come from.

Types of Transitions

PowerPoint organizes its 50-plus built-in slide transitions into five different categories:

▶ **Fades and Dissolves.** The tasteful transitions in this category include Fade Smoothly, Fade Through Black, Cut, Cut Through Black, and Dissolve.

▶ **Wipes.** Wipe transitions make your slides appear from one or more directions, as though you were wiping slide content on with a rag. The impressive number of transitions in this category include Wipe Down, Wipe Left, Wipe Right, Wipe Up, Wedge, Uncover Down, Uncover Left, Uncover Right, Uncover Up, and many more.

- **Push and Cover.** Similar to Wipes transitions, these transitions make slide content appear from one or more directions. The difference is that Push and Cover transitions appear to push old slides out of the way as new slides appear. The transitions in this category include Push Down, Push Left, Push Right, Push Up, Cover Down, Cover Left, Cover Right, Cover Up, Cover Left-Down, Cover Left-Up, Cover Right-Down, and Cover Right-Up.

- **Stripes and Bars.** The transitions in this category cause slides to appear a strip or chunk at a time. They include Blinds Horizontal, Blinds Vertical, Checkerboard Across, Checkerboard Down, Comb Horizontal, and Comb Vertical.

- **Random.** This category includes two Stripes-and-Bars-like transitions, Random Bars Horizontal and Random Bars Vertical (both of which cause slides to appear one strip at a time). It also includes the Random transition, which tells PowerPoint to pick your transition. Because a good presenter consciously chooses every aspect of her presentation to support her message, you'll almost never want to use the Random transition.

Adding Transitions Between Slides

Transition effects look impressive, but adding them to your slideshow is no more difficult than, say, applying a font or choosing a bullet point style. Your tools are all in one place—the Animations tab shown in Figure 10-1. Open a slideshow with two or more slides in it, and then follow the steps described next.

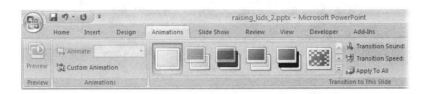

Figure 10-1. Until you tell it otherwise, PowerPoint assumes you don't want a slide transition applied to any of your slides. The Animations tab shows you five popular slide transitions. You can mouse over them to get a description of each as well as an instant preview, or you can click More (the down arrow) to see the 52 additional slide transitions.

1. **In Normal view, select the second slide in your presentation (or the slide you want to add a transition *to*).**

   On the Slides tab, PowerPoint highlights the selected slide. The slide's contents appear in the slide editing area.

2. **On the Animations tab, head to the "Transition to This Slide" section and click the More down arrow on the far right.**

   A transition gallery similar to Figure 10-2 appears.

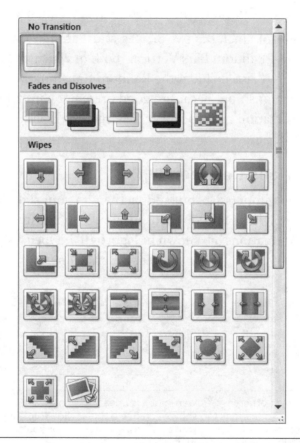

Figure 10-2. PowerPoint 2003 listed the names of slide transitions and you had to click a name to see the transition in action. In PowerPoint 2007, it's the other way around. You see an illustrative thumbnail of the transition in this gallery. Mousing over a thumbnail displays the transition the name and a live preview.

3. **Mouse slowly over each transition option.**

   As your cursor passes over each transition option, PowerPoint displays the name of that option (such as Blinds Horizontal, Checkerboard Down, or Dissolve) and previews the option in the slide editing area.

4. **Click the transition you want.**

   PowerPoint previews the transition in the slide editing area. On the Slides tab, PowerPoint displays the star-shaped Play Animations icon directly beneath the slide number (Figure 10-3).

Figure 10-3. A star displayed under a slide number on the Slides tab or in Slideshow View lets you know that PowerPoint has successfully applied an animated effect to that slide. Clicking the star previews the effect.

5. **To set transition speed, on the Animations ribbon, head to the Transition to this Slide section, and click the Transition Speed drop-down menu (Figure 10-1) and choose Slow, Medium, or Fast.**

   Out of the box, PowerPoint assumes you want your transition to move as quickly as possible.

6. **Tell PowerPoint how you want to advance from slide to slide.**

   If you want to do it manually, go to Animations → Transition to This Slide and turn on the On Mouse Click checkbox. To have slides advance automatically, turn on the Automatically After checkbox, and then enter the number of seconds you want PowerPoint to pause before it moves on.

7. **If you want every slide in your slideshow to have the same slide transition, select Animations → Transition to This Slide → Apply To All.**

   On the Slides tab, PowerPoint displays stars beneath every slide number. (If you change your mind after you apply a slide transition to your entire slideshow, click Undo.)

   ___ **NOTE** ___

   If you've already applied a slide transition to all of the slides in your slideshow and then change how the transition looks, behaves, or sounds, you need to click Apply To All *again* to tell PowerPoint to update the transition for all of the slides.

8. **Run your slideshow to preview the transition.**

   PowerPoint gives you two additional ways to preview your slide transition: by heading to the Animations ribbon and clicking Preview → Preview, or heading to the Slides tab and clicking the star beneath the slide number. But make sure you run the entire slideshow, too, and not just that one slide; doing so lets you double-check that you've added the transition you want to the slides you want.

GETTING HELP

- ▶ Getting Help from PowerPoint
- ▶ Getting Help from Microsoft
- ▶ Getting Help from the PowerPoint Community

IN A LOT OF WAYS, POWERPOINT 2007 IS EASIER TO WORK WITH than its predecessors—after you get the hang of it. (And after you've had a chance to read this book, of course.) But sooner or later, you're going to run into a snag and need some help—and getting you that help is what this appendix is all about.

Help with PowerPoint starts right there in the program's window and extends into the far reaches of the Internet. There are descriptive screen tips that pop up when you mouse over the item in question, help screens stored on your computer and on Microsoft's Web site, and a vast community of PowerPoint experts on message boards and Web sites.

Getting Help from PowerPoint

In PowerPoint 2007, help's never far away. In fact, the program gives you a helpful description of just about every item onscreen before you even click it—in the form of a screen tip. You can also get help from wherever you are inside PowerPoint by displaying the Microsoft Office PowerPoint Help window.

Displaying Screen Tips

To get help on a specific button, menu, or dialog box option, first mouse over the option. A good-sized screen tip pops up with a description of the item, and advice on where to get further help (Figure A-1).

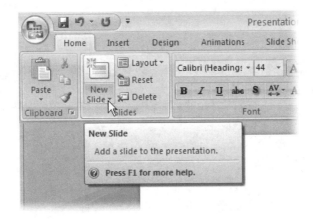

Figure A-1. Not every screen tip you see contains a link you can click to get more help, but many do. New in Office 2007, this contextual help system was designed to whisk you directly to help articles describing the thing you're trying to do (instead of the old approach, which forced you to hunt for the right article yourself).

Searching Help Topics

To open the Help window, click the Help icon located in the upper right of the screen (Figure A-1). This icon's always visible in the top-right corner the PowerPoint interface, no matter which tab you're on. Just as in older versions of the product, Power-Point gives you an alternate way to display the help window: by pressing F1.

Either way, the Microsoft Office PowerPoint Help window shown in Figure A-2 appears. PowerPoint help launches in its own window, which means it doesn't automatically disappear when you go back to working in PowerPoint. (Minimizing the help window and clicking the pushpin icon keeps it handily in sight when you go back to work.)

Figure A-1. The question-mark icon shown here (the international symbol for help) replaces the Help menu that was included in earlier versions of PowerPoint.

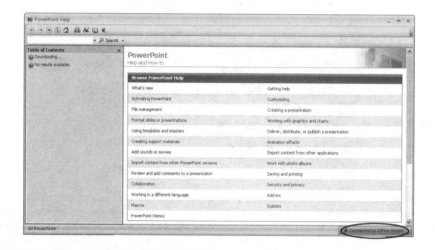

Figure A-2. PowerPoint lets you access the latest and greatest online help, or just the help files you installed on your computer when you installed PowerPoint. Head to the bottom of the window to change this setting.

In the Search box, type the word or phrase you need help with and click Search. You can also click any of the links in the Table of Contents pane to search for a word or phrase. PowerPoint displays a list of topics and topic-related links in the right-hand side of the Help window. You may have to repeat this step several times to zero in on the information you want.

Out of the box, PowerPoint assumes you want to see online help files, which are more numerous than the ones installed on your computer. You can tell PowerPoint whether you want it to search online help files or not. (Unless your Internet connection is down or is very, very slow, you want to search online.) To do so:

- **To tell PowerPoint to access online help files:** At the bottom of the Help window, click the down-arrow next to Offline and, from the menu that appears, choose "Show content from the Internet." When you do, Offline changes to Connected, and PowerPoint attempts to access your Internet connection. If it can't get online, you'll get an error message.

- **To restrict PowerPoint access to the help files stored on your computer:** Click the down-arrow next to Connected and choose "Only show content from this computer." When you do, Connected changes to Offline.

___ NOTE _____

To get help while you're running a slideshow, right-click anywhere on the slide. When you do, a menu of options appears (unless the slideshow creator turned it off using kiosk mode, as described on page 199). In the PowerPoint Options dialog box (Figure A-3), many of the options include help icons.

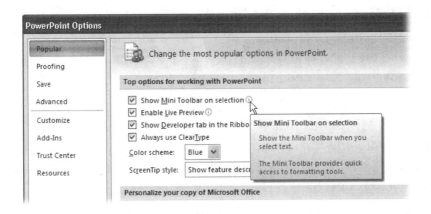

Figure A-3. Figuring out what you can expect when you set an option in PowerPoint can be challenging. Fortunately, many of the options include Help icons you can mouse over to see a meaty description.

Getting Help from Microsoft

Although getting help directly from Microsoft is neither cheap nor easy, you can do it, as you'll see in the following sections.

Help for Folks Familiar with PowerPoint 2003

Because PowerPoint 2007 looks so much different from earlier versions of the program, Microsoft maintains the Microsoft Office PowerPoint 2007 Highlights Web site, which offers a tutorial as well as a well-designed, 12-minute animated demo showing PowerPoint 2007 in action (*www.microsoft.com/office/preview/programs/ powerpoint/highlights.mspx*).

Tutorials

The folks at Microsoft have created several dozen interactive tutorials in Power-Point, some of which address PowerPoint topics (such as adding animated effects to your slideshow). To see a list of these tutorials, head to Microsoft's Office training center, *http://office.microsoft.com/en-us/training*, and search for "PowerPoint 2007."

Online Articles, FAQs, and More

The Microsoft Technical Communities Web site (*www.microsoft.com/communities/ default.mspx*) is the place to find user groups, technical chats, Web casts, a 24/7-accessible knowledge base, and to find out about PowerPoint-related events and training.

You can also try Microsoft's Help and Support site for PowerPoint, *http:// support.microsoft.com/ph/2522*, which organizes questions (and answers) by topic and lists important security updates you can download to help keep your copy of PowerPoint (and your computer) healthy and virus-free.

If it's creating PowerPoint macros you're interested in, start with the PowerPoint Developer Portal (*http://msdn.microsoft.com/office/program/powerpoint/ default.aspx*), which offers links to a VBA language reference as well as articles written especially for VBA programmers.

Forums

Microsoft maintains a public PowerPoint forum (*www.microsoft.com/office/comm-unity/en-us/default.mspx?lang=en&cr=US&dg=microsoft.public.powerpoint*) where anyone can ask a question (and anyone can answer). Although this forum isn't moderated by actual Microsoft employees, it *is* monitored by knowledgeable PowerPoint gurus.

Direct Person-to-Person Help

Sometimes, nothing wil do but asking a real, live technical support person for help. The prices for contacting Microsoft (see the site *http://office.microsoft.com/en-us/contactus.aspx?Sitename=1*) start at $35 per email or phone call and go up from there—so you probably want to exhaust the options described in the preceding sections before you begin the process.

Getting Help from the PowerPoint Community

With an estimated 600 million folks just like you using PowerPoint to pound out everything from business presentations to school reports, sermons, prosecuting arguments, and who-knows-what-else, odds are good that whatever problem you've run into is one that someone else (or a whole lot of someone else's) has already run into and solved.

Useful PowerPoint resources abound on the Web; here are a handful of the best:

▶ **The PowerPoint FAQ** (*www.rdpslides.com/pptfaq*): Created and maintained by PPTools (a company that also develops PowerPoint add-in programs), this site is so rich with practical advice, tips, and tricks that Microsoft's own PowerPoint site links to it.

▶ **MasterView International** (*www.masterviews.com/index.htm*): This site's articles, forums, links to blogs, and free online newsletter all focus on designing and managing effective PowerPoint presentations for international audiences.

▶ **Michael Hyatt's Working Smart** (*www.michaelhyatt.com/workingsmart/ microsoft_powerpoint*) is an intelligent, well-written blog that address not just the technical aspects of PowerPoint, but the meatier issues of designing and delivering effective presentations.

INDEX

Symbols

COLOPHON

Mary Brady was the production editor for *PowerPoint 2007 for Starters: The Missing Manual*. Sanders Kleinfeld and Adam Witwer provided quality control. Dawn Mann wrote the index.

The cover of this book is based on a series design originally created by David Freedman and modified by Mike Kohnke, Karen Montgomery, and Fitch (*www.fitch.com*). Back cover design, dog illustration, and color selection by Fitch.

Tom Ingalls designed the interior layout, which was modified by Ron Bilodeau. Robert Romano and Jessamyn Read produced the illustrations.

Related Titles from O'Reilly

Missing Manuals

Access 2003 for Starters: The Missing Manual

Access 2007 for Starters: The Missing Manual

Access 2007: The Missing Manual

AppleScript: The Missing Manual

AppleWorks 6: The Missing Manual

CSS: The Missing Manual

Creating Web Sites: The Missing Manual

Digital Photography: The Missing Manual

Dreamweaver 8: The Missing Manual

eBay: The Missing Manual

Excel 2003 for Starters: The Missing Manual

Excel 2007 for Starters: The Missing Manual

Excel 2007: The Missing Manual

FileMaker Pro 8: The Missing Manual

Flash 8: The Missing Manual

FrontPage 2003: The Missing Manual

GarageBand 2: The Missing Manual

Google: The Missing Manual, 2nd Edition

Home Networking: The Missing Manual

iMovie HD 6: The Missing Manual

iPhoto 6: The Missing Manual

iPod: The Missing Manual, 5th Edition

Mac OS X: The Missing Manual, Tiger Edition

Office 2004 for Macintosh: The Missing Manual

PCs: The Missing Manual

Photoshop Elements 5: The Missing Manual

PowerPoint 2007 for Starters: The Missing Manual

PowerPoint 2007: The Missing Manual

QuickBooks 2006: The Missing Manual

Quicken 2006 for Starters: The Missing Manual

Switching to the Mac: The Missing Manual, Tiger Edition

The Internet: The Missing Manual

Windows 2000 Pro: The Missing Manual

Windows XP for Starters: The Missing Manual

Windows XP Home Edition: The Missing Manual, 2nd Edition

Windows XP Pro: The Missing Manual, 2nd Edition

Windows Vista: The Missing Manual

Windows Vista for Starters: The Missing Manual

Word 2007: The Missing Manual

Other O'Reilly Titles

Excel 2007 Pocket Reference

Writing Excel Macros with VBA, 2nd edition

Excel Hacks

Analyzing Business Data with Excel

Excel Scientific and Engineering Cookbook

Better than e-books

Buy *PowerPoint 2007 for Starters: The Missing Manual*
and access the digital edition FREE on Safari for 45 days.

Go to www.oreilly.com/go/safarienabled
and type in coupon code EOMEBWH

Search
thousands of
top tech books

Download
whole chapters

Cut and Paste
code examples

Find
answers fast

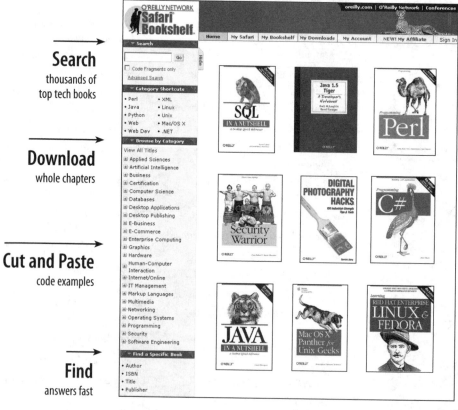

Search Safari! The premier electronic reference
library for programmers and IT professionals.